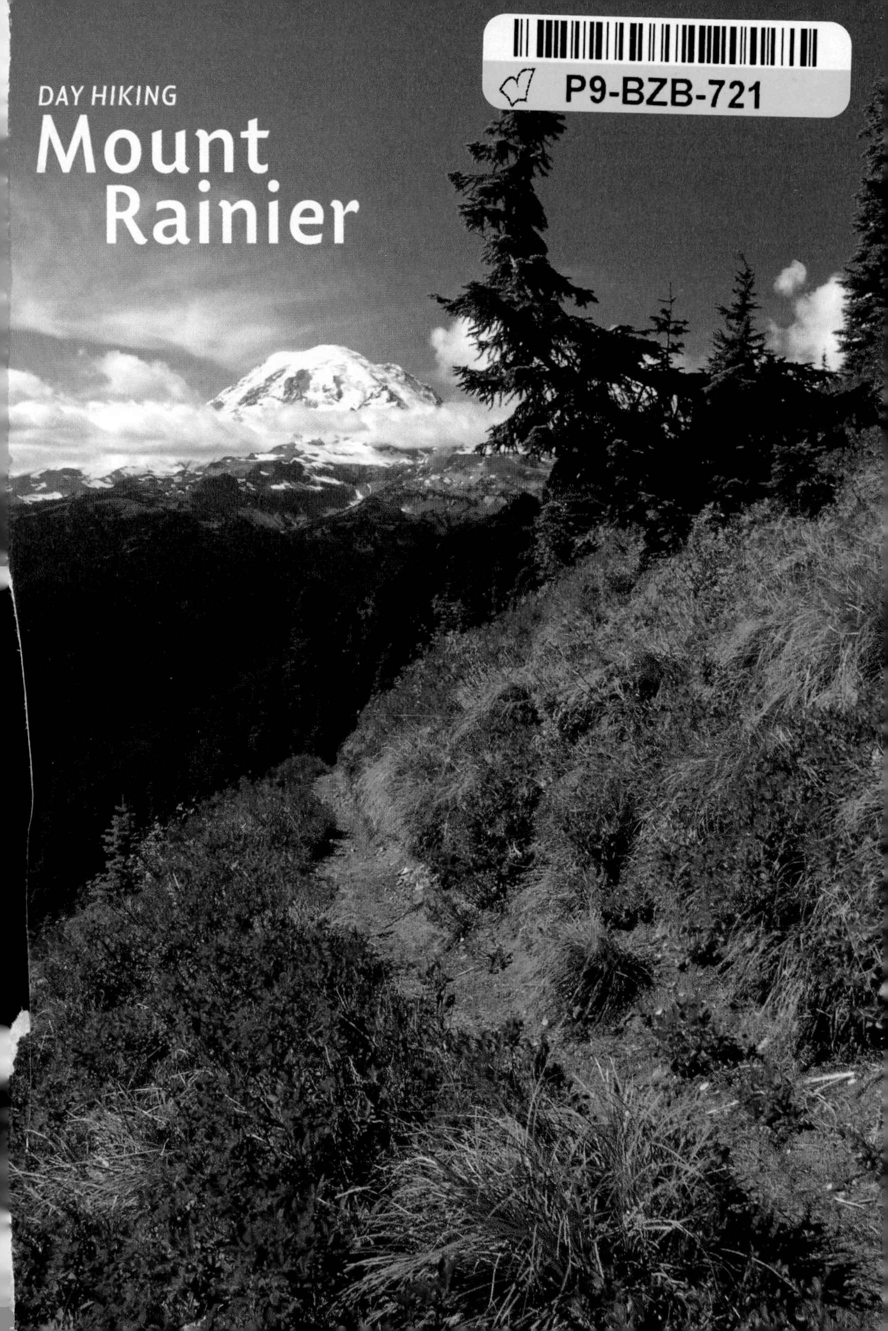
DAY HIKING
Mount
Rainier
P9-BZB-721

Previous page: Vivid colors of fall along the upper Shriner Peak trail with views of Mount Rainier

Above: Deep purple of the aging western trillium in late spring

Opposite: The vanilla-leaf-lined Eastside Trail passing through stands of Pacific silver firs

Below: It really is a mirror... famous Mirror Lake reflecting the beauty of Mount Rainier and surrounding alpine fir trees.

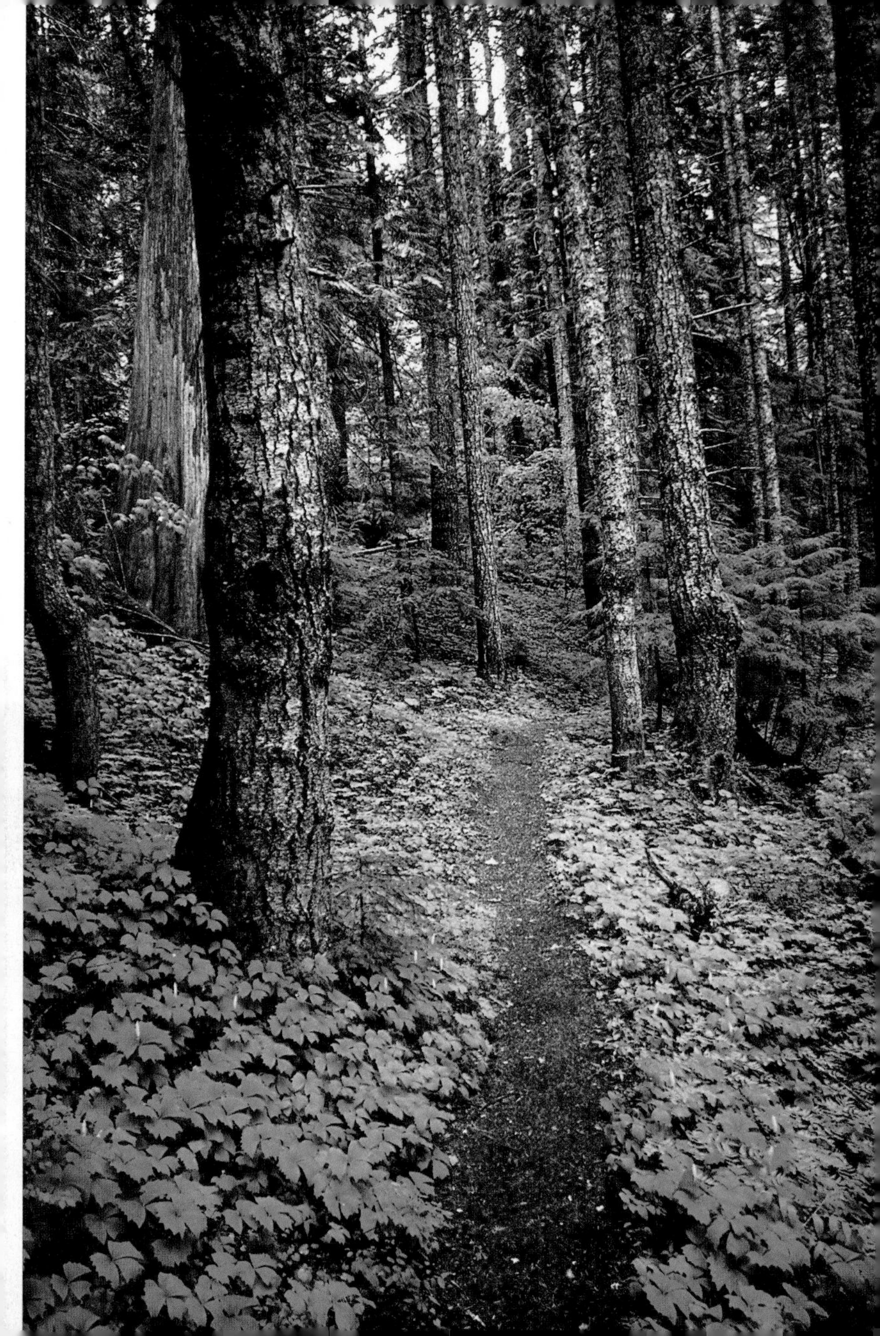

Left: Bold autumn colors carpeting the meadows around Van Trump Park

Below: Sunset on Mount Rainier from Alta Vista

Top: Aerial view of a space ship . . . otherwise known as a lenticular cloud over Mount Rainier. It'll be raining within 24 hours!

Right: A solid carpet of avalanche lilies, a showcase wildflower of Mount Rainier National Park

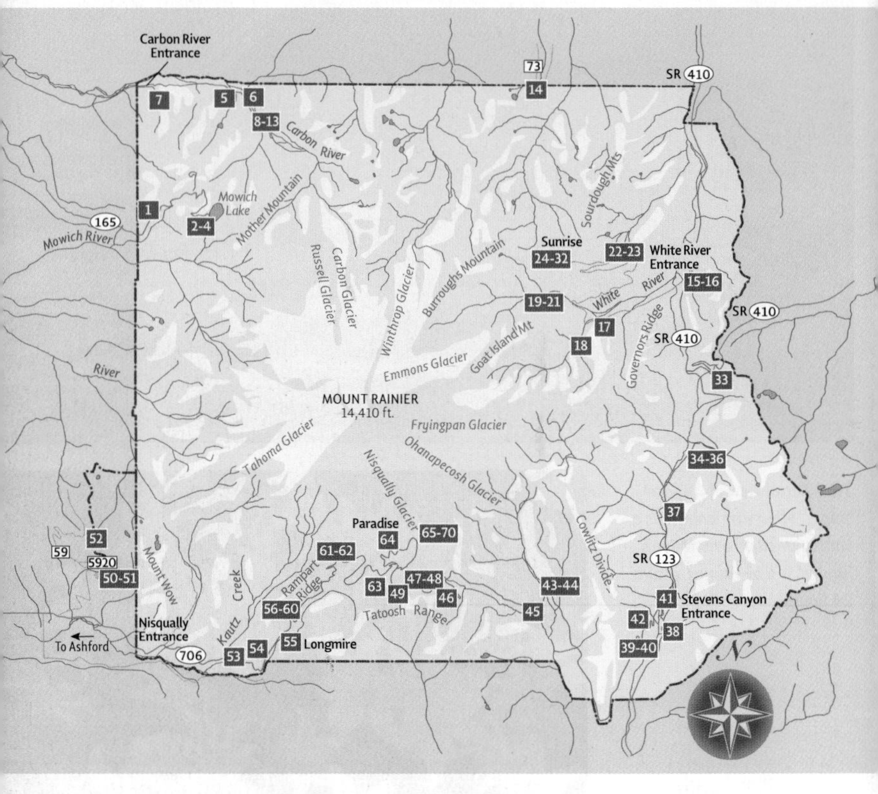

LEGEND

Symbol		Symbol		Symbol	
SR 410	State Highway	1	Hike Number		Summit
	Secondary Road	T	Trailhead		River/Lake
	Unpaved Road		Hiking Route		Campground
24	Forest Road		Other Trail		Backcountry Campsite
	Park Boundary		Bridge		Picnic Area
	Ranger Station	) (	Pass/Saddle		

Opposite: Fog lifts to allow enjoyment of "the reflection" at Reflection Lakes.

DAY HIKING Mount Rainier

National Park Trails

Dan A. Nelson
photography by
Alan L. Bauer

THE MOUNTAINEERS BOOKS

THE MOUNTAINEERS BOOKS
is the nonprofit publishing arm of The Mountaineers Club, an organization founded in 1906 and dedicated to the exploration, preservation, and enjoyment of outdoor and wilderness areas.

1001 SW Klickitat Way, Suite 201, Seattle, WA 98134

First edition, 2008

Manufactured in Canada

Copy Editor: Kris Fulsaas
Cover and Book Design: The Mountaineers Books
Layout: Peggy Egerdahl
Cartographer: Moore Creative Designs

Cover photograph: *Dennis and Michael hike down the Crystal Peak trail with stunning views of Mount Rainier and the White River Valley before them.*
Frontispiece: *A doe gently walks through crimson-colored huckleberries near Alta Vista.*

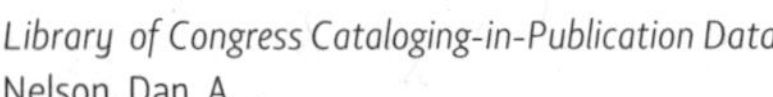

Maps shown in this book were produced using *National Geographic*'s TOPO! software. For more information, go to *www.nationalgeographic.com/topo.*

Library of Congress Cataloging-in-Publication Data
Nelson, Dan A.
Day hiking Mount Rainier: national park trails / Dan A. Nelson; photography by Alan L. Bauer. —1st ed.
p. cm.
Includes index.
ISBN 978-1-59485-060-8 (ppb)
1. Hiking—Washington (State)—Mount Rainier National Park—Guidebooks. 2. Trails—Washington (State)—Mount Rainier National Park—Guidebooks. 3. Mount Rainier National Park (Wash.)—Guidebooks. I. Bauer, Alan. II. Title.
GV199.42.W22M685 2008
796.5109797'782—dc22
2007041731

 Printed on recycled paper

In memory of

Greg Ball and Ira Spring,

trail champions

whom we proudly called

colleagues, trail companions, and friends

Table of Contents

Longmire

Paradise

A Quick Guide to the Hikes

ROUTE NAME	TRAILHEAD WAYPOINT	RATING	DIFFICULTY	MILES	ELEV. GAIN
CARBON RIVER AND MOWICH LAKE					
1. Paul Peak	N46 56.097, W121 54.409	2	2	5.6	1050
2. Tolmie Peak Lookout	N46 55.962, W121 51.817	4	3	7.5	1100
3. Spray Park	N46 55.962, W121 51.817	5	4	7	1600
4. Mowich River	N46 55.962, W121 51.817	3	4	7	2400
5. Green Lake	N46 59.546, W121 51.034	3	3	4	1300
6. Chenuis Falls	N46 59.437, W121 50.640	3	1	1	50
7. Carbon River Rain Forest Nature Trail	N46 58.625, W121 49.892	3	1	0.5	80
8. Carbon Glacier	N46 58.625, W121 49.892	4	3	6.5	1000
9. Moraine Park–Mystic Lake	N46 58.625, W121 49.892	5	5	15.6	3650
10. Ipsut Falls	N46 58.625, W121 49.892	3	1	1.4	300
11. Ipsut Pass	N46 58.625, W121 49.892	3	3	8	2800
12. Seattle Park	N46 58.625, W121 49.892	5	5	12	2850
13. Yellowstone Cliffs and Windy Gap	N46 58.625, W121 49.892	5	5	13	3500
WHITE RIVER					
14. Grand Park	N46 59.777, W121 38.480	4	4	9	1100
15. Crystal Lakes	N46 55.364, W121 32.017	3	4	6	2300
16. Crystal Peak	N46 55.364, W121 32.017	3	4	8	3100
17. Owyhigh Lakes	N46 53.431, W121 35.807	3	4	8	1650
18. Panhandle Gap	N46 53.302, W121 36.662	5	5	12	2950
19. Glacier Basin	N46 54.129, W121 38.621	4	4	6	1600
20. Emmons Glacier View	N46 54.129, W121 38.621	3	2	3	900
21. White River to Sunrise	N46 54.129, W121 38.621	3	4	6	2100
SUNRISE					
22. Sunrise Lake	N46 55.053, W121 35.268	2	2	1.5	425
23. Palisades Lakes	N46 55.053, W121 35.268	4	3	7.5	500
24. Sourdough Ridge	N46 54.877, W121 38.540	4	2	2.5	400
25. Fremont Lookout	N46 54.877, W121 38.540	4	3	5.6	800
26. Berkeley Park	N46 54.877, W121 38.540	4	3	7	900
27. Skyscraper Mountain	N46 54.877, W121 38.540	5	4	8.5	1078
28. Burroughs Mountain	N46 54.877, W121 38.540	4	4	7.4	1000

HIGH POINT	KID-FRIENDLY	WILDLIFE	HISTORIC	VIEWS	WATERFALLS	ENDANGERED	LAKE
4200		X					
5900	X		X	X			X
6400		X		X	X		X
5000		X					X
3400	X				X	X	X
2200	X				X		
1960	X						
3400	X		X				
6000				X			X
2650	X				X		
5150				X	X		
5200		X					
5800		X					X
5600		X		X		X	X
5828		X		X			X
6595		X		X		X	
5400	X	X					X
6800		X		X			
5900			X	X			
5200				X			
6400		X					X
6150	X	X					X
6150		X					X
6800	X	X		X			
7200	X	X	X	X			X
6800		X		X			X
7078		X		X			X
7400		X		X			X

ROUTE NAME	TRAILHEAD WAYPOINT	RATING	DIFFICULTY	MILES	ELEV. GAIN
29. Shadow Lake–Sunrise Camp Loop	N46 54.877 W121 38.540	4	2	3.5	200
30. Forest Lake	N46 54.877, W121 38.540	3	3	5	1000
31. Dege Peak	N46 54.877, W121 38.540	3	2	4	600
32. Silver Forest–Emmons Vista	N46 54.877, W121 38.540	3	1	2.4	200
CAYUSE PASS					
33. Tipsoo Lake–Naches Peak Loop	N46 52.041, W121 31.055	4	2	3	600
34. Deer Creek Falls	N46 50.012, W121 32.107	3	2	1	300
35. Deer Creek Falls to Owyhigh Lakes	N46 50.012, W121 32.107	3	4	10	2200
36. Deer Creek to Tipsoo Lake	N46 50.012, W121 32.107	2	4	10	2100
37. Shriner Peak	N46 48.106, W121 33.305	5	5	8.5	3434
38. Laughingwater Creek to Three Lakes	N46 45.094, W121 33.429	4	4	12	2800
39. Ohanapecosh Hot Springs	N46 43.983, W121 34.157	2	1	1	50
40. Silver Falls Loop	N46 43.983, W121 34.157	3	2	3	200
STEVENS CANYON					
41. Grove of the Patriarchs Loop	N46 45.478, W121 33.454	3	1	1.5	50
42. Ollalie Creek Camp	N46 45.373, W121 33.765	3	3	5.6	1600
43. Box Canyon and Nickel Creek	N46 45.918, W121 38.169	3	2	2	400
44. Indian Bar–Cowlitz Divide	N46 45.918, W121 38.169	5	5	15	2900
45. Stevens Canyon Waterfalls	N46 45.610, W121 38.344	4	4	7	700
46. Bench and Snow Lakes	N46 45.610, W121 38.344	3	2	2.6	300
47. Louise Lake	N46 46.132, W121 43.442	2	2	2	300
48. Faraway Rock	N46 46.132, W121 43.442	2	2	2	300
49. Pinnacle Saddle	N46 46.097, W121 43.885	5	4	3.5	1150
LONGMIRE					
50. Mount Beljica	N46 46.405, W121 56.674	3	3	4	1100
51. Gobblers Knob	N46 46.405, W121 56.674	3	4	10	1100
52. Glacier View	N46 46.405, W121 56.674	3	3	6	900
53. Kautz Creek	N46 44.181, W121 51.333	3	5	12	3100
54. Twin Firs Loop	N46 44.062, W121 50.327	2	1	0.5	50

HIGH POINT	KID-FRIENDLY	WILDLIFE	HISTORIC	VIEWS	WATERFALLS	ENDANGERED	LAKE
6400	X	X	X		X		X
6800		X				X	
7006	X	X	X	X			
6400	X		X	X			
5849	X		X				
3200	X			X	X		X
5400			X	X	X	X	X
5296		X	X			X	
5834			X	X			
4880					X		
1900	X		X				
2100	X			X	X		
2200	X						
3900		X					
3400	X	X					
5914			X	X	X		
3750				X	X		
4679			X		X		X
4880	X				X		X
5210	X		X		X		
6000			X				
5478		X	X	X			X
5485			X	X			X
5450			X	X			
5600			X	X		X	
2550	X						

ROUTE NAME	TRAILHEAD WAYPOINT	RATING	DIFFICULTY	MILES	ELEV. GAIN
55. Eagle Peak	N46 44.909, W121 48.468	3	4	7	2950
56. Trail of the Shadows	N46 44.980, W121 48.639	2	1	1	20
57. Rampart Ridge Loop	N46 44.980, W121 48.639	3	3	4.5	1300
58. Pyramid Creek Camp	N46 44.980, W121 48.639	2	3	6.6	1060
59. Indian Henrys Hunting Ground	N46 44.980, W121 48.639	5	5	12.6	2500
60. Carter Falls	N46 44.980, W121 48.639	3	2	7.2	9000
61. Comet Falls	N46 46.742, W121 46.938	4	4	5	1200
62. Van Trump Park	N46 46.742, W121 46.938	5	5	7	2300
PARADISE					
63. Narada Falls to Reflection Lakes	N46 46.516, W121 44.793	2	3	3	500
64. Nisqually Vista Loop	N46 47.088, W121 44.487	3	1	1.4	200
65. Alta Vista Loop	N46 47.162, W121 44.099	3	1	1.5	540
66. Golden Gate	N46 47.162, W121 44.099	4	3	3.2	1000
67. Mazama Ridge	N46 47.162, W121 44.099	4	3	7	600
68. Skyline Trail Loop	N46 47.162, W121 44.099	4	4	6	1400
69. Glacier Vista–Panorama Point	N46 47.162, W121 44.099	4	3	5	1300
70. Camp Muir	N46 47.162, W121 44.099	5	5	10	4600

HIGH POINT	KID-FRIENDLY	WILDLIFE	HISTORIC	VIEWS	WATERFALLS	ENDANGERED	LAKE
5650				X		X	
2770	X	X	X				
4080				X			
3860			X				
5300		X	X	X			X
3650	X				X		
4875					X		
5900		X		X	X		
4900					X		X
5400	X			X			X
5940					X		
6400				X	X		
5850	X	X		X	X		X
6800			X	X	X		
6700				X			
10,000				X			

Introduction

Mount Rainier stands as the most recognizable feature in Washington's diverse landscape. At 14,411 feet, this mighty mountain towers nearly 8000 feet over its neighboring peaks, which makes it visible from nearly every corner of the state. The mountain has been a standard feature of Washington's history well before it was "discovered" by Captain George Vancouver. Native tribes on both sides of the Cascades, as well as those living far south in present-day Oregon, included the mountain in their stories and legends.

But though the mountain's presence has been a constant throughout human history in the region, that presence has also been an ever-changing one. Mighty Mount Rainier is, after all, an active volcano and, more importantly (on a human scale, at least), it's an imposing geologic feature whose sheer size and prominence not only attracts strong weather systems but also helps create wild weather. This is important for recreationists to keep in mind. Despite what your schoolteachers may have taught, geologic change isn't so much a matter of slow, steady change. Rather, it's like a war: long, boring periods of calm are broken by random moments of extreme activity, sheer chaos, and ruin.

The latest of these chaotic moments occurred during November 2006. Record rainfall and gale-force winds wreaked havoc on the environs of Mount Rainier National Park, changing the courses of rivers, toppling acres of trees, moving mountains of mud, and destroying a great deal of the man-made structures within the national park. Roads were washed out, bridges and footlogs swept away, trails blocked by windfalls, and even destroyed one entire campground—Sunrise Camp, which was swept away by the raging Nisqually River. Even as this book is being completed, we still don't know when all the extensive damage done by those early winter storms will be repaired. We do know most trails are open, though sections may be very rough for the next few years.

Still, hikers should understand that trails aren't static features on the ground. Time and weather do bring changes—sometimes quickly and dramatically. By understanding that, and accepting route changes and obstacles as they come, hikers can rest assured that their trail adventures will be outstanding in this wonderful wild country.

Mount Rainier National Park offers some of the most spectacular and diverse backcountry found in this nation. Wilderness enthusiasts from Bob Marshall to John Muir have praised the beauty and unique splendor of the park's meadows, forests, and glacier basins. Muir called Rainier's array of wildflower meadows the most superb subalpine gardens he had ever encountered. The park sports vast fields of flower parklands, from the broad, sloping fields of Spray Park to the gaudy colors that fill the cirque of Indian Bar Camp, to the huge, flat, mountaintop meadow of Grand Park. In addition to the meadows, there are more than one hundred waterfalls within the park (some estimates run as high as 162 falls)—fifty-two of which are prominent enough to warrant names. You'll also find nearly three hundred lakes and more than one hundred named peaks within the park. Finally, the park has one of the world's largest glacier systems

Opposite: Dennis crosses the Ohanapecosh River suspension bridge to access the Grove of the Patriarchs—the same bridge that was severely damaged in the November 2006 floods.

found on a single peak. About 9 percent of the total park surface is covered in glacial ice. There are twenty-seven individual glaciers and fifty permanent snowfields within the park. All told, snow and ice permanently covers more than 22,000 acres of land.

In short, Mount Rainier National Park offers more than grand views of the mighty mountain. Many of the hikes you'll find in this book provide few, or no, views of the big mountain itself, yet all offer incredible scenery and wonderful wilderness exploration.

THE MOUNTAIN'S HISTORY

Before it was Rainier, this grand mountain was known to local tribes as Tahoma (or one of many variations of this name), which reportedly means "breast of milk-white waters" or perhaps simply "great white mountain."

This latter meaning seems most likely, since it was also a description used independently by early European explorers. Indeed, the first account of the mountain, by Captain George Vancouver, describes Rainier as "the round snowy mountain..." The mountain was formally "discovered" by Vancouver while his ship lay at anchor near what is now Port Townsend. From his ship's deck, he sighted the big, snowcapped peak on the southeastern horizon. On May 8, 1792, Vancouver wrote in his journal entry about the sighting:

> *"The weather was serene and pleasant, and the country continued to exhibit, between us and the eastern snowy range, the same luxuriant appearance. At its northern extremity, Mount Baker bore by the compass N22°E; the round snowy mountain, now forming its southern extremity and which, after my friend Rear Admiral Rainier, I distinguish by the name of Mount Rainier, bore N(S)42°E."*

Since that first written description, Mount Rainier has captured the hearts of men and women who ventured out to the wild Washington Territory. In 1849 the United States established Fort Steilacoom near present-day Tacoma, to help protect settlers against Indians who fought the loss of their lands. Following the Indian War of 1855, areas beyond the Puget Sound lowlands were open for greater exploration. In 1857 a young lieutenant from Fort Steilacoom decided to try for the summit of the mountain that dominated the eastern skyline. Lt. A. V. Kautz set out with an army surgeon from Fort Bellingham, four soldiers, and a Nisqually Indian guide. The Kautz party failed in its summit bid but did get farther up the mountain than any other American party. Kautz Creek along the southwestern side of the mountain still bears the lieutenant's name.

The next recorded summit attempt occurred thirteen years later. This time, Hazard Stevens and P. B. Van Trump successfully summitted on August 17, 1870. James Longmire served as a pack master on that trip, helping get Stevens and Van Trump to the base of the mountain. Another thirteen years would pass before Longmire himself summitted in 1883, with Van Trump, and on their return from the top, they discovered the meadows and hot springs of what is now the Longmire area .

Longmire returned to the area and established a hotel and spa at the hot springs, launching the tourism business that grew around the southwest corner of the mountain. As more and more people discovered the splendor of this remarkable mountain, the move to preserve the mountain was born.

In 1893 President Benjamin Harrison created the Pacific Forest Reserve, which included much of what is now Mount Rainier National Park and the adjacent national forestland. Four years later, Present Grover Cleveland signed an order changing the name to the Mount Rainier Forest Preserve, and on March 2, 1899, President William McKinley signed into law the establishment of Mount Rainier National Park—just the fifth national park in the United States. (The other four were Yellowstone National Park, 1872; Sequoia National Park, 1890; General Grant National Park, 1890; and Yosemite National Park, 1890. In 1940 General Grant National Park was incorporated into Kings Canyon National Park.)

As a national park, Mount Rainier received a great deal of attention. Roads were built to help guide visitors to some of the most remarkable portions of the park. In the 1930s, the Civilian Conservation Corp (CCC) began their efforts, and much of their work still stands today. Indeed, Mount Rainier National Park holds one of the great collections of intact and still functioning CCC projects in the country. The CCC built things, from lodges to trails, to last. Many of the rock walls lining the road to Paradise were made by CCCers—the intricate rock work is best viewed at the Narada Falls parking area.

Not all the developments were beneficial, though. Through the 1920s, '30s, and '40s, the Paradise area was overrun by tourists. The beautiful meadows were buried every summer under cities of tents. There was even a golf course set up in the meadows. Those campsites, putting greens, and car parks were all removed in later years, fortunately, and the glorious meadows were restored to their native beauty. Similar overdevelopment and subsequent return to nature occurred in the Sunrise area—though the golf course there was much smaller!

Today, some park visitors bemoan the "overdevelopment" of the backcountry. The lower trails near Paradise are paved, and other trails are generally broad and well maintained. Backpackers are restricted, for the most part, to established backcountry campsites. But the country is still wild, the trails can still be rough and even treacherous, and the scenery is as spectacular as it was when Vancouver first sighted the big mountain more than two hundred years ago.

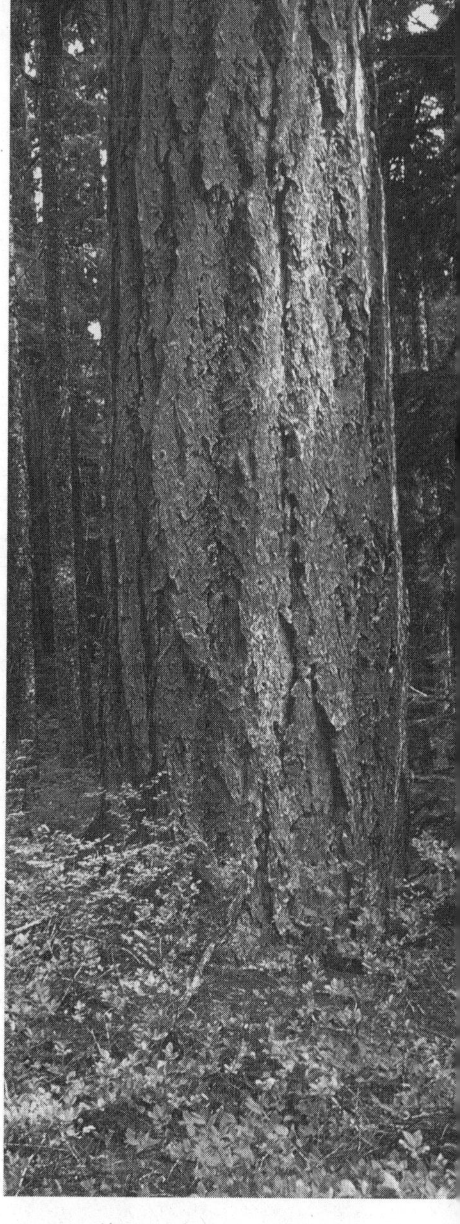

Douglas fir along the trail above Chinook Creek on the way to Owyhigh Lakes

USING THIS BOOK

These Day Hiking guidebooks strike a fine balance. They were developed to be as easy to use as possible while still providing enough detail to help you explore a region. As a result, these guidebooks include all the information you need to find and enjoy the hikes, but they leave enough room for you to make your own discoveries as you venture into areas new to you.

What the Ratings Mean

Every trail described in this book features a detailed "trails facts" section. Not all of the details here are facts, however.

Each hike starts with two subjective ratings: each has an overall **rating** of one to five stars for its overall appeal, and each route's **difficulty** is rated on a scale of 1 to 5. This is subjective, based on the author's impressions of each route, but the ratings do follow a formula of sorts. The overall rating is based on scenic beauty, natural wonder, and other unique qualities, such as solitude potential and wildlife-viewing opportunities.

- ***** Unmatched hiking adventure; great scenic beauty and wonderful trail experience!
- **** Excellent experience sure to please all.
- *** A great hike, with one or more fabulous features to enjoy.
- ** May lack the "killer view" features but offers lots of little moments to enjoy.
- * Worth doing as a refreshing wild-country walk, especially if you are in the vicinity.

The difficulty rating is based on trail length, the steepness of the trail, and how strenuous it is to hike. Generally, trails that are rated more difficult (4 or 5) are longer and steeper than average. But it's not a simple equation. A short, steep trail over talus slopes may be rated 5, whereas a long, smooth trail with little elevation gain may be rated 2.

- 5 Extremely difficult: Excessive elevation gain, and/or more than 6 miles one-way, and/or bushwhacking required.
- 4 Difficult: Some steep sections, possibly rough trail or poorly maintained trail.

Always check for flood damage: the Carbon River Road in December 2006.

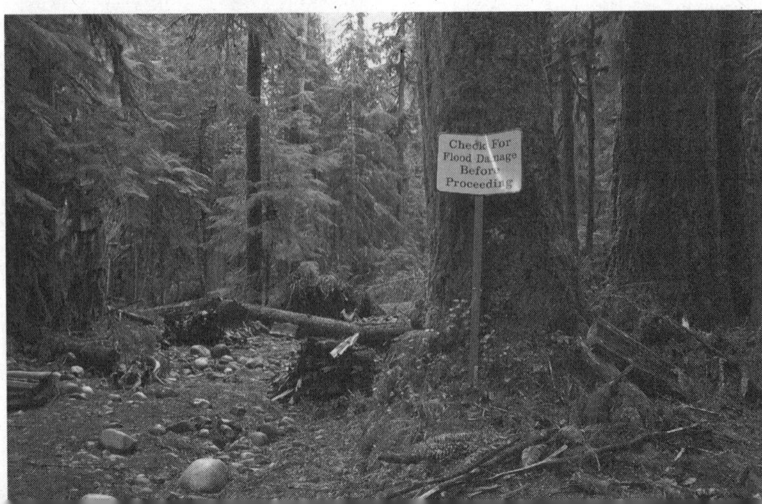

3 Moderate: A good workout, but no real problems.
2 Moderately easy: Relatively flat or short, with good trail.
1 Easy: A relaxing stroll in the woods.

To help explain how those difficulty ratings were arrived at, you'll also find the following information:

Round-trip mileage: The distances given are not always exact mileages (round-trip unless otherwise noted as one-way)—trails weren't measured with calibrated instruments—but the mileages are those used by cartographers and land managers (who have measured many of the trails).

Elevation gain: The elevation gains report the cumulative difference between the high and low points on the route—in other words, the total amount you will go up on a hike (given in feet).

High point: It's worth noting that not all high points (also given in feet) are at the end of a trail—a route may run over a high ridge before dropping to a lake basin, for instance.

Season: Many trails can be enjoyed from the time they lose their winter snowpack right up until they are buried in fresh snow the following fall. But snowpacks vary from year to year, so a trail that is open in May one year may be snow-covered until mid-July the next. The hiking season for each trail is an estimate, but before you venture out, it's worth contacting the land manager to get current conditions.

Profiles: Each hike's relative elevation changes are shown in feet over the hike's mileage—usually one-way.

Maps: The maps you'll want to have on your hike are listed next. Hikes in this guidebook typically reference Green Trails maps, which are based on the standard 7.5-minute U.S. Geological Survey topographical maps. Green Trails maps are available at most outdoor retailers in the state, as well as at many National Park Service and U.S. Forest Service visitor centers.

Contact: Here you'll find phone and web information for each trail's governing agency so you can get current trail conditions.

Notes: Next are quick notes, in some cases, that might be pertinent to your planning, such as annual road closures or trail restrictions.

GPS coordinates: For each trailhead, the GPS coordinates are provided—use this both to get to the trail and to help you get back to your car if you get caught out in a storm or wander off the trail.

Following these detailed "trail facts," the route descriptions themselves provide a basic overview of what you might find on your hike, directions to get you to the trailhead, and in some cases additional highlights beyond the actual trails you'll be exploring.

Icons and trail introduction: This is a quick overview of what each trail has to offer, including icons to help you quickly determine the following:

 kid-friendly

 dog-friendly (Note: This icon seldom appears in this book because dogs are prohibited on all trails within Mount Rainier National Park except on the Pacific Crest Trail.)

 wildlife viewing

 historic

 exceptional views

 views of waterfall(s)

 endangered trail

 saved trail

A world of glacial ice peeks through the clouds.

Getting there: Directions to the trailhead are from the nearest large town or geographic location or feature.

On the trail: Detailed descriptions of the hiking route tell you some of the things you might find along the way, including geographic features, scenic views, potential flora and fauna, and more.

Extending your trip: For those looking to go farther and do more than the recommended outing, details are provided on how to add miles or even days to the hike. You might also find brief descriptions of additional trail miles and/or camping options.

Of course, even with all of this, you'll need some information long before you ever leave home. So as you plan your trips, consider the following several issues.

PERMITS, REGULATIONS, AND PARK FEES

You can't set foot out your door these days without first making sure you're not breaking the rules. In an effort to keep our wilderness areas wild and our trails safe and well maintained, the land managers—especially the National Park Service and the U.S. Forest Service—have implemented a sometimes complex set of rules and regulations governing the use of public lands.

Within Mount Rainier National Park, the system is fairly simple. To enter the park at one of the main gateways (Nisqually Entrance, Stevens Canyon Entrance, White River Entrance, or Carbon River Entrance), you'll pay a vehicle entry fee of $15 for private noncommercial vehicles or $5 per visitor on foot, bicycle, or motorcycle. The fee provides access for seven days. Frequent visitors can opt instead for an annual pass for $30—this pass covers the entry fee for the pass holder, the pass holder's vehicle, and any passengers. Day hikers require no other permit, though backpackers will have to pick up a free wilderness camping permit from any of the park's ranger stations.

WEATHER

Mountain weather in general is famously unpredictable, but Mount Rainier's 8000-foot prominence over its neighboring peaks makes it a magnet for extreme weather. The big peak stretches up so far above the surrounding Cascades that it captures weather that streams over the top of the lesser mountains. As a result, Mount Rainer can host howling blizzards in July and torrential downpours in August. The mountain recently lost its standing as "snowiest place on earth" to Mount Baker to the north, but the mountain regularly records nearly 1000 inches of snow per year. (The record for annual snowfall is 1140 inches, set at Mount Baker during the winter of 1998–99. Prior to that year, Mount Rainier held the record, with 1122 inches.) One of the reasons for the big annual accumulations is the tendency for snow to fall periodically throughout the year. As I researched the routes for this book, I experienced snowfall during every month of the year. So prudent hikers must plan for extreme weather, even if they're heading out on just a short day hike. (See also "Mount Rainier: The Weather-Maker" in the Longmire section).

But unexpected rain and snow is just part of the story. During the summer months, when the warm air of the lower Cascades rises up and hits the cool, moist air surrounding the upper slopes of Rainier, thunderstorms can develop quickly. Hikers must be aware of this potential because thunderstorms can develop very quickly, with little warning, and a hiker stuck high on the mountain's flanks becomes a good target for a lightning bolt (see "All Lit Up" for how to avoid this).

ROAD AND TRAIL CONDITIONS

Trails in general change little year to year. Though they truly are man-made structures in rugged wilderness settings, trails are quite durable. But change can and does occur, and sometimes it occurs very quickly.

ALL LIT UP

The following are suggestions for reducing the dangers of lightning should thunderstorms be forecast or develop while you are in the mountains:

- Use a NOAA weather radio (a radio tuned in to one of the national weather forecast frequencies) to keep abreast of the latest weather information.
- Avoid travel on mountain tops and ridge crests.
- Stay well away from bodies of water.
- If your hair stands on end or you feel static shocks, move immediately—the static electricity you feel could very well be a precursor to a lightning strike.
- If there is a shelter or building nearby, get into it. Don't take shelter under trees, however, especially in open areas.
- If there is no shelter available and lightning is flashing, remove your pack (the metal stays or frame are natural conductors of electricity) and crouch down, balancing on the balls of your feet until the lightning clears the area.

One brutal storm can alter a river's course, washing out sections of trail in moments. Wind can drop trees across trails by the hundreds, making the paths unhikeable. And snow can obliterate trails well into the heart of summer.

Access roads face similar threats and, in fact, are more susceptible to washouts and closures than the trails themselves. For instance, the massive rains of November 2006 created unprecedented floods in the national park. Roads, trails, and even a campground washed away. The Carbon River Road and Cayuse Pass Highway (State Route 123) are especially prone to temporary closures due to flooding.

Because there really is no such thing as a flat trail in the Mount Rainier area, trails are susceptible to water damage, too. Trail treads erode, bridges and footlogs wash out, and windfall trees block routes after every large storm. Fortunately, repairs take place regularly, and for that we can thank the countless volunteers who donate tens of thousands of hours to trail maintenance each year. The Washington Trails Association (WTA) alone coordinates upward of 60,000 hours of volunteer trail maintenance each year in Washington State, and Mount Rainier National Park benefits from a good portion of that effort.

As massive as the volunteer efforts have become, there is always a need for more. Our wilderness trail system faces increasing threats, including (but by no means limited to) ever-shrinking trail funding, inappropriate trail uses, and conflicting land-management policies and practices.

With this in mind, this guide includes several trails that are threatened and in danger of becoming unhikeable. These "endangered trails" are marked with the special icon shown at the start of this paragraph.

On the other hand, we've also been blessed with some great trail successes in recent years, thanks in large part to that massive volunteer movement spearheaded by WTA. These "saved trails" are marked with the icon shown at the start of this paragraph. As you enjoy these saved trails, stop to consider the contributions made by your fellow hikers that helped protect our trail resources.

WILDERNESS ETHICS

As wonderful as volunteer trail maintenance programs are, they aren't the only way to help save our trails. Indeed, these on-the-ground efforts provide quality trails today, but to ensure the long-term survival of our trails—and the wildlands they cross—we all must embrace and practice sound wilderness ethics.

Strong, positive wilderness ethics include making sure you leave the wilderness as pure as or purer than it was when you found it. As the adage says, "Take only pictures, leave only footprints."

But sound wilderness ethics go deeper than that, beyond simply picking up after ourselves when we go for a hike. Wilderness ethics must carry over into our daily lives. We need to ensure that our elected officials and public land managers recognize and respond to our wilderness needs and desires. If we hike the trails on the weekend but let the wilderness go neglected—or, worse, allow it to be abused—on the weekdays, we'll soon find our weekend haunts diminished or destroyed.

TRAIL GIANTS

I want to add a personal note here. As I began my career as a guidebook author, I was blessed with the opportunity to learn from the men and women who helped launch the guidebook genre for The Mountaineers Books. Throughout the 1990s, I enjoyed many conversations with Ira Spring—we would talk for hours

Encroaching clear-cuts on the western national park boundary seen from the summit of Glacier View

about our favorite trails and how we needed to diligently fight for those trails. I exchanged frequent correspondence with Harvey Manning, debating the best means of saving wildlands. I was advised and mentored by Louise Marshall. I worked alongside Greg Ball—founder of the WTA's volunteer trail maintenance program—for more than a decade.

In short, I served my apprenticeship with masters of the trail trade. From them, and from my own experiences exploring the wonderful wildlands of Washington, I discovered the pressing need for individual activism. When hikers get complacent, trails suffer. We must, in the words of the legendary Ira Spring, "get people onto trails. They need to bond with the wilderness." This green bonding, as Ira called it, is essential in building public support for trails and trail funding.

As you get out and hike the trails described here, consider that many of these trails would have long ago ceased to exist without the phenomenal efforts of people such as Ira Spring, Harvey Manning, Louise Marshall, and Greg Ball, not to mention the scores of unnamed hikers who joined them in their push for wildland protection, trail funding, and strong environmental stewardship programs.

When you get home, bear in mind these people's actions and then sit down and write a letter to your congressperson asking for better trail funding. Call your local Forest Service office to say that you've enjoyed the trails in their jurisdiction and that you want these routes to remain wild and accessible for use by you and your children.

And if you're not already a member, consider joining an organization devoted to wilderness, backcountry trails, or other wild-country issues. Organizations including The Mountaineers Club, Washington Trails Association, Volunteers for Outdoor Washington, the Cascade chapter of the Sierra Club, Conservation Northwest, the Cascade Land Conservancy, and countless others (see the appendix at the back of this book) leverage individual contributions and efforts to help ensure the future of our trails and the wonderful wilderness legacy we've inherited.

TRAIL ETIQUETTE

Everyone who enjoys backcountry trails should recognize their responsibility to those trails and to other trail users. We each must work to preserve the tranquility of wildlands by being sensitive not only to the environment but to other trail users as well.

Share the Trails

The trails in this book are used by a very large number of hikers, as well as by other users, including climbers, trail runners, and horse riders (allowed only on some trails within the park). When you encounter other hikers and trail users, please follow the trail-tested rules of practicing common sense and exercising simple courtesy. It's hard to overstate just how vital these two things—common sense and courtesy—are to maintaining an enjoyable, safe, and friendly situation when different types of trail users meet. See "The Golden Rules of Trail Etiquette" for what you can do during trail encounters to make everyone's trip more enjoyable.

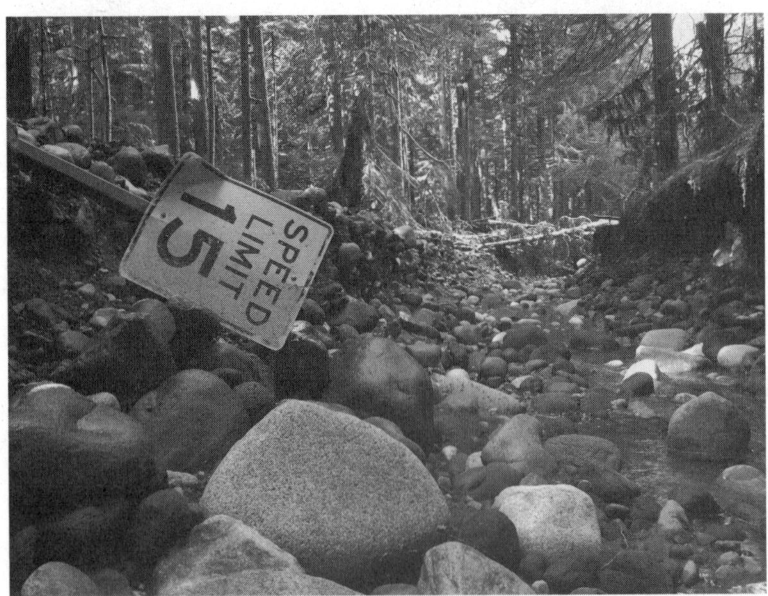

Where the road used to be: the Carbon River Road near Ipsut Creek Campground after the November 2006 floods

THE GOLDEN RULES OF TRAIL ETIQUETTE

Below are just a few of the things you can do to maintain a safe and harmonious trail environment. And while not every situation is addressed by these rules, you can avoid problems by always remembering that common sense and courtesy are in order.

- **Yield right-of-way.** When two or more hikers meet, the uphill hiker has the right-of-way. There are two general reasons for this. First, on steep ascents, hikers may be watching the trail and not notice the approach of descending hikers until they are face-to-face. More important, it is easier for descending hikers to break their stride and step off the trail than it is for those who have gotten into a good climbing rhythm. But by all means, if you are the uphill trekker and you wish to grant passage to oncoming hikers, go right ahead with this act of trail kindness.
- **Move off-trail when yielding.** When a hiker meets other user groups (such as bicyclists or horseback riders), the hiker should move off the trail. This is because hikers are more mobile and flexible than other users, making it easier for them to step off the trail.
- **Step downhill when encountering horses.** When a hiker meets horseback riders, the hiker should step off the downhill side of the trail, unless the terrain makes this difficult or dangerous. In that case, move to the uphill side of the trail, but crouch down a bit so you don't tower over the horses' heads. Also, make yourself visible so as not to spook the big beasties, and talk in a normal voice to the riders. This calms the horses. If you're hiking with a dog, keep your buddy under control.
- **Stay on trails** and practicing minimum impact. Don't cut switchbacks, take shortcuts, or make new trails. If your destination is off-trail, stick to snow and rock when possible so as not to damage fragile alpine meadows. Spread out when traveling off-trail; if you're hiking in a group, don't hike in a line, as this greatly increases the chance of compacting thin soils and crushing delicate plant environments.
- **Obey the rules** specific to the trail you are visiting. Many trails are closed to certain types of use, including hiking with dogs or riding horses.
- **Stay in control when hiking with dogs.** Hikers who take their dogs on the trails should have their dog on a leash or under very strict voice command at all times. **Note:** This Trail Etiquette rule is rendered moot in most of this book since dogs are prohibited on all trails within Mount Rainier National Park (as they are in all national parks).
- **Avoid disturbing wildlife,** especially in winter and in calving areas. Observe from a distance, resisting the urge to move closer to wildlife (use your telephoto lens). This not only keeps you safer, but it prevents the animal from having to exert itself unnecessarily to flee from you.
- **Take only photographs.** Leave all natural things, features, and historic artifacts as you found them, for others to enjoy.
- **Never roll rocks off trails or cliffs.** You risk endangering lives below you.

A female blue "sooty" grouse near Pinnacle Saddle

Pack It Out

Also part of trail etiquette is packing out everything you packed in, even biodegradable things such as apple cores. The phrase "leave only footprints, take only pictures" is a worthy slogan to live by when visiting the wilderness.

Practice Backcountry Bathroom Etiquette

Another important Leave No Trace principle focuses on the business of taking care of personal business. The first rule of backcountry bathroom etiquette says that if an outhouse exists, use it. This seems obvious, but all too often, folks find that backcountry toilets are dark, dank affairs and they choose to use the woods rather than the rickety wooden structure provided. It may be easier on your nose to head off into the woods, but this disperses human waste around popular areas. Privies, on the other hand, concentrate the waste and thus minimize contamination of area waters. The outhouses get even higher environmental marks if they feature removable holding tanks that can be air-lifted out. These johns and their accompanying stacks of tanks aren't exactly aesthetically pleasing, but having an ugly outhouse tucked into a corner of the woods is better than finding toilet paper (or worse) strewn about.

When privies aren't provided, the key factor to consider is location. You'll want to choose a site at least 200 to 300 feet from water, campsites, and trails. A location well out of sight of trails and viewpoints will give you privacy and reduce the odds of other hikers stumbling onto the site after you leave. Other factors to consider are ecological: surrounding vegetation and some direct sunlight will aid decomposition.

Once you pick your place, start digging. The idea is to make like a cat and bury your waste. You need to dig down through the organic duff into the mineral soil below—a hole 6 to 8 inches deep is usually adequate. When you've taken care of business, refill the hole and camouflage it with rocks and sticks—this helps prevent other humans, or animals, from digging in the same location before decomposition has done its job. And pack out your used toilet paper—don't bury it.

Cleanup

When washing your hands, first rinse off as much dust and dirt as you can in just plain water. If you still feel the need for a soapy wash, collect a pot of water from a lake or stream and move at least 100 feet away. Apply a tiny bit of biodegradable soap to your hands, dribble on a little water, and lather up. Use a bandanna or towel to wipe away most of the soap, and then rinse with the water in the pot. Be sure to discard any wash water at least 100 feet away from natural water sources.

WATER

You'll want to treat your drinking water in the backcountry. Wherever humans have gone, germs have gone with them—and humans have gone just about everywhere. That means that even the most pristine mountain stream may harbor microscopic nasties such as *Giardia* cysts, *Cryptosporidium*, or *E. coli.*

Treating water can be as simple as boiling it, chemically purifying it (adding tiny iodine tablets), or pumping it through one of the new-generation water filter or purifiers. (**Note:** Pump units labeled as filters generally remove everything but viruses, which are too small to be filtered out. Pumps labeled as purifiers use a chemical element—usually iodine—to render viruses inactive after all the other bugs are filtered out.) Never drink untreated water, or your intestines will never forgive you.

WILDLIFE

Bears

There are an estimated 30,000 to 35,000 black bears in Washington, and the big bruins can be found in every corner of the state. The central and southern Cascades are especially attractive to the solitude-seeking bears. Watching bears graze through a rich huckleberry field or seeing them flip dead logs in search of grubs can be an exciting and rewarding experience—provided, of course, that you aren't in the same berry patch.

Bears tend to prefer solitude to human company and will generally flee long before you have a chance to get too close (see "Bear in Mind"). There are times, however, when bears either don't hear hikers approaching or they are more interested in defending their food source—or their young—than they are in avoiding a confrontation. These instances are rare, and there are things you can do to minimize the odds of an encounter with an aggressive bear (see "The Bear Essentials").

Cougars

Very few hikers ever see a cougar in the wild. Not only are these big cats some of the most solitary, shyest animals in the woods, but there are just 2500 to 3000 of them roaming the entire state of Washington. Still, cougars and hikers do sometimes encounter each other (see "This Is Cougar Country"). In these cases, hikers should, in my opinion, count their blessings—they will likely never see a more majestic animal than a wild cougar.

To make sure the encounter is a positive one, hikers must understand the cats. Cougars are shy but very curious. They will follow hikers simply to see what kind of beasts we are, but they very rarely (as in, almost never) attack adult humans. See "Cool Cats" for how to make the most of your luck.

GEAR

No hiker should venture far up a trail without being properly equipped, starting with the feet. A good pair of boots can make the difference between a wonderful hike and a horrible death march. Keep your feet happy, and you'll be happy.

BEAR IN MIND

Here are some suggestions for helping to avoid running into an aggressive bear:

- Hike in a group and only during daylight hours.
- Talk or sing as you hike. If a bear hears you coming, it will usually avoid you. When surprised, however, a bear may feel threatened. So make noises that will identify you as a human—talk, sing, rattle pebbles in a tin can—especially when hiking near a river or stream (which can mask more subtle sounds that might normally alert a bear to your presence).
- Be aware of the environment around you, and know how to identify bear sign. Overturned rocks and torn-up deadwood logs often are the result of a bear searching for grubs. Berry bushes stripped of berries—with leaves, branches, and berries littering the ground under the bushes—show where a bear has fed. Bears will often leave claw marks on trees, and since they use trees as scratching posts, fur in the rough bark of a tree is a sign that says "a bear was here!" Tracks and scat are the most common signs of a bear's recent presence.
- Stay away from abundant food sources and dead animals. Black bears are opportunistic and will scavenge food. A bear that finds a dead deer will hang around until the meat is gone, and it will defend that food against any perceived threat.
- Keep dogs leashed and under control. Many bear encounters have resulted from unleashed dogs chasing a bear: The bear gets angry and turns on the dog. The dog gets scared and runs for help (back to its owner). And the bear follows right back into the dog owner's lap.
- Leave scented items at home—perfume, hair spray, cologne, and scented soaps. Using scented sprays and body lotions makes you smell like a big, tasty treat.
- **Clean fish away from camp.** Never clean fish within 100 feet of camp.

But you can't talk about boots without talking about socks. There's only one rule here: wear whatever is most comfortable, unless it's cotton. The corollary to that rule is this: never wear cotton.

Cotton is a wonderful fabric when your life isn't on the line—it's soft, light, and airy. But get it wet, and it stays wet. That means blisters on your feet. Wet cotton also lacks any insulation value. In fact, get it wet, and it sucks away your body heat, leaving you susceptible to hypothermia. So leave your cotton socks, cotton underwear, and even the cotton T-shirts at home. The only cotton I carry on the trail is my trusty pink bandanna (pink because nobody else I know carries pink, so I always know which is mine).

While the list of what to pack varies from hiker to hiker, there are a few things each and every one of us should have in our packs. For instance, every hiker who ventures more than a few hundred yards away from the road should be prepared to spend the night under the stars (or under the clouds, as may be more likely)—just in case. Mountain storms can whip up in a hurry, catching sunny-day hikers by surprise. What was an easy-to-follow trail during a calm, clear day can disappear into a confusing world of fog and rain—or even snow—in a windy tempest. Therefore, every member of the party should pack the Ten Essentials, as well as a few other items that aren't necessarily essential but would be good to have on hand in an emergency. (Also see "Day Hiker's Checklist.")

The Ten Essentials

1. **Navigation (map and compass):** Carry a topographic map of the area you plan to be in, and know how to read it. Likewise, carry a compass—and again, make sure you know how to use it.
2. **Sun protection (sunglasses and sunscreen):** In addition to sunglasses and sunscreen (SPF 15 or better), take along physical sun barriers such as a wide-brimmed hat, a long-sleeved shirt, and long pants.
3. **Insulation (extra clothing):** This means you should have more clothing with you than you would wear during the worst weather of the planned outing. If you get injured or lost, you won't be moving around and generating heat, so you'll need to be able to bundle up.
4. **Illumination (flashlight or headlamp):** If you're caught after dark, you'll need a headlamp or flashlight to be able to follow the trail. If you're forced to spend the night outdoors, you'll need it to set up an emergency camp, gather wood, and so on. Carry extra batteries and a spare bulb too.
5. **First-aid supplies:** Nothing elaborate is needed—especially if you're unsure how to use less familiar items. Make sure you have adhesive bandages, gauze bandages, some aspirin, and so on, and carry any personal medications you need in case you get caught out longer than expected. At minimum, a Red Cross first-aid training course is recommended. Better still, sign up for a Mountaineering Oriented First Aid course (MOFA) if you'll be spending a lot of time in the woods.
6. **Fire (firestarter and matches):** An emergency campfire provides warmth, but it also has a calming effect on most people. Without one, the night can be cold, dark, and intimidating. With one,

Lupine leaf munchies for a hoary marmot near the Golden Gate trail

the night is held at arm's length. A candle or tube of firestarting ribbon is essential for starting a fire with wet wood. And of course matches are an important part of this essential. You can't start a fire without them. Pack them in a waterproof container and/or buy the waterproof-windproof variety. Book matches are useless in wind or wet weather, and disposable lighters can be unreliable.

7. **Repair kit and tools (including a knife):** A pocketknife is helpful; a multitool is better. You never know when you might need a small pair of pliers or scissors, both of which are commonly found on compact multitools. A basic repair kit includes such things as a 20-foot length of nylon cord, a small roll of duct tape, some 1-inch webbing and extra webbing buckles (to fix broken pack straps), and a small tube of superglue.
8. **Nutrition (extra food):** Pack enough snacks so that you'll have leftovers after an uneventful trip—those leftovers will keep you fed and fueled during an emergency.
9. **Hydration (extra water):** Figure what you'll drink between water sources, and then add an extra liter. If you plan on relying on wilderness water sources, be sure to include some method of purification, whether a chemical additive, such as iodine, or a filtration device.
10. **Emergency shelter:** This can be as simple as a few extra-large garbage bags or something more efficient, such as a reflective space blanket or tube tent.

TRAILHEAD CONCERNS

Sadly, the topic of trailhead and trail crime must be addressed. As urban areas continuously encroach upon our green spaces, societal ills follow along.

But by and large, our hiking trails are safe places—far safer than most city streets. Common sense and vigilance, however, are still in order. This is true for all hikers, but particularly so for solo hikers.

Be aware of your surroundings at all times. Leave your itinerary with someone back home. If something doesn't feel right, it probably isn't. Take action by leaving the place or situation immediately. But remember, most hikers are friendly, decent people. Some may be a little introverted, but that's no cause for worry.

COOL CATS

If you encounter a cougar, remember that these animals rely on prey that can't, or won't, fight back. So as soon as you see the cat, take the following precautions:

- **Do not run!** Running may trigger a cougar's attack instinct.
- Stand up and face it. Virtually every recorded cougar attack on humans has been a predator-prey attack. If you appear as another aggressive predator rather than as prey, the cougar will likely back down.
- Try to appear large. Wave your arms or a jacket over your head.
- Pick up children and small dogs. They're more likely to be attacked than a large adult, since the cougar will identify them as easier prey.
- Maintain eye contact with the animal. The cougar will interpret this as a show of dominance on your part.
- Back away slowly if you can safely do so. Don't turn your back on a cougar!

Where the road used to be: now a finger of the Carbon River flows in the old roadbed of the Carbon River Road.

By far your biggest concern should be with trailhead theft. Car break-ins are a far too common occurrence at some of our trailheads. Do not—absolutely under any circumstances—leave anything of value in your vehicle while out hiking. Take your wallet, cell phone, and listening devices with you, or better yet, don't bring them along in the first place. Don't leave anything in your car that may appear valuable. A duffle bag on the backseat may contain only dirty T-shirts, but a thief may think there's a laptop in it. If you do leave a duffle of clothes in the car, unzip it so prowlers can see that it does indeed have just clothes inside. Save yourself the hassle of returning to a busted window by not giving criminals a reason to clout your car.

If you arrive at a trailhead and someone looks suspicious, don't discount your intuition. Take notes on the person and his or her vehicle. Record the license plate and report the behavior to the authorities. Don't confront the person. Leave and go to another trail.

Although most car break-ins are crimes of opportunity, organized bands intent on stealing personal identification have also been known to target parked cars at trailheads. While some trailheads are regularly targeted and others rarely, if at all, there's no sure way of preventing this from happening to you other than being dropped off at the trailhead or taking the bus (rarely is either an option). But you can make your car less of a target by not leaving anything of value in it.

ENJOY THE TRAILS

Above all else, I hope you can safely enjoy the trails in this book. These trails exist for our enjoyment and for the enjoyment of future generations. We can use them and protect them at the same time if we are careful with our actions and forthright with our demands on Con-

DAY HIKER'S CHECKLIST

ALWAYS CARRY THE TEN ESSENTIALS

- See the list in the *Introduction*.

THE BASICS

- Day pack (just big enough to carry all your gear)

CLOTHING

- Polyester or nylon shorts or pants
- Short-sleeved shirt
- Long-sleeved shirt
- Wicking long underwear
- Non-cotton underwear
- Bandanna

OUTERWEAR

- Warm pants (fleece or microfleece)
- Fleece jacket or wool sweater
- Raingear
- Wide-brimmed hat (for sun or rain)
- Fleece or stocking hat (for warmth)
- Gloves (fleece or wool and shell)

FOOTWEAR

- Hiking boots
- Hiking socks (not cotton!). Carry one extra pair. When your feet are soaked with sweat, change into the clean pair, then rinse out the dirty pair and hang them on the back of your pack to dry. Repeat as often as necessary during the hike.
- Liner socks
- Extra laces
- Gaiters
- Moleskin (for prevention of blisters) and Second Skin (for treatment of blisters). Carry both in your first-aid kit.

OPTIONAL GEAR

- Camera
- Binoculars
- Reading material
- Fishing equipment
- Field guides (for nature study)
- Head net or mosquito net suit

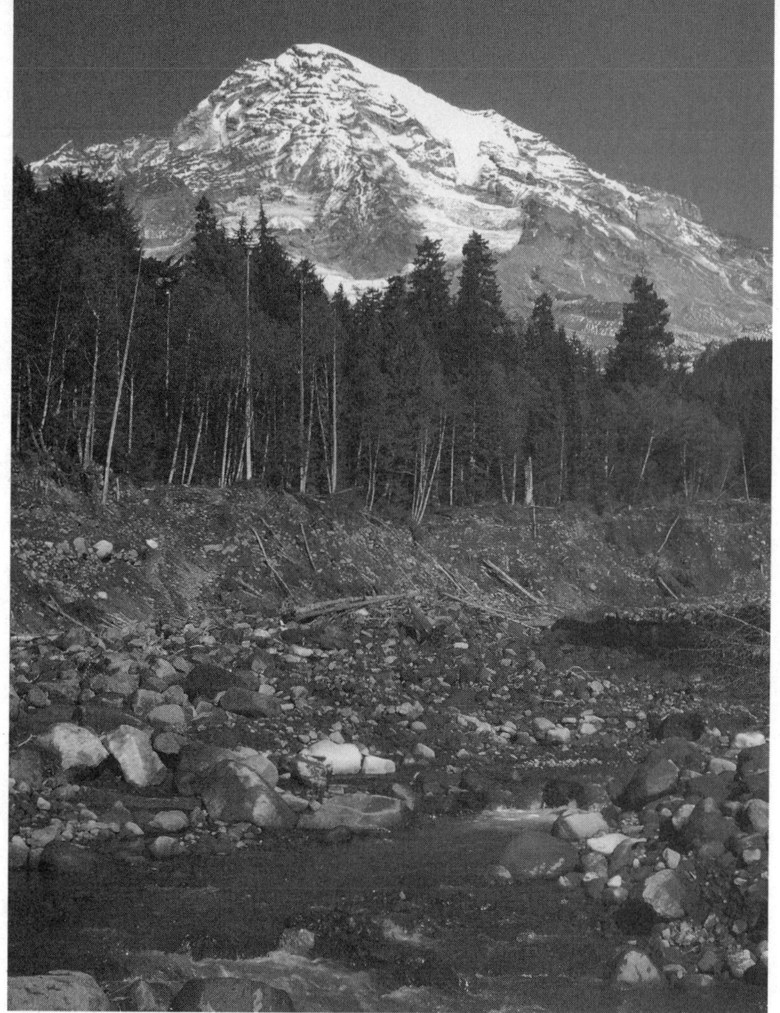

Kautz Creek and Mount Rainier seen as you cross the wide bed of Kautz Creek hiking toward Pyramid Creek Camp

gress to continue and further the protection of our country's wildlands.

Throughout the twentieth century, wilderness lovers helped secure protection for the lands we enjoy today. As we enter the twenty-first century, we must see to it that those protections continue and that the last bits of wildlands are also preserved for the enjoyment of future generations.

Please, if you enjoy these trails, get involved. Something as simple as writing a letter to Congress can make a big difference.

A NOTE ABOUT SAFETY

Safety is an important concern in all outdoor activities. No guidebook can alert you to every hazard or anticipate the limitations of every reader. Therefore, the descriptions of roads, trails, routes, and natural features in this book are not representations that a particular place or excursion will be safe for your party. When you follow any of the routes described in this book, you assume responsibility for your own safety. Under normal conditions, such excursions require the usual attention to traffic, road and trail conditions, weather, terrain, the capabilities of your party, and other factors. Keeping informed on current conditions and exercising common sense are the keys to a safe, enjoyable outing.

The Mountaineers Books

Opposite: Old mossy footbridge along the Carbon Rainforest Loop trail

carbon river and mowich lake

Though the northwest corner of Mount Rainier National Park boasts a rich history of human development and exploitation, it also offers the most remote and pristine wilderness experience in the park. Throughout the early twentieth century, miners poked and prodded the hills of the upper Carbon and Mowich river basins, searching for everything from gold to coal. But though the miners certainly left a mark, nature is quick to reclaim its own, and most of those early developments have nearly disappeared. Forests covered cabins, rivers washed away old mine sites, and roads eroded back into the hillsides. Today, this region offers hikers long walks on quiet trails. The best chance for solitude in the park can be found here, on the remote trails high above the Carbon River or beyond the shores of Mowich Lake. This is also one of the best places to encounter shy wildlife. Black bears frequent the berry-rich meadows, and mountain goats scamper through the rocky slopes above the subalpine fields.

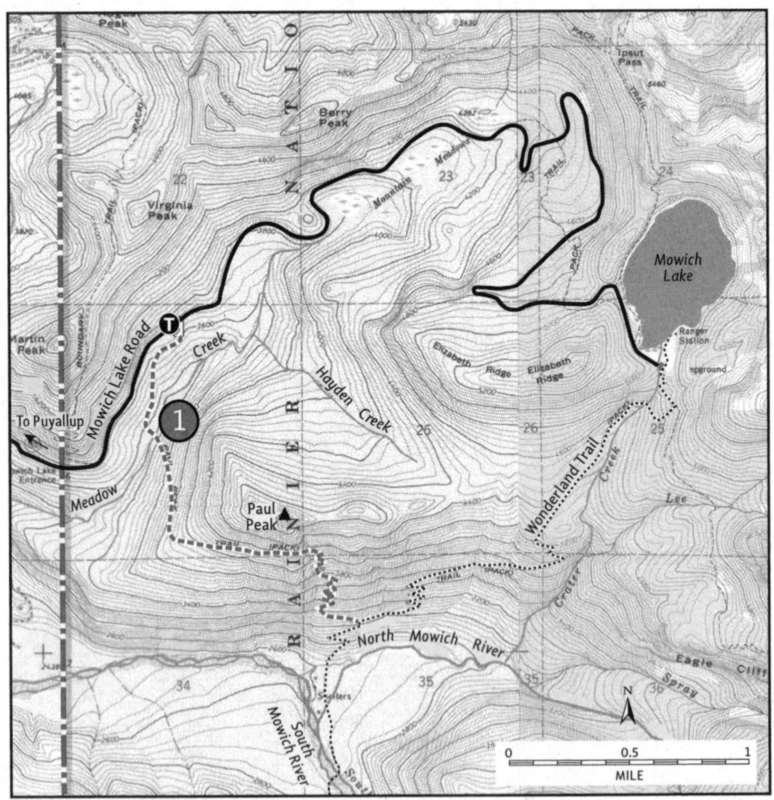

1 Paul Peak

RATING/ DIFFICULTY	ROUND-TRIP	ELEV GAIN/ HIGH POINT	SEASON
**/2	5.6 miles	1050 feet/ 4200 feet	May–Nov

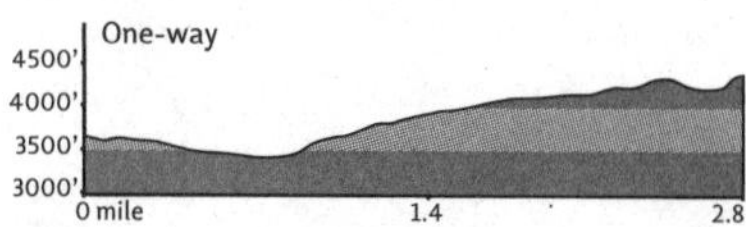

Maps: Green Trails Mount Rainier West, No. 269; **Contact:** Carbon River Ranger Station, (360) 829-9639; **GPS:** N46 56.097, W121 54.409

Although this trail is within Mount Rainier National Park, limited views of the big mountain are found on this route. In fact, there are few sweeping panoramic views. Fortunately, the forest is a wonderful example of mixed old-growth, with cedar, Douglas fir, hemlock, and a few bigleaf-maples tossed in for good measure. Camp-robber jays, ptarmigans, grouse, hares, red foxes, coyotes, and cougars patrol the area. Best of all, this trail—one of the easiest to reach in the northwest corner of the park—is one of the most lightly used. As a result, hikers can frequently find peaceful solitude on this often-overlooked trail. Walk quietly, and you might encounter some of the beings that do share the trail with you: small birds and other beasts of the forest.

GETTING THERE

From Puyallup, drive 13 miles east on State Route 410 to Buckley. Turn right (south) onto SR 165 and proceed through Carbonado. Just beyond the Carbon River Gorge bridge, bear right onto Mowich Lake Road. Follow the road about 11 miles to the park boundary. Just 0.5 mile inside the signed boundary, find the trailhead on the right.

Golden-crowned sparrow on the tip of an alpine fir

ON THE TRAIL

The trail begins with a gradual drop of a couple hundred feet in the first 0.5 mile before the trail crosses the beautiful Meadow Creek at 3450 feet. The bridge over the creek often is visited by small birds that use it as a perch as they flit around the creek, searching for insects to eat. Pause for a moment of quiet reflection at the creekside, and you might hear the twitter of the birds or possibly even see them dipping for aquatic bugs.

The trail stays fairly level from the creek crossing, following the hillside south another 0.5 mile before curving east along the flank of Paul Peak. As you cross a broad area of blown-down timber on the steep slope, you'll find a grand view of Mount Rainier as well as a sweeping panorama

Opening in the forest along the Paul Peak trail down at the South Mowich River

of the South Mowich River drainage. At 2.8 miles (3500 feet), the trail joins the Wonderland Trail. Your best bet for a modest, quiet outing is to turn around here and return the way you came.

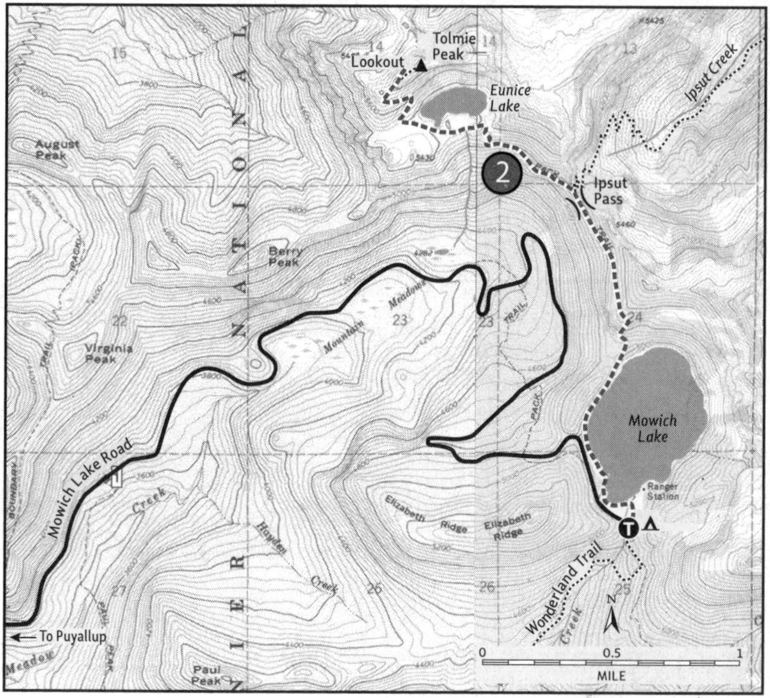

EXTENDING YOUR TRIP

If you turn right on the Wonderland Trail, you'll drop into a long set of switchbacks down to the Mowich River in less than 0.5 mile, at about the point where the North and South forks merge. If you turn left onto the Wonderland Trail, you can hike another 3 miles through this wonderful forest before reaching Mowich Lake (Hike 4)—a good option if you can arrange a ride there.

2 Tolmie Peak Lookout

RATING/ DIFFICULTY	ROUND-TRIP	ELEV GAIN/ HIGH POINT	SEASON
****/3	7.5 miles	1100 feet/ 5900 feet	June–Sept

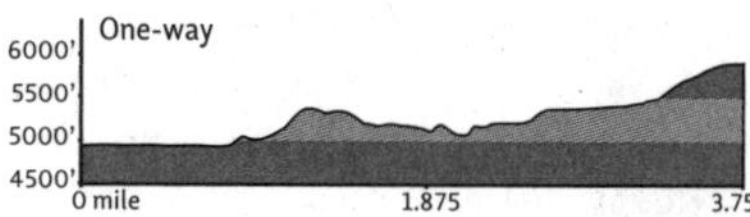

Maps: Green Trails Mount Rainier West, No. 269; **Contact:** Carbon River Ranger Station, (360) 829-9639; **GPS:** N46 55.962, W121 51.817

Cirrus clouds over Mount Rainier seen from Tolmie Peak

Bring the kids for this one so they can join everyone else's kids in trooping up to see grand views at a lovely alpine lake, with none of those raspy-looking backpacker types fouling the air along the trail. Tolmie Peak is a day-hiker's special. It's about the right distance, offers the right touch of outdoor magic at its destination, and has been ruled off-limits to overnighters.

GETTING THERE

From Puyallup, drive 13 miles east on State Route 410 to Buckley. Turn right (south) onto SR 165 and proceed through Carbonado. Just beyond the Carbon River Gorge bridge, bear right onto Mowich Lake Road. Follow the road about 17 miles to its end and find the trailhead on the left (north) side of the road, near Mowich Lake.

ON THE TRAIL

The trail meanders about 1.75 miles to Ipsut Pass (elevation 5100 feet), where more ambitious hikers can continue north along Ipsut Creek to the Carbon River (Hike 11) and the Wonderland Trail.

Stay left and walk just 0.8 mile to Eunice Lake, which offers grand views of Tolmie Peak and its lookout tower, not to mention a little molehill to the east known as Tahoma. Cinch down your knapsack and head on up the trail, climbing steeply another mile to Tolmie Peak, where the panorama is worth every one of the painful steps it took to get here. An old fire lookout cabin still stands atop the ridge knoll west of the true summit of Tolmie Peak. These high, lonesome watch stations have been replaced by satellites and computers, but at times you might still find a volunteer at the lookout cabin. If so, take the time to check out the historic old work room.

3 Spray Park

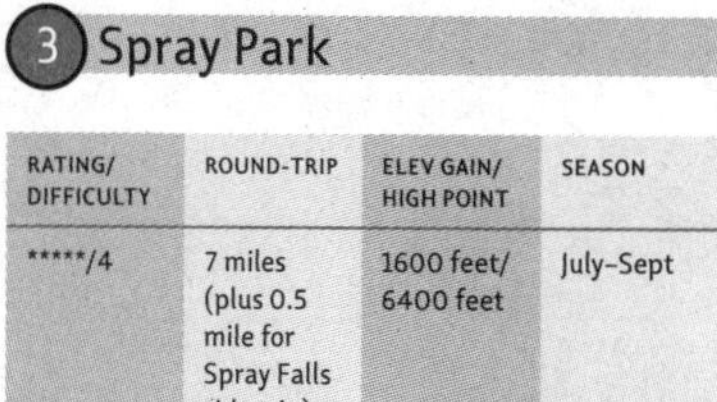

RATING/ DIFFICULTY	ROUND-TRIP	ELEV GAIN/ HIGH POINT	SEASON
*****/4	7 miles (plus 0.5 mile for Spray Falls side trip)	1600 feet/ 6400 feet	July–Sept

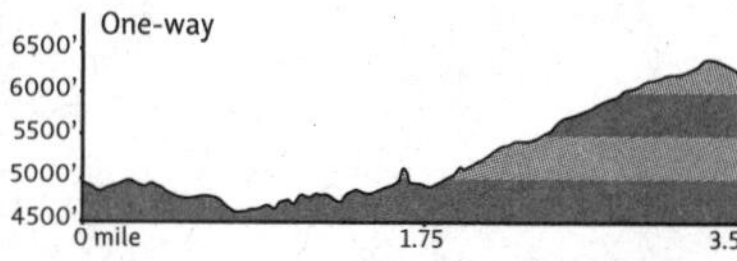

Maps: Green Trails Mount Rainier West, No. 269; **Contact:** Carbon River Ranger Station, (360) 829-9639; **GPS:** N46 55.962, W121 51.817

In many ways, you never recover from your first walk into Spray Park. The trail isn't difficult to follow. It's just difficult to forget. The 3.5-mile walk leads to seemingly endless open meadows of heather and alpine blossoms that tease the nose, ease the mind, and tickle the imagination. The place is a virtual lily

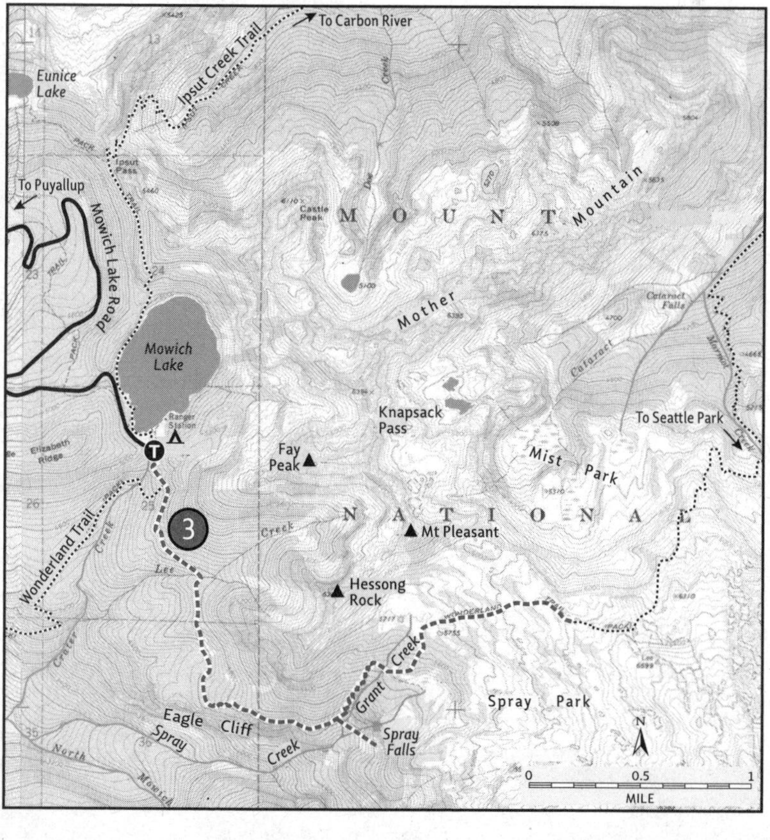

factory. The so-called park itself—actually a vast corridor of open meadows interspersed among rocky moraines, lingering snow patches, whistling marmots, and sun-basking hikers—is a wonder to behold in the summer, truly qualifying as one of Rainier's most magnificent day-hike destinations.

GETTING THERE

From Puyallup, drive 13 miles east on State Route 410 to Buckley. Turn right (south) onto SR 165 and proceed through Carbonado. Just beyond the Carbon River Gorge bridge, bear right onto Mowich Lake Road. Follow the road about 17 miles to its end; the trailhead is at the far end of the Mowich Lake Campground.

ON THE TRAIL

Even though the Mowich entrance to Rainier is a lesser-used, backdoor way into the park, this trail also can be (understandably) quite crowded. But Spray Park is a broad enough area, rife with so many hidden pockets of meadow between rock formations, that it's still possible to grab some solitude among the blossoms.

From Mowich Lake, the trail drops quickly (less than 0.1 mile) to a junction with the Wonderland Trail and then climbs gradually for the next 1.7 miles through sun-filled forests. At this point, you'll find a broad side trail on the right leading a short 0.25 mile down to Spray Falls, a worthwhile side trip (seriously, do *not* skip this side trip).

After your 0.5-mile excursion to the falls, continue climbing as the trail turns steeply upward through a series of switchbacks. At about 2.5 miles from the trailhead, you'll climb out of the switchbacks and move across Grant Creek. The forest opens onto increasingly broad clearings and meadows, providing views of Hessong Rock (6385 feet) to the north and the hulk of Mount Rainier to the southeast.

The trail continues to climb, more gradually now, through broad fields of flowers. Stop anywhere along here—there are endless options for picnic spots with grand views. To find the best views, though, push on to the spine of the rocky ridge separating Spray Park from Seattle Park to the east. Here, at around 3.5 miles out, you'll find a cool rock garden at 6400 feet.

EXTENDING YOUR TRIP

Continue northeast from Spray Park along the Wonderland Trail for 2.5 miles and then southwest on the Ipsut Creek Trail for a 5-mile walk back to the Mowich Lake parking lot. The total mileage for this tough-to-beat loop is about 15.5 miles. Your feet might not be glad you did it, but your soul will.

4 Mowich River

RATING/ DIFFICULTY	ROUND-TRIP	ELEV GAIN/ HIGH POINT	SEASON
***/4	7 miles	2400 feet/ 5000 feet	June–Nov

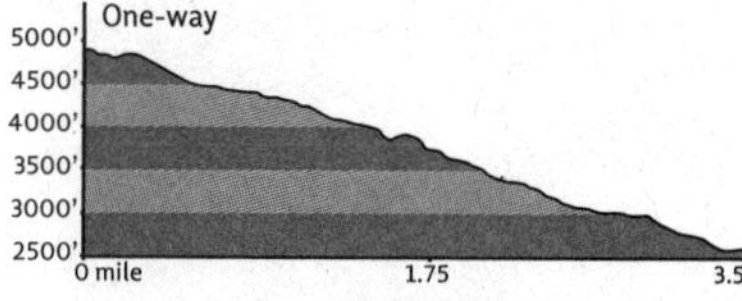

Maps: Green Trails Mount Rainier West, No. 269; **Contact:** Carbon River Ranger Station, (360) 829-9639; **GPS:** N46 55.962, W121 51.817

Lake to river, this route descends through lush old forests that provide cool relief from hot summer days. Following

Opposite: Dan hikes through the first openings into Spray Park through autumn colors and opening views.

the Wonderland Trail south, the trail skirts Crater Creek before traversing the flank of Paul Peak to finally drop into the Mowich River basin, near the junction of the North and South forks of that broad glacial stream. You'll find no views until you stand on the gravel bars in the riverbed, but you will experience forest primeval. Look for wildflowers such as Indian pipe, trillium, and beargrass. There are mushrooms aplenty along the route too—be sure you know which are safe before even thinking about picking them. Black-tailed deer and black bears are commonly seen here, but the most likely critters you'll encounter are grouse—listen for their whomp, whomp, whomps—and squirrels.

GETTING THERE

From Puyallup, drive 13 miles east on State Route 410 to Buckley. Turn right (south) onto SR 165 and proceed through Carbonado. Just beyond the Carbon River Gorge bridge, bear right onto Mowich Lake Road. Follow the road about 17 miles to its end; the trailhead is at the far end of the Mowich Lake Campground.

ON THE TRAIL

From Mowich Lake, find the Wonderland Trail access path on the south side of the parking lot, and after a short walk through the woods, veer right when you hit the true Wonderland. This leads out across Crater Creek about 0.5 mile from the parking lot, then you descend gradually through the forest, between Crater Creek and Elizabeth Ridge. The trees here are largely hemlock and Douglas fir, some of ancient lineage. Long beards of lichen hang from many of the lower branches, and birds twitter and trill in the undergrowth. If you are here in the twilight hours around dusk or

Logs and debris clog the North Mowich River after the November 2006 floods—many choices for logs to use for new footbridges!

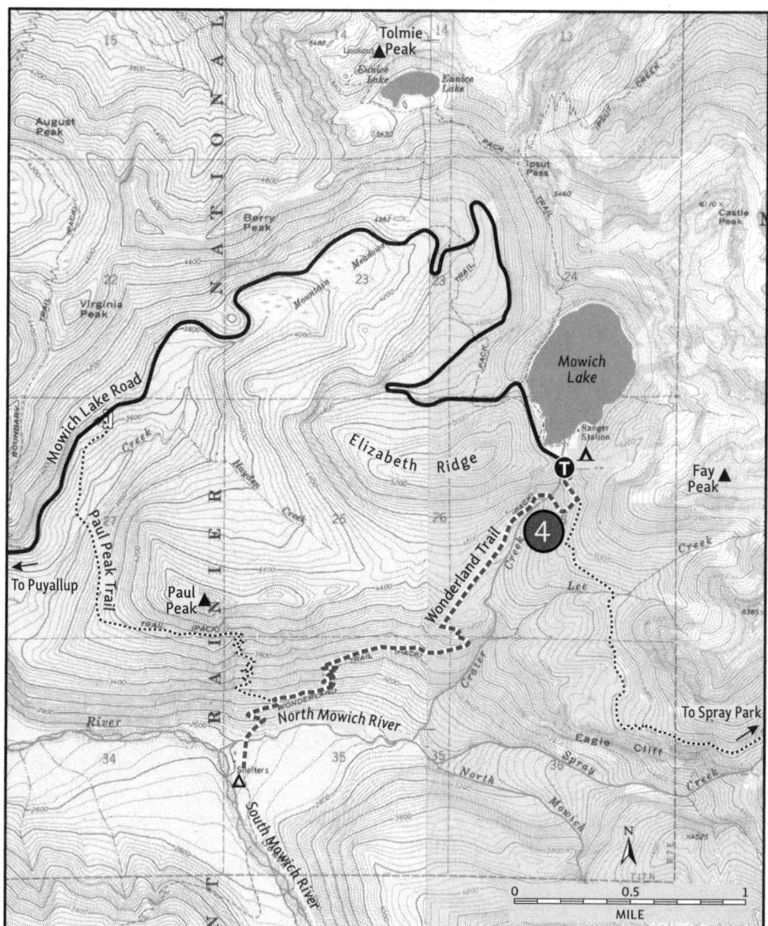

dawn, you might even see bats flying fast and silently through the trees, snatching insects out of the air as if by magic.

About 1.5 miles out, the tail cuts back toward the creek—not quite reaching the tumbling waters, though, before switching back to the west for a long, gentle traverse along the steep slope of Paul Peak. About 0.5 mile later, the trail drops in a series of switchbacks that burn up several hundred feet of elevation before tapering off for a final sidehill run to a trail junction at 3 miles, just above the North Mowich River. Turn left to drop into the river basin and in less than 0.5 mile, cross the river to find the Mowich River backcountry campsite on the peninsula between the North and South forks. Stay and rest in this forest camp before returning the way you came.

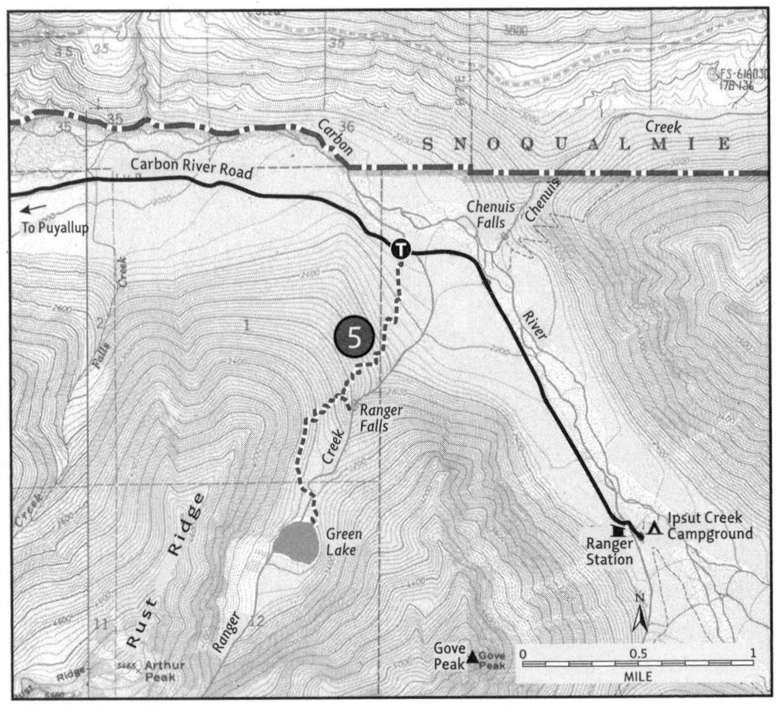

EXTENDING YOUR TRIP

You can return to the trail junction above the river in less than 0.5 mile, then follow the Paul Peak Trail (Hike 1) 2.8 miles to the road, if you can arrange a vehicle shuttle.

5 Green Lake

RATING/ DIFFICULTY	ROUND-TRIP	ELEV GAIN/ HIGH POINT	SEASON
***/3	4 miles	1300 feet/ 3400 feet	May–Nov

One-way

3500'
3000'
2500'
2000'
0 mile
1.0
2.0

Maps: Green Trails Mount Rainier West, No. 269; **Contact:** Carbon River Ranger Station, (360) 829-9639; **GPS:** N46 59.546, W121 51.034

Think Mount Rainier, and the images that instantly come to mind usually include open meadows, wildflowers, glaciers, and grand views. Green Lake, though, proves there's more to the park than that. This wonderful trail stays with the cool shadows of deep old-growth forests. You'll explore the quiet waters of a cool mountain stream and the deep, dark pool of a forested lake. No sweeping vistas. No

Ranger Falls after a light mid-winter dusting of snow

alpine meadows. No glaciated peaks. Just rich forest ecosystems and trout-rich waters.

GETTING THERE

From Puyallup, drive 13 miles east on State Route 410 to Buckley. Turn right (south) onto SR 165. Proceed to the bridge over the Carbon River Gorge and then bear left to Mount Rainier National Park's Carbon River Entrance. Proceed 3 miles to the trailhead on the right. **Note:** Due to 2006 flood damage, it may be necessary to walk the road from the point of the first damage, just inside the park boundary. Please contact the park service for current information prior to your hike.

ON THE TRAIL

From the trailhead, it's an easy, 1-mile-long walk through spectacular old-growth forest to spellbinding Ranger Creek Falls, just off

As close as you can get to Chenius Falls when floods have taken the footbridge out—always check if the bridges are in!

the main trail. Stop and enjoy the pounding waters of the falls before moving back up the forest path as it continues upward on a gradual incline toward Green Lake. About 1 mile past the falls, you'll suddenly find yourself stepping out of forest onto the lakeshore. The trees push right down to the water's edge, and frequently they fall into the deep waters, taking the woods right into the lake.

Enjoy it with the kids—they'll relish a cool (!) dip in the lake on a hot summer day. Just be sure to warn them of underwater logs so they don't dive and get tangled in the submerged branches.

The trail faces perennial threats due to the frequent flooding damage to the Carbon River Road. That road provides access to the trailhead, and because this quiet one-way trail lacks the high-profile grandeur of some other area trails, the Carbon River Road frequently is last to be repaired. The trail today remains in good form, but hikers need to keep using it—even during those periodic road closures (at these times, a short mountain bike ride gets to the trailhead with no trouble), to ensure its longevity.

6 Chenuis Falls

RATING/ DIFFICULTY	ROUND-TRIP	ELEV GAIN/ HIGH POINT	SEASON
***/1	1 mile	50 feet/ 2200 feet	June–Nov

Maps: Green Trails Mount Rainier West, No. 269; **Contact:** Carbon River Ranger Station, (360) 829-9639; **GPS:** N46 59.437, W121 50.640

Chenuis Creek stair-steps down a series of rocky platforms to form the multitiered Chenuis Falls. The short trail leading to the noisy cascade is perfect for families or for visiting relatives who want to experience the diverse beauty of Mount Rainier National Park without excessive effort. The short hike can be combined with one or more of the other short routes in the Carbon River area to create a day of adventure without overtiring anyone.

GETTING THERE

From Puyallup, drive 13 miles east on State Route 410 to Buckley. Turn right (south) onto SR 165. Proceed to the bridge over the Carbon River Gorge and then bear left to Mount Rainier National Park's Carbon River Entrance. Proceed 3.5 miles to the trailhead on the left. **Note:** Due to 2006 flood damage, it may be necessary to walk the road from the point of the first damage, just inside the park boundary. Please contact the park service for current information prior to your hike.

ON THE TRAIL

From the parking area along the Carbon River Road, follow the trail as it drops 50 feet in less than 0.25 mile to the banks of the river itself. You then climb onto a footbridge and trudge across the churning waters before climbing away from the Carbon River. The trail, well shaded by cedars and maples, angles into the Chenuis Creek valley and, at about 0.5 mile from the trailhead, ends at the falls themselves. The crystal-clear water tumbling down the rocky ledges is a nice change from the milky waters of the silt-rich Carbon. The trail fades into the forest beyond this point and isn't worth trying to follow.

Note that this route potentially is accessible by mid-March, though the footbridge over the Carbon River frequently is damaged by winter floods, and repairs usually aren't completed until late May or June. If you plan to visit in late spring or early summer, call ahead to see if the trail is open.

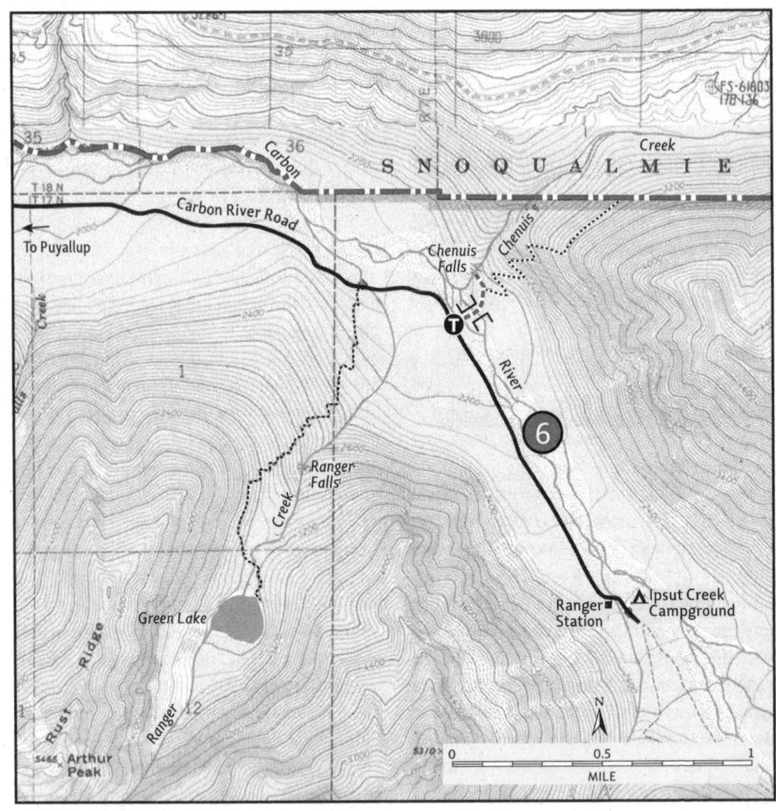

7 Carbon River Rain Forest Nature Trail

RATING/ DIFFICULTY	ROUND-TRIP	ELEV GAIN/ HIGH POINT	SEASON
***/1	0.5 mile	80 feet/ 1960 feet	June–Nov

Maps: Green Trails Mount Rainier West, No. 269; **Contact:** Carbon River Ranger Station, (360) 829-9639; **GPS:** N46 58.625, W121 49.892

There aren't many examples of temperate rain forest left standing in the southern Cascades. Most of these moss-laden cathedral forests are found on the Olympic Peninsula or along the Coastal Range of Oregon. To be sure, there are old-growth forest stands throughout the Cascades, but very few are of the rain-forest variety. Here is one of those last remnants of the ancient lowland rain forests. Massive cedars and hemlocks fill the valley floor around

Opposite: Moss-lined trail is the norm along the Carbon Rainforest Loop.

the floodplain of the Carbon River. A blanket of moss covers the forest floor, while lichens drape from hanging branches and ferns sprout from nearly every surface. Bring the kids and let them explore the micro-ecosystems under the dripping leaves and in the mossy hollows.

GETTING THERE

From Puyallup, drive 13 miles east on State Route 410 to Buckley. Turn right (south) onto SR 165. Proceed to the bridge over the Carbon River Gorge and then bear left to Mount Rainier National Park's Carbon River Entrance. Find the trailhead parking area just inside the park boundary.

ON THE TRAIL

This self-guided nature trail is a wonderful place to bring the kids. They'll marvel at the tree frogs and lizards that thrive in this damp forest. Bring your binoculars, too, so you

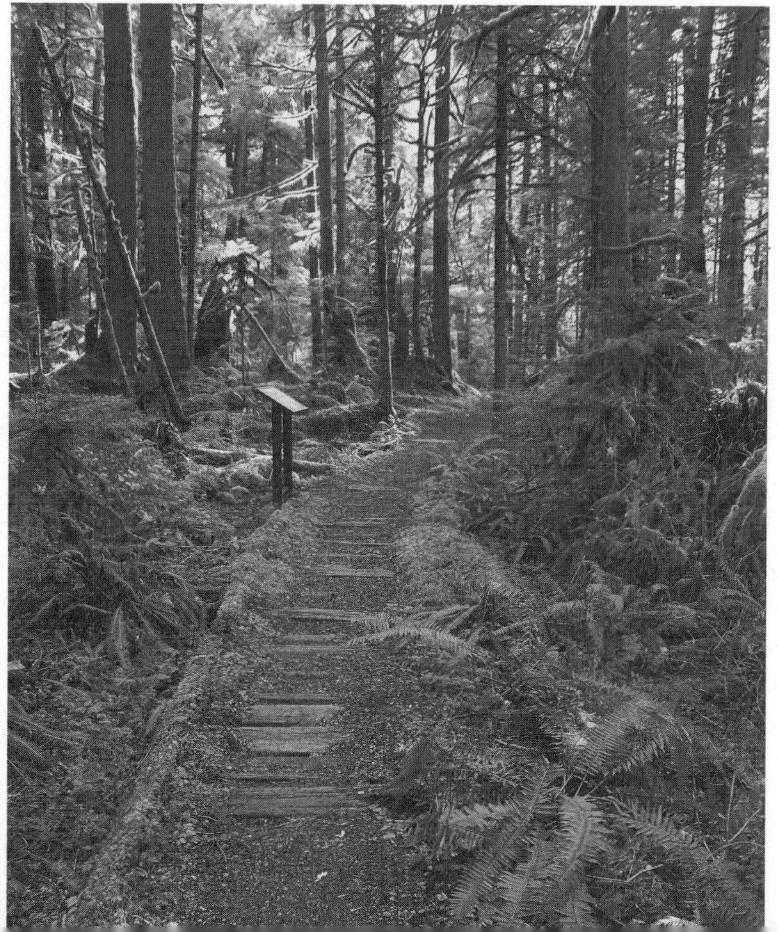

can examine the birds that dart through the trees—hunting the same bugs that are being pursued by those amphibians and reptiles (and some of the birds will be hunting those amphibians and reptiles, too).

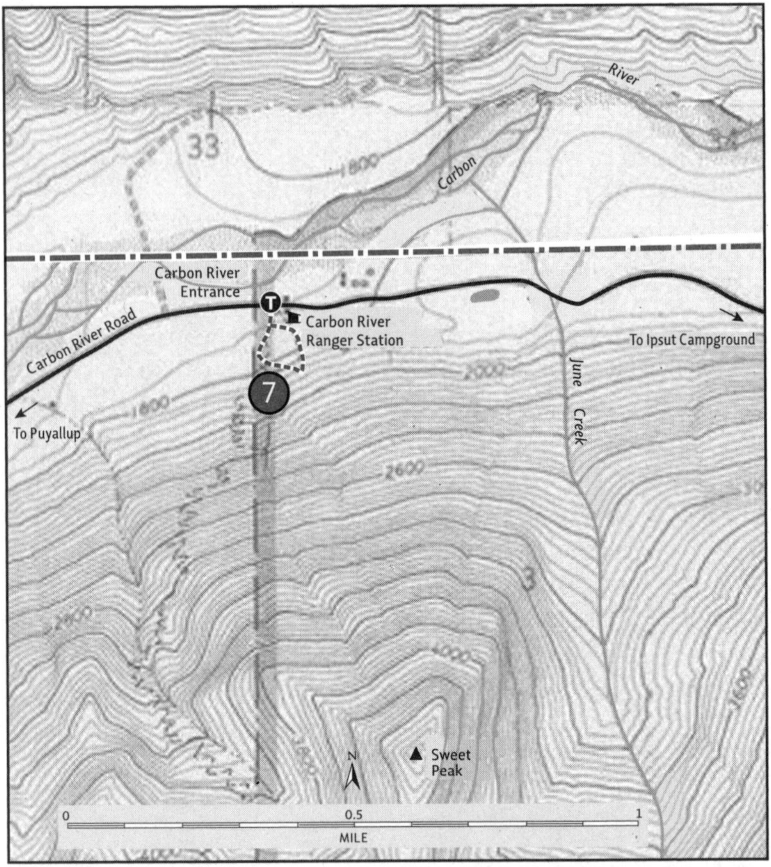

The trail loops 0.5 mile through the marshy forest, with signage spaced throughout to help educate and entertain forest visitors. Combine this walk with the Chenuis Falls hike if you need more mileage to fully stretch your legs.

8 Carbon Glacier

RATING/ DIFFICULTY	ROUND-TRIP	ELEV GAIN/ HIGH POINT	SEASON
****/3	6.5 miles	1000 feet/ 3400 feet	May–Nov

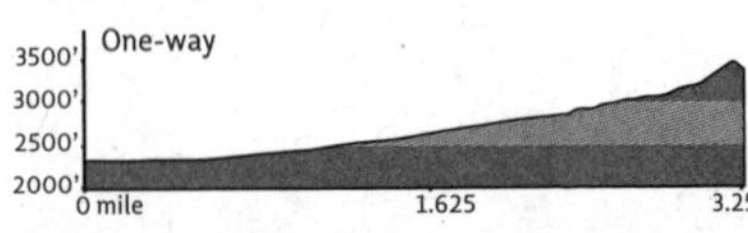

Maps: Green Trails Mount Rainier West, No. 269; **Contact:** Carbon River Ranger Station, (360) 829-9639; **GPS:** N46 58.625, W121 49.892

Though the trail is lovely, it's not exactly a thrill—not until you reach the end of the route. There, you'll find yourself swinging on a cable suspension bridge and cooling your heels on an actual glacier. Getting to those highlights, you'll trek along an old miners' road paralleling the Carbon River upstream. This frothy river boasts some serious white water, but it's not because of the rapids (which are generally small and not too frothy). Rather, the whiteness of the water comes from all the powder-fine silt ground up by the moving glacier. This water, known as "glacier milk," is deathly cold (remember, it's melted glacier ice from just a few miles upstream), so regardless of the heat, steer clear of the river itself.

GETTING THERE

From Puyallup, drive 13 miles east on State Route 410 to Buckley. Turn right (south) onto SR 165. Proceed to the bridge over the Carbon River Gorge and then bear left to Mount Rainier National Park's Carbon River Entrance. Proceed 5 miles to the trailhead at the road's end at Ipsut Creek Campground. **Note:** Due to 2006 flood damage, it may be necessary to walk the road from the point of the first damage, just inside the park boundary. Please contact the park service for current information prior to your hike.

ON THE TRAIL

The trail follows an old road built by early twentieth-century miners up the south bank of the Carbon River. The broad trail leads gradually upward 2 miles from Ipsut Creek Campground to a junction with the Northern Loop Trail. This side trail drops off the left side of the main trail, into the river channel. Trail crews replace or realign a series of precarious footlogs and narrow bridges each season as the braided river shifts each year.

Don't worry about those crossings, though, as our trail continues south along the bank of the Carbon. In another mile, you encounter another fork in the trail. To the right, the trail climbs up the Cataract Creek valley (Hike 12). Take the trail to the left, which rolls up onto

A lenticular cloud towers over Mount Rainier above the Carbon Glacier.

a narrow bridge suspended over the Carbon. Thick steel cables hold the bridge deck suspended over the rushing ice water, but the long span is still a bouncing adventure. The bridge is well anchored, however, so cross in confidence. Be sure to stop midbridge, however, to look upstream to the stark face of the Carbon Glacier.

Once safely across, turn right and follow the moraine steeply upward to an excellent viewpoint of the glacier, the lowest-elevation glacier in the Lower 48 states and one of the more melt-resistant ice fingers on Rainier. Most people stop here at about 3.25 miles; the trail beyond shows why, as it gets steep, rocky, and downright ornery for approximately the next mile up to Dick Creek Camp (see Hike 9).

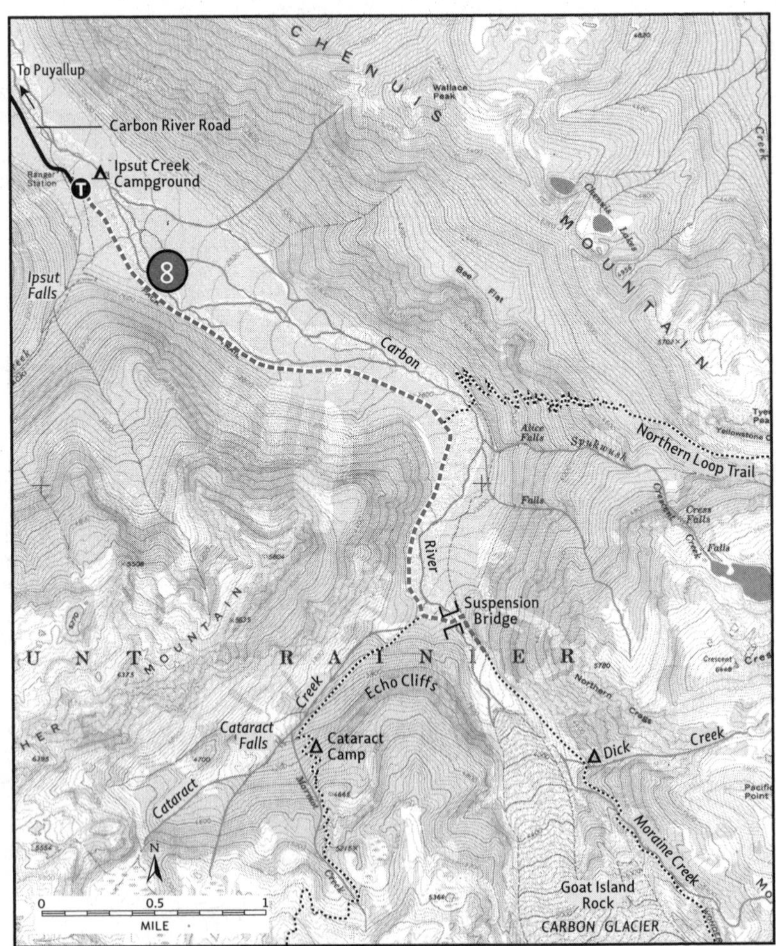

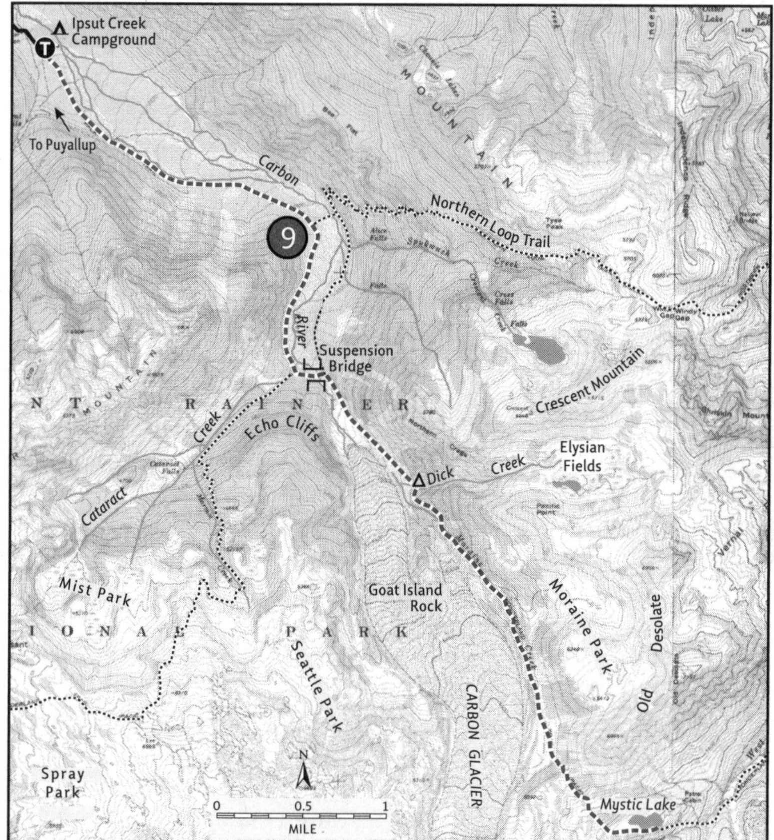

GETTING THERE

From Puyallup, drive 13 miles east on State Route 410 to Buckley. Turn right (south) onto SR 165. Proceed to the bridge over the Carbon River Gorge and then bear left to Mount Rainier National Park's Carbon River Entrance. Proceed 5 miles to the trailhead at the road's end at Ipsut Creek Campground. **Note:** Due to 2006 flood damage, it may be necessary to walk the road from the point of the first damage, just inside the park boundary. Please contact the park service for current information prior to your hike.

ON THE TRAIL

The Carbon Glacier Trail, actually part of Rainier's Wonderland Trail, leads gradually upward 2 miles from Ipsut Creek Campground to a junction with the Northern Loop Trail and then turns upward along the Carbon River to a junction with the Spray Park–Seattle Park Trail at about 3 miles. Turn left to cross the spring suspension bridge over the Carbon River, then go right to climb up the lateral moraine kicked out the side of Carbon Glacier. About 0.5 mile from the bridge, take

Massive old-growth trees near Ipsut Falls

a moment to stop and enjoy the views of this, the lowest-elevation glacier in the Lower 48 states (see Hike 8).

From this point, the trail gets serious, climbing steeply—ruthlessly—for another mile to Dick Creek backcountry campsite. The climbing slows a bit past Dick Creek, but the route continues steadily upward alongside the glacier—staying well above the glacier itself—another 3 miles. It is in this stretch that you'll enjoy the flower meadows of Moraine Park. The broadest fields are well above the trail on the lower flank of Old Desolate peak, but the trail provides plenty of opportunity to enjoy the flowers at the forest fringe.

At 6.5 miles out, the trail angles away from the glacier basin and climbs, steeply again, into the more open terrain. At 7 miles, you'll find yourself in increasingly expansive meadows, and at 7.8 miles, you'll tiptoe into the Mystic Lake basin.

10 Ipsut Falls

RATING/ DIFFICULTY	ROUND-TRIP	ELEV GAIN/ HIGH POINT	SEASON
***/1	1.4 miles	300 feet/ 2650 feet	May–Nov

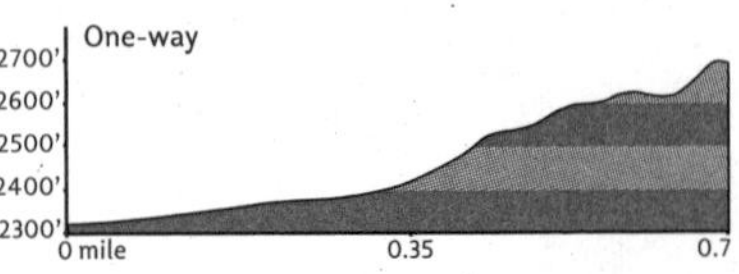

Maps: Green Trails Mount Rainier West, No. 269; **Contact:** Carbon River Ranger Station, (360) 829-9639; **GPS:** N46 58.625, W121 49.892

Kids will love this route, which features a short exploration of a lush old-growth forest and leads to a pretty waterfall in a forest dell. The route stays well within the cool shade of the forest, with nice views of the Carbon River as well as Ipsut Creek. This area is frequented by both black-tailed deer and Rocky Mountain elk, so keep an eye open and you might see one or more of the big beasts browsing through the woods or sipping from the waterways.

GETTING THERE

From Puyallup, drive 13 miles east on State Route 410 to Buckley. Turn right (south) onto SR 165. Proceed to the bridge over the Carbon River Gorge and then bear left to Mount Rainier National Park's Carbon River Entrance. Proceed 5 miles to the trailhead at the road's end at Ipsut Creek Campground. **Note:** Due to 2006 flood damage, it may be necessary to walk the road from the point of the first damage, just inside the park boundary. Please contact the park service for current information prior to your hike.

ON THE TRAIL

From the trailhead at the campground, follow the Carbon River Trail south into the forest. You'll weave through the trees for more than 0.5 mile, usually well back from the Carbon River, though frequently within hearing distance of the churning water. Deer love this browse-rich section of forest since it provides good cover as well as abundant food and water, so have the kids keep their eyes open for movement in the woods around you, and they might see a stag staring back at you. Or maybe even a delicate doe with fawn. (Blacktails are very small deer in general, and the does can be dainty little ladies.)

At 0.5 mile out, veer right as the trail angles up the Ipsut Creek Valley, and in just 0.2 mile—just as the trail starts to climb—go right onto a side trail to cut over to the Ipsut Falls viewpoint. Enjoy the spectacle of the churning cascade before heading back.

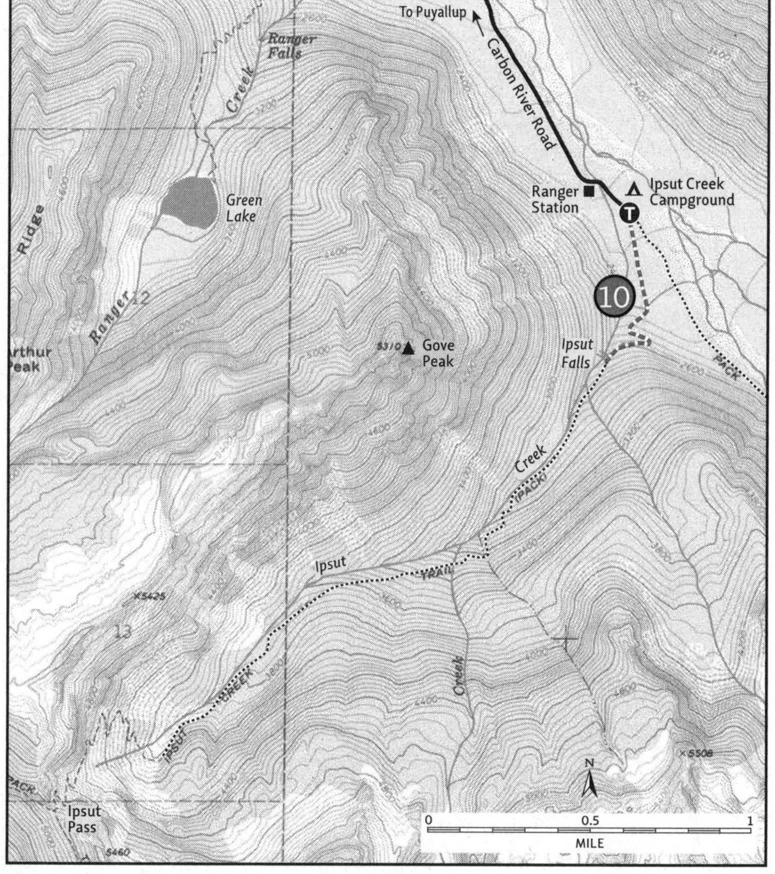

11 Ipsut Pass

RATING/ DIFFICULTY	ROUND-TRIP	ELEV GAIN/ HIGH POINT	SEASON
***/3	8 miles	2800 feet/ 5150 feet	June–Oct

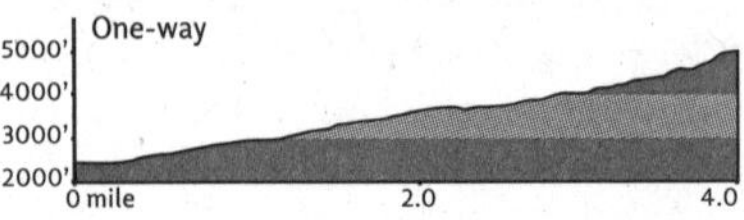

Maps: Green Trails Mount Rainier West, No. 269; **Contact:** Carbon River Ranger Station, (360) 829-9639; **GPS:** N46 58.625, W121 49.892

The State of Alaska is a big, brash place full of larger-than-life people, places, and things. That being the case, you'd think the world's largest Alaska yellow cedar would exist in Alaska, right? Wrong. Alaska may be a land of big

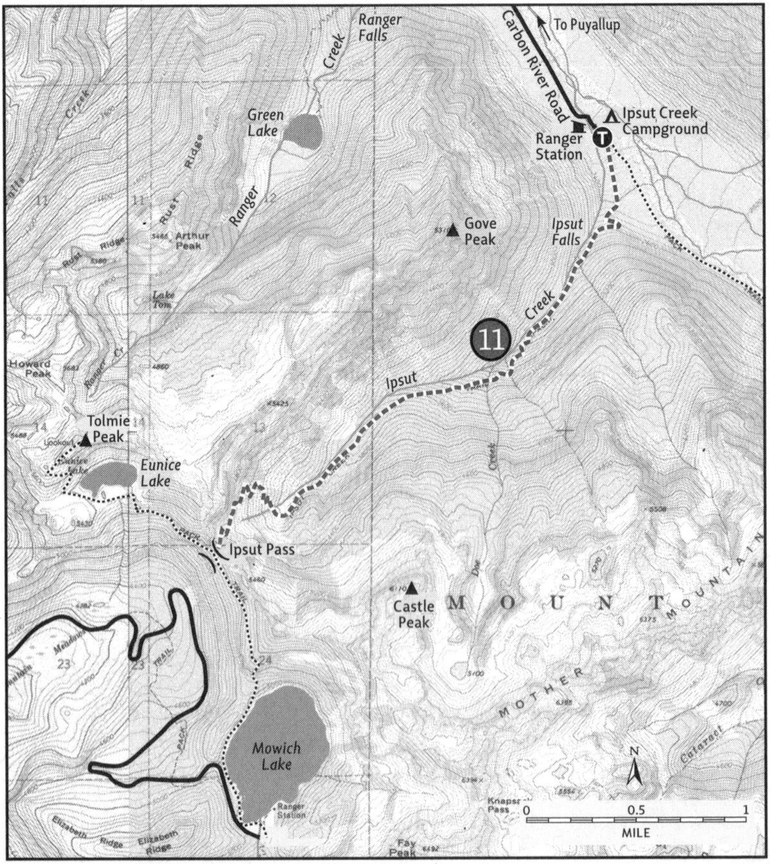

View down the Ipsut Creek Valley from Ipsut Pass

mountains, big bears, and big egos, but if you want big trees—especially big Alaska yellow cedars—look no further than Ipsut Creek. Halfway up this valley hike you'll encounter the world's largest Alaska yellow cedar, though this centuries-old tree is just one of many massive trees on this woodland hike. Besides the cathedral forests, you'll also find fantastic views and sprawling meadows on this walk, though these come only at the end.

GETTING THERE

From Puyallup, drive 13 miles east on State Route 410 to Buckley. Turn right (south) onto SR 165. Proceed to the bridge over the Carbon River Gorge and then bear left to Mount Rainier National Park's Carbon River Entrance. Proceed 5 miles to the trailhead at the road's end at Ipsut Creek Campground. **Note:** Due to 2006 flood damage, it may be necessary to walk the road from the point of the first damage, just inside the park boundary. Please contact the park service for current information prior to your hike.

ON THE TRAIL

Start up the Carbon River Trail as it weaves through the moss-laden forests adjacent to the Carbon River. At about 0.5 mile, veer right as the trail angles up the Ipsut Creek Valley. Before the trail really starts to climb, you can duck off on a short side track to view Ipsut Falls (Hike 10). Past the falls, the trail climbs moderately through an impressive forest of old-growth Douglas firs and western hemlocks. For the next couple of miles, the trail stays well within earshot, if not eyesight, of Ipsut Creek.

At around 2.7 miles from the trailhead, the forest thins and opens first onto a series of broad clearings, then open hillside meadows. Near the 3-mile mark, the path passes a stand of subalpine trees. These high-elevation trees are smaller than their lowland cousins but no less ancient. Here you'll find the big Alaska yellow cedar.

Continuing on past the well-marked world-record tree, the trail runs into a series of steep switchbacks weaving upward through a cliff band to reach Ipsut Pass at 5100 feet elevation. This pass separates the Carbon Valley from the Mowich Valley. From the pass, find limited views of Tolmie Peak and Mother Mountain. Peer down through the trees toward Eunice Lake and Mowich Lake. Then head back the way you came.

EXTENDING YOUR TRIP

You can continue north 2 miles to Eunice Lake and Tolmie Peak Lookout or south 1.75 miles to Mowich Lake (both in Hike 2).

Mama bear and her twin cubs roaming up the slope away from the photographer in Seattle Park

12 Seattle Park

RATING/ DIFFICULTY	ROUND-TRIP	ELEV GAIN/ HIGH POINT	SEASON
*****/5	12 miles	2850 feet/ 5200 feet	June–Oct

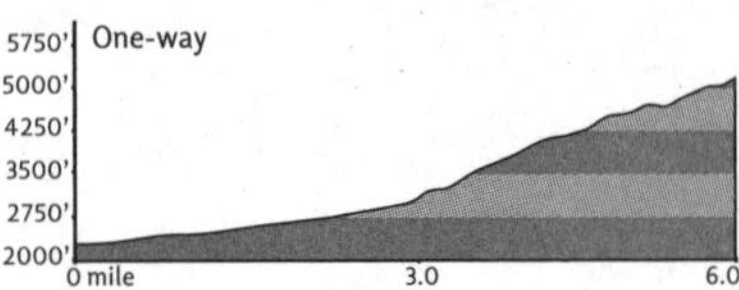

Maps: Green Trails Mount Rainier West, No. 269; **Contact:** Carbon River Ranger Station, (360) 829-9639; **GPS:** N46 58.625, W121 49.892

Skyscrapers. Noisy, raucous crowds. Air traffic heavy enough to have you ducking your head at times. About what you'd expect in Seattle, and exactly what you get in Seattle Park—and that's a good thing. The skyscrapers here are towering peaks and jagged rocks. The raucous crowds are colonies of marmots. And the hair-raising air traffic? Gray jays, eagles, ravens, and hawks. The Seattle Park Trail starts in lush old-growth forest and climbs into some of the most spectacular parkland you'll find on the flanks of Mount Rainier. The area is rich in wildlife. Coyotes and bobcats hunt those marmots, as do enormous golden eagles. Mountain goats and black-tailed deer browse those meadows, and so to do lumbering black bears. I've even seen red foxes prancing through the fields, scarfing down mice and voles.

GETTING THERE

From Puyallup, drive 13 miles east on State Route 410 to Buckley. Turn right (south) onto SR 165. Proceed to the bridge over the Carbon River Gorge and then bear left to Mount Rainier National Park's Carbon River Entrance. Proceed 5 miles to the trailhead at the road's

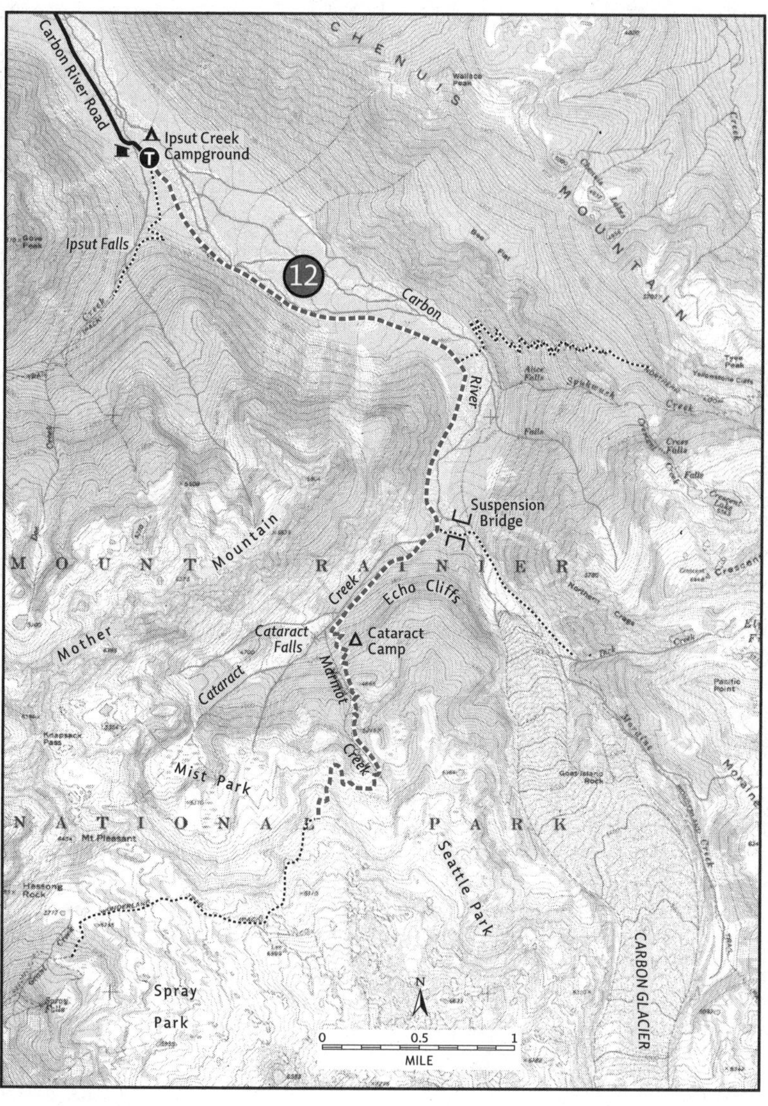
Carbon River Road
Ipsut Creek Campground
Ipsut Falls
12
Carbon
River
CHENUIS MOUNTAIN
Suspension Bridge
MOUNT RAINIER NATIONAL PARK
Mother Mountain
Creek
Echo Cliffs
Cataract Falls
Cataract Camp
Cataract
Marmot Creek
Mist Park
Seattle Park
Spray Park
CARBON GLACIER
N
0 0.5 1
MILE

THIS IS COUGAR COUNTRY

While eastern Washington is clearly cougar country (home to Washington State University), so are the central Cascades. But the cougars that roam these hills don't don crimson and gray! They're wild cats. And they're proliferating. Cougar populations throughout the state have been increasing. No surprise: so have sightings.

Still, cougar encounters are rare. Keep in mind that fewer than twenty fatal cougar attacks have occurred in the United States since the early twentieth century (on the other hand, more than fifty people are killed, on average, by deer each year—most in auto collisions with the deer). You can minimize the already slim chances of having a cougar encounter by doing the following:

- Don't hike or run alone (runners look like fleeing prey to a predator).
- Keep children within sight and close at all times (small humans are more likely prey).
- Avoid dead animals; cougars return to killed prey to continue feeding.
- Keep dogs on leash and under control. A cougar may attack a loose, solitary dog, but a leashed dog next to you makes two foes for the cougar to deal with—and cougars are too smart to take on two aggressive animals at once.
- Be alert to your surroundings.
- Use a walking stick.

Just in case you do have a run-in with this elusive predator, it's important to know how to react. Cougars are curious animals. They may appear threatening when they are only being inquisitive. By making the cougar think you are a bigger, meaner critter than it is, you will be able to avoid an attack (the big cats realize that there is enough easy prey out there that they don't have to mess with something that will fight back). If the cat you encounter acts aggressively, take these steps:

- Don't turn your back on or take your eyes off the cougar.
- Remain standing.
- Throw things, provided you don't have to bend over to pick them up. If you have a water bottle on your belt, chuck it at the cat. Throw your camera, wave your hiking stick, and if the cat gets close enough, whack it hard with your hiking staff (I know of two cases in which women delivered good, hard whacks across the nose of aggressive-acting cougars, and the cats immediately turned tail and ran away).
- Shout loudly.
- Fight back aggressively.

end at Ipsut Creek Campground. **Note:** Due to 2006 flood damage, it may be necessary to walk the road from the point of the first damage, just inside the park boundary. Please contact the park service for current information prior to your hike.

ON THE TRAIL

Follow the Carbon River Trail upstream for 3 nearly flat miles. When you reach the suspension bridge crossing the river (see Hike 8), turn right so that, instead of crossing the swinging bridge, you head up the Cataract

Creek valley. You now start climbing. As you climb, you'll note the areas of windfalls in the forest—windstorms periodically blast down this valley and have toppled several stands of trees along the way.

After just 1.5 miles of slogging uphill, look for Cataract Camp in a clearing on the left. This backcountry camp is one of the designated stopping points for backpackers. It makes a nice place for a rest for day hikers, too, since you'll find water (from Marmot Creek, a tributary of Cataract Creek) and sunshine after having spent the last few hours hiking under the forest canopy.

Once past Cataract Camp, the trail enters a series of meadows broken by stands of forest. From here on, the higher you go, the bigger and broader the meadow clearings. Finally, at 6 miles, you cross the upper reaches of Marmot Creek and stroll out into the sprawling meadows of lower Seattle Park (5200 feet). Stop here to rest and enjoy the alpine beauty before returning.

EXTENDING YOUR TRIP

If after 6 miles you still have the energy to explore, push on up the trail and, in less than 0.5 mile, you'll reach the transition zone between subalpine and alpine environments, leaving behind the green meadows and entering the world of rock and ice. At 1 mile past Marmot Creek (7 miles from the trailhead), you'll reach the 6400-foot ridge crest that separates Seattle Park from Spray Park (Hike 3).

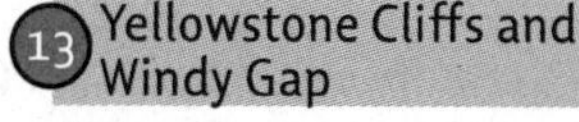

13 Yellowstone Cliffs and Windy Gap

RATING/ DIFFICULTY	ROUND-TRIP	ELEV GAIN/ HIGH POINT	SEASON
*****/5	13 miles	3500 feet/ 5800 feet	June–Oct

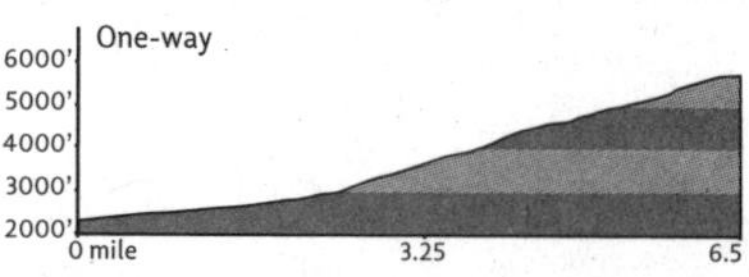

Maps: Green Trails Mount Rainier West, No. 269; **Contact:** Carbon River Ranger Station, (360) 829-9639; **GPS:** N46 58.625, W121 49.892

Windy Gap may be the most underrated trail destination in Mount Rainier National Park. Part of the reason for that is the fact that Seattle Park and Spray Park, found just to the southwest, offer equally lovely scenery with less of a workout. It could be because from Windy Gap itself, Mount Rainier can't be seen. Or it could be that the brutal climb to the gap scares most hikers off. Regardless of the reason, the fact remains that the broad meadowlands of Windy Gap and the long, stark face of Yellowstone Cliffs offer stunningly beautiful scenery with a high probability of solitude.

GETTING THERE

From Puyallup, drive 13 miles east on State Route 410 to Buckley. Turn right (south) onto SR 165. Proceed to the bridge over the Carbon River Gorge and then bear left to Mount Rainier National Park's Carbon River Entrance. Proceed 5 miles to the trailhead at the road's end at Ipsut Creek Campground. **Note:** Due to 2006 flood damage, it may be necessary to walk the road from the point of the first damage, just inside the park boundary. Please contact the park service for current information prior to your hike.

ON THE TRAIL

Hike up the Carbon River Trail from the east end of the campground, and in just 2 miles look for a side trail to the left. This is the

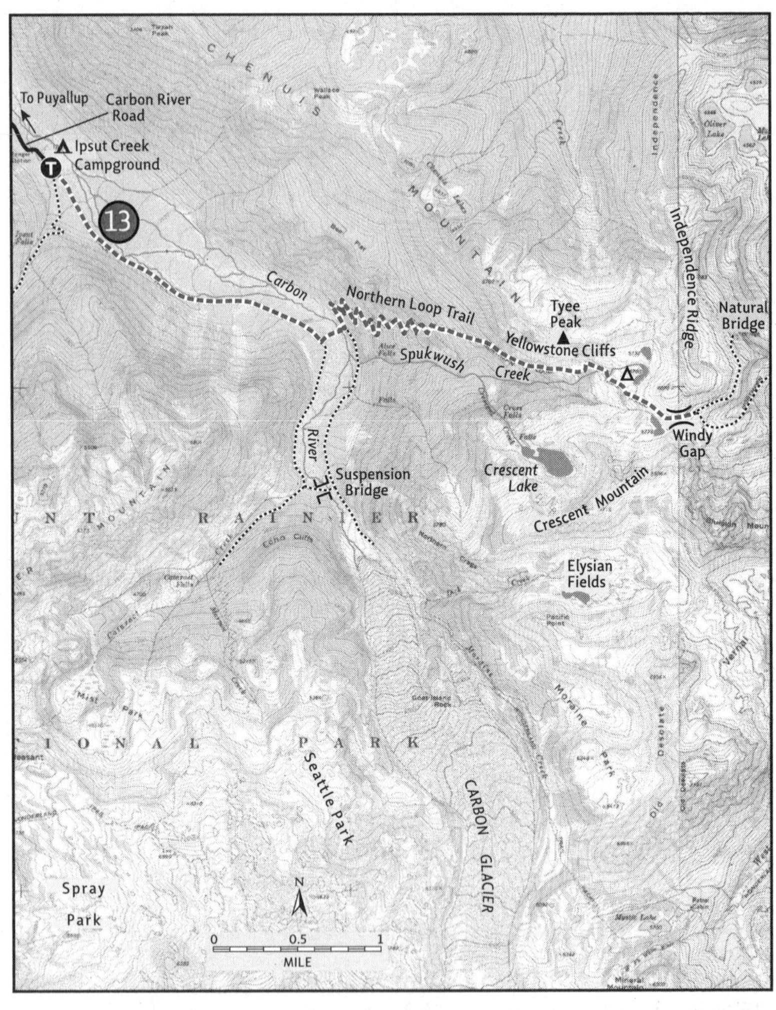

official start of the Northern Loop Trail, but because there is not a true bridge across the river here—just a series of long footlogs that have a tendency to wash out in the spring—hikers might have to push on to the Carbon River suspension bridge at 3 miles to cross the river, then backtrack down the opposite shore to the start of the loop trail (this detour adds about 2 miles to the one-way mileage).

Assuming you can cross the river at the lower point, however, find the trail on the northeastern shore and start a long, steep climb through a seemingly endless series of switchbacks. This punishing climb will tax even the

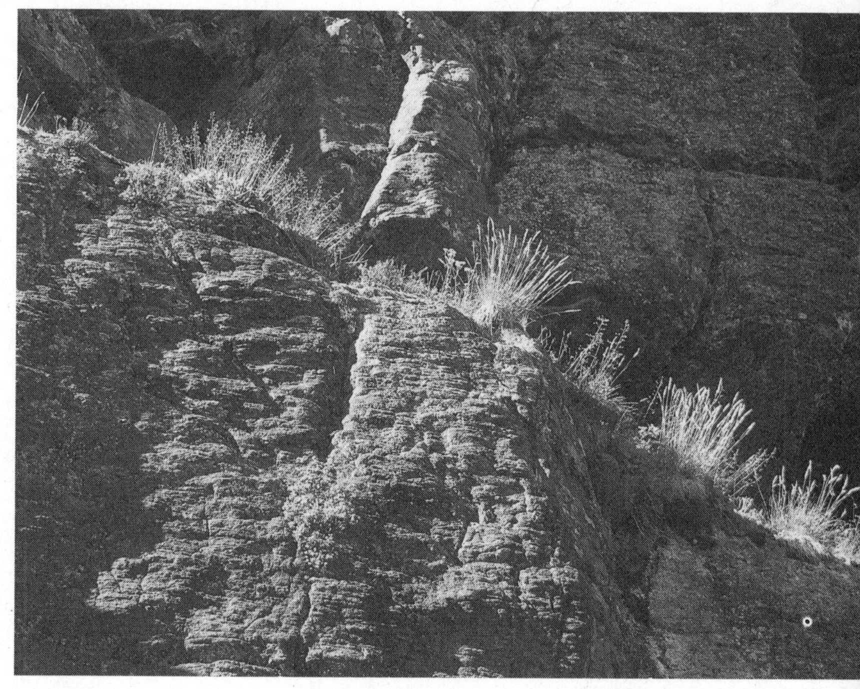

Dried flowers and grasses growing right out of the rocky cliffs

strongest hiker as it gains a whopping 3000 feet in just over 3 miles. The good news is, the climb is through heavy, cool forest most of the way, and as you near the top, the forest opens on broad meadows and windswept ridges.

At about 5 miles from the start (via the lower river crossing), you reach Yellowstone Cliffs. The cliffs are a tall wall of yellow-tinged rocks towering over a long, sloping meadowland. Deer and mountain goats share this area, with the goats preferring the rocks and the meadows atop them and the deer favoring the meadows abutting the forests below the cliffs. A fine campsite is nestled in the trees near Spukwush Creek, with good views of the cliffs and the meadows.

Continuing on past the cliffs, the trail keeps climbing, now in the broad meadows, for another 1.5 miles to the U-shaped basin of Windy Gap (at 6.5 miles from the road end). Plant life is sparser here, with just a bit of heather and grasses pushing up through the rocks and around the edges of the many little tarns that dot the gap. A perpetual breeze blows through the gap (hence the name), but there's not much of a view.

If you have the time and inclination, an off-trail scramble is worthwhile here. Climb the rocky slope on the south side of the gap to attain the ridge crest above. Here, you can peer down to the west on the sapphire-blue waters of Crescent Lake and south to the emerald-green plain of the Elysian Fields. Towering above the fields is mighty Mount Rainier.

EXTENDING YOUR TRIP

It's well worth the time to venture another long mile along the Northern Loop Trail and then just over a half-mile northeast on a side trail to a viewpoint of the Natural Bridge, a massive rock arch across a ravine. For an even longer adventure, continue east from here to hike Rainier's Northern Loop, which leads to Grand Park (Hike 14) and then the Fire Creek and Berkeley camps near Sunrise; it then swings back west on the Wonderland Trail over Skyscraper Pass to Granite Creek Park, the Winthrop Glacier, Mystic Lake, and (ultimately) the start at Ipsut Creek Campground. The total loop is about 35 miles and leads through some of the most unspoiled and untrammeled alpine areas of the park. Allow four or five days, but if you've got a week, you'll be glad you took it. Upper portions of this trail are snow-covered until midsummer.

Opposite: Grand Park in its complete glory filled with lupines and bistort

white river

One of the largest herds of Rocky Mountain elk in Washington calls the upper White River valley home. The big beasts—called *wapiti* by Native Americans—range from the rocky banks of the White River to the high alpine meadows on the flanks of Sunrise Ridge and Crystal Mountain. The southeast end of the valley also hosts one of the largest herds of mountain goats in Mount Rainier National Park. Scores of the snowy-fleeced beasts can be found on the rocky flanks of Barrier Peak and Tamanos Mountain and especially around the Panhandle Gap area on Rainier's northeastern flank. But there's more than ungulates to see in this wild region. Crashing rivers, thundering falls, sparkling lakes, sprawling alpine meadows, and stark glacier basins make this corner of the park a fantastic hiking destination.

14 Grand Park

RATING/ DIFFICULTY	ROUND-TRIP	ELEV GAIN/ HIGH POINT	SEASON
****/4	9 miles	1100 feet/ 5600 feet	July–Oct

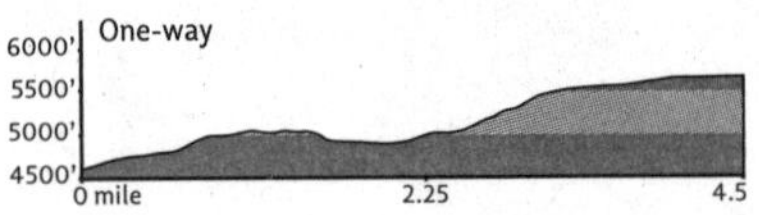

Maps: Green Trails Mount Rainier East, No. 270; **Contact:** Sunrise Ranger Station, (360) 663-2425; for road information, contact Snoqualmie Ranger District, (425) 888-1421; **GPS:** N46 59.777, W121 38.480

***Ain't it Grand!** When viewed from a distant vantage point, Grand Park looks as though a scythe sheared off the top of a mountain, leaving a flat, mesalike meadow sprawling across the forested horizon. Stroll into the meadows at the fringe of the broad, table-flat plateau of Grand Park, and it seems as if the vast field of wildflowers stretches endlessly before you. The meadows are occasionally broken by small stands of woodlands, several of which are "silver forests"—the still-standing weathered-gray skeletons of trees killed by forest fire. The "official" access to Grand Park requires a long 14-mile round-trip hike in from Sunrise. That's a beautiful trail, but that long walk gets you only to the edge of the meadows. Better to visit Grand Park by the backdoor.*

GETTING THERE

From Enumclaw, drive east 24 miles on State Route 410 to a junction with Forest Road 73. Turn right (south) and drive 6 miles to a bridge over Huckleberry Creek. There is a gate here, frequently closed and locked in winter (contact the Snoqualmie Ranger District to check road accessibility prior to your trip). Proceed over the bridge and continue another 2.5 miles to a road junction. Turn right here and at 10 miles from SR 410, park at the unsigned trailhead near the Eleanor Creek bridge.

ON THE TRAIL

As you start into this hike, note that the section of trail from the trailhead to Lake Eleanor just inside the national park boundary was built by boots. It was created mostly by anglers looking for fast access to the fish in Lake Eleanor. Today, though, so many hikers have trod this trail that the "boot-built" section is in better condition than most officially built trails in the surrounding national forest.

The trail angles southwest from the trailhead, rolling upward through cool forest, running up the Eleanor Creek basin. The trail crosses over into Mount Rainier National Park in about 0.25 mile, then reaches Lake Eleanor (elevation 4985 feet) at 1 mile.

From the lake, the trail climbs to the east

A hiker crossing the massive meadows of mile-long Grand Park

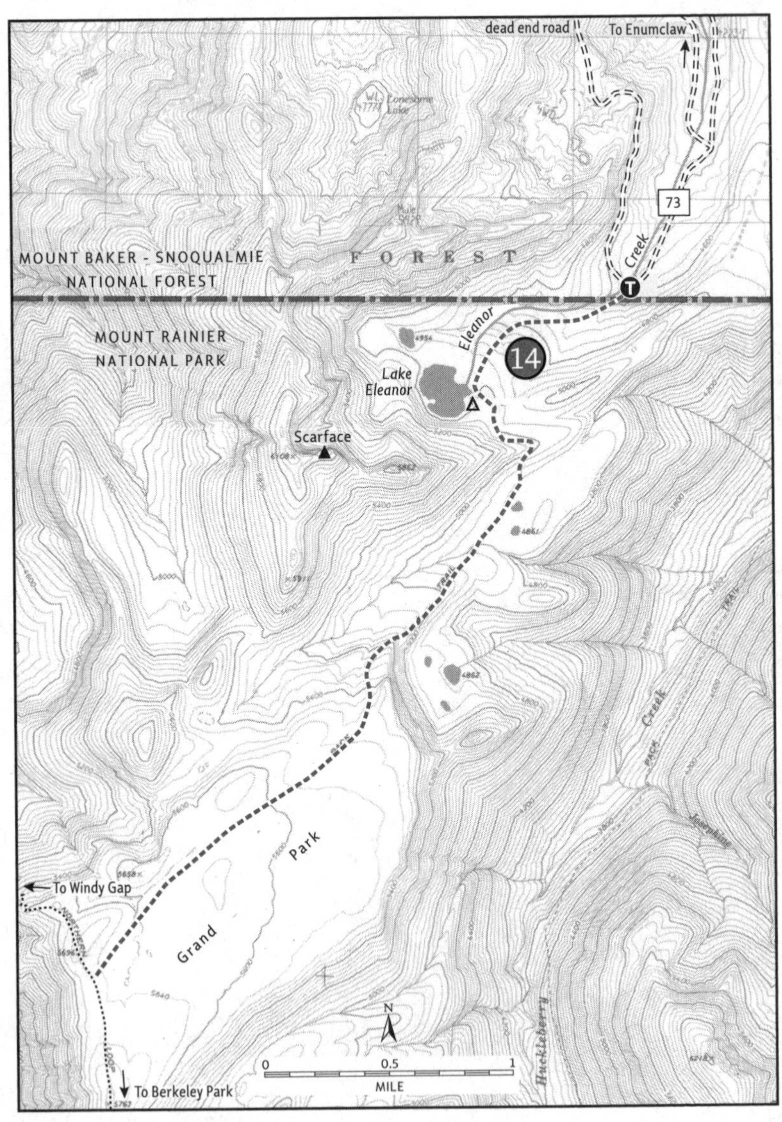

over a low ridge, then turns southwest again upward through the forest to a modest meadow at about 1.5 miles. Look for deer and even elk (from the huge White River herd) in this forage-rich meadow before continuing onward and upward. Another mile of forest walking leads to the start of increasingly open forest glades and small meadows.

At 3 miles out, the forest clearings merge into the start of the broad meadows of Grand Park. Follow the trail as it hugs the western edge of the park and at 3.5 miles, stop for the first fantastic views of Mount Rainier. You can amble out into the meadows to find the best photographic vantage points or continue to follow the trail along its southwesterly route to get the full grandeur of Grand Park. The meadows continue on for more than 1 mile, and you'll hit a trail junction at 4.5 miles. This is a great place to turn back.

EXTENDING YOUR TRIP

If you want more mileage, at the trail junction turn left (south) onto the Northern Loop Trail and follow it about 0.75 mile as it skirts the southwestern edge of the Grand Park meadows. Continue on another 3 miles past the end of the meadows, the trail climbing moderately as it sweeps around the head of Cold Basin before ascending to Berkeley Park. **Note:** If you want to camp along this route, you'll need to get a backcountry permit from the Park Service. Official camps are available at Lake Eleanor and Berkeley Park.

From the trail junction in Grand Park, you could also turn right (north) on the Northern Loop Trail and hike 4 miles to Windy Gap (Hike 13).

15 Crystal Lakes

RATING/ DIFFICULTY	ROUND-TRIP	ELEV GAIN/ HIGH POINT	SEASON
***/4	6 miles	2300 feet/ 5828 feet	June–Oct

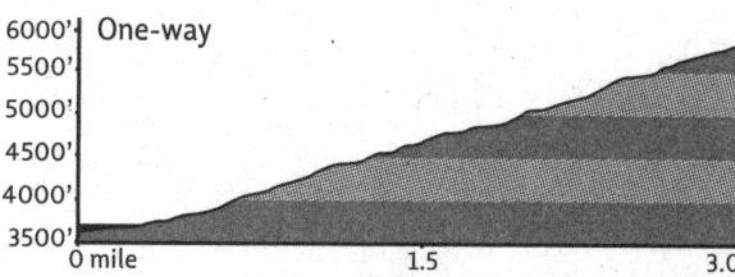

Upper Crystal Lake basin

Maps: Green Trails Mount Rainier East, No. 270; **Contact:** Sunrise Ranger Station, (360) 663-2425; **GPS:** N46 55.364, W121 32.017

These beautiful lakes are nestled in a green bowl beneath high, craggy peaks. You might encounter a few elk, maybe a mountain goat or two, and possibly even a black bear. The latter is especially likely in late summer when the plethora of purple fruit—succulent huckleberries!—ripens up. That's all you'll find here. If you need more natural beauty, you're out of luck. You won't find many trails that offer wilderness like this.

GETTING THERE

From Enumclaw, drive east 42 miles on State Route 410 to the trailhead parking lot on the

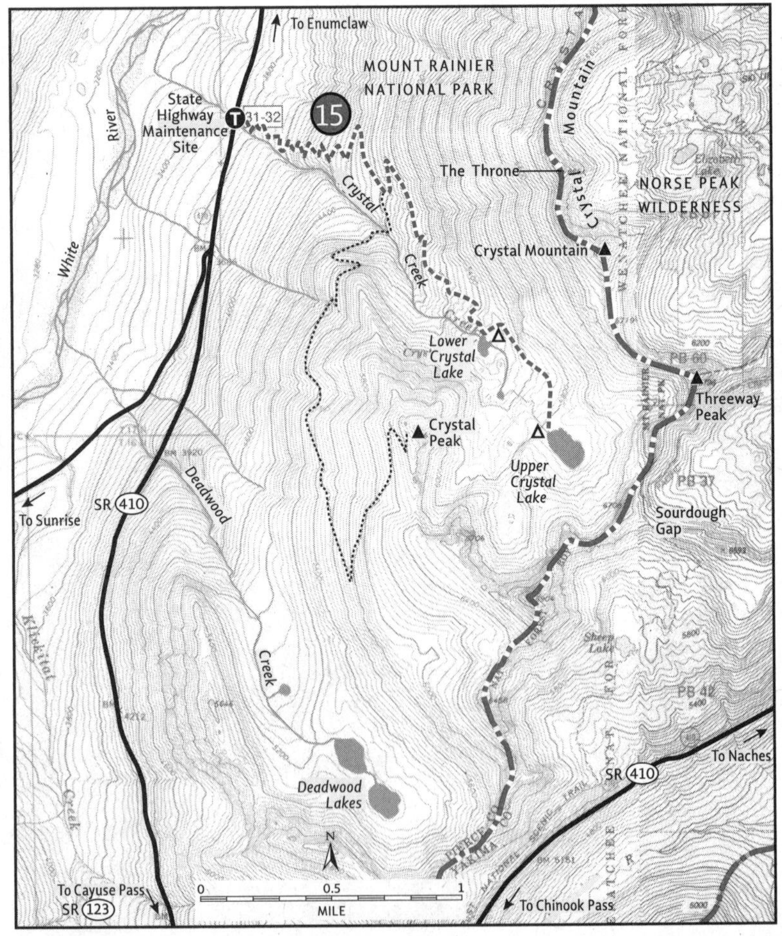

right, just 4.5 miles after passing through the park's entryway arch.

ON THE TRAIL

The trail climbs steeply away from the highway, piercing dense old forest as it climbs. That's a good thing, since the tight forest canopy provides welcome shade as you sweat up a long series of switchbacks in the first 1.5 miles. At that point, the trail splits; the right fork leads to Crystal Peak (Hike 16).

Go left on a trail that sweeps out across a broad avalanche slope before switching back to recross the slide zone, then angling up into the Crystal Creek valley. At 2.5 miles, after another short series of switchbacks, you find yourself at Lower Crystal Lake Camp (5400). The small tarn here is pretty but not spectacular. Better to keep on moving.

A short 0.5 mile gets you to the upper lake (5828 feet) and its bigger backcountry camp. Here, you have a broad, clear-watered lake and stunning views. Mount Rainier is blocked by Crystal Peak, but that's okay. The ring of rock surrounding the lake basin is plenty impressive. Stands of trees dot the heather and huckleberry meadows flanking the lake, and high above the basin stands The Throne, Crystal Mountain, Threeway Peak, Sourdough Gap, and Crystal Peak. The trail ends at the lake, so stop to swim or at least to soak your feet while enjoying lunch before heading back down the trail.

16 Crystal Peak

RATING/ DIFFICULTY	ROUND-TRIP	ELEV GAIN/ HIGH POINT	SEASON
***/4	8 miles	3100 feet/ 6595 feet	June–Oct

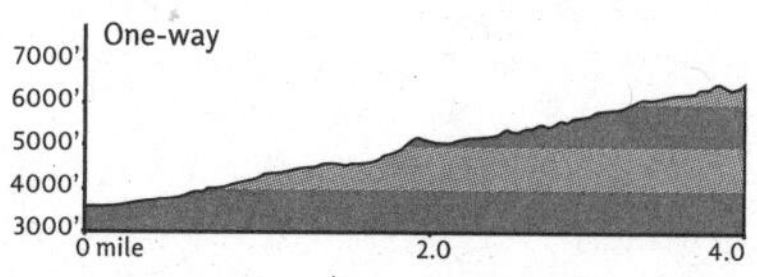

Maps: Green Trails Mount Rainier East, No. 270; **Contact:** Sunrise Ranger Station, (360) 663-2425; **GPS:** N46 55.364, W121 32.017

Grand views await you here, as Crystal Peak stands between the stunning spires of the Norse Peak Wilderness and the mighty summit of Mount Rainier's northeastern

The White River lined with fall yellow color seen from the Crystal Peak trail

Dennis and Michael hike down the Crystal Peak trail with stunning views of Mount Rainier in their faces.

flank. You might encounter elk; you'll surely see soaring hawks and/or eagles; and if you time it right, you'll be waist deep in huckleberries on the upper slopes of the peak. If the berries aren't ripe yet, no worries—you'll find wildflowers in bloom along the way.

GETTING THERE

From Enumclaw, drive east 42 miles on State Route 410 to the trailhead parking lot on the right, just 4.5 miles after passing through the park's entryway arch.

ON THE TRAIL

Tighten your laces, and then head up from the highway. The trail pitches steeply upward immediately, climbing through a long series of switchbacks in the first 1.5 miles. The forest is close and well shaded, so even on the hottest summer days the route is relatively cool.

At 1.5 miles, the trail splits; the left fork heads to Crystal Lakes (Hike 15). To the right is a rough boot-built trail. Take that right turn and start a long, sweeping traverse south along the flank of Crystal Peak. The path crosses Crystal Creek and continues under the forest canopy for another mile or so, but then it begins to open up and, at around 2.75 miles, you run into some open hillside meadows. Look for ripening berries along these sun-drenched slopes.

At 3 miles, the trail switches back and starts a steeper climb. The final mile rolls steeply upward through heather and wildflower meadows to the summit of the peak. Once upon a time, a fire lookout tower stood here—you might still find some fragments of the steel cable that secured the tower on the wind-blasted peak.

As you might expect from an old lookout site, the views here are phenomenal. The panoramic wonder spreads out in 360 degrees, with Mount Rainier dominating the scenery, though the view across the White River valley to the Sourdough Mountains is also spectacular.

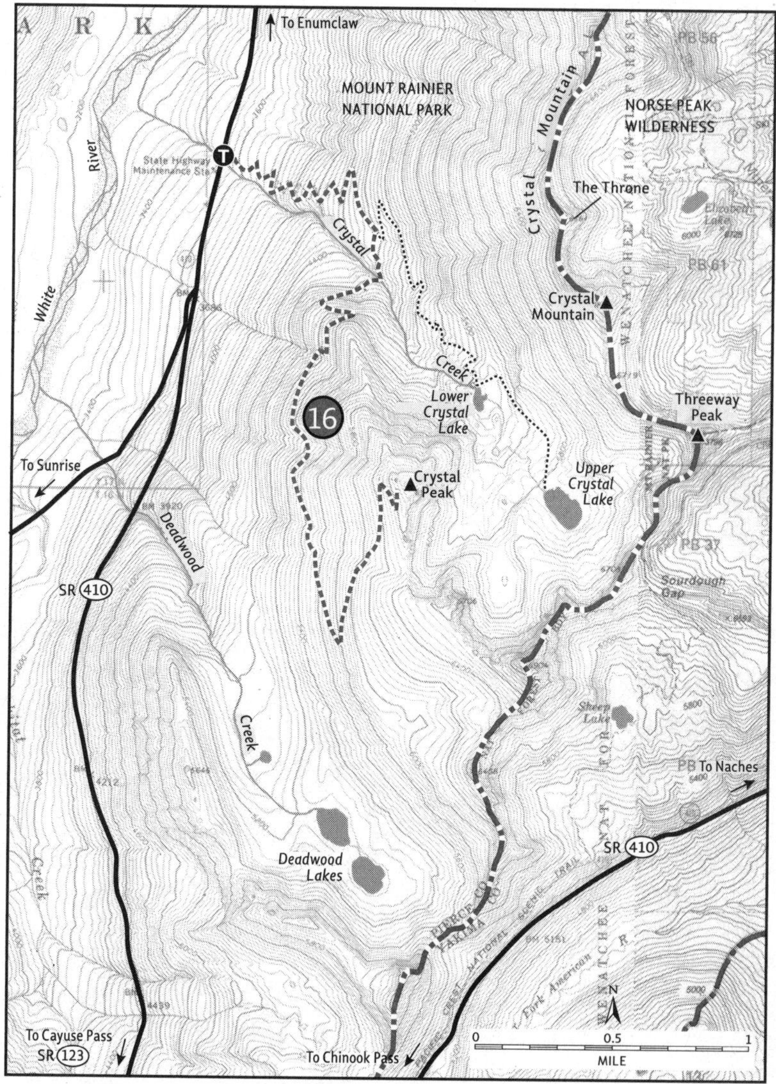
To Enumclaw
MOUNT RAINIER
NATIONAL PARK
NORSE PEAK
WILDERNESS
River
White
Crystal
Creek
Crystal Mountain
The Throne
Crystal
Mountain
Lower
Crystal
Lake
16
Threeway
Peak
To Sunrise
Crystal
Peak
Upper
Crystal
Lake
Deadwood
SR 410
Sourdough
Gap
Sheep
Lake
Creek
To Naches
SR 410
Deadwood
Lakes
To Cayuse Pass
SR 123
To Chinook Pass
0
0.5
1
MILE
N

17 Owyhigh Lakes

RATING/ DIFFICULTY	ROUND-TRIP	ELEV GAIN/ HIGH POINT	SEASON
***/4	8 miles	1650 feet/ 5400 feet	July–Oct

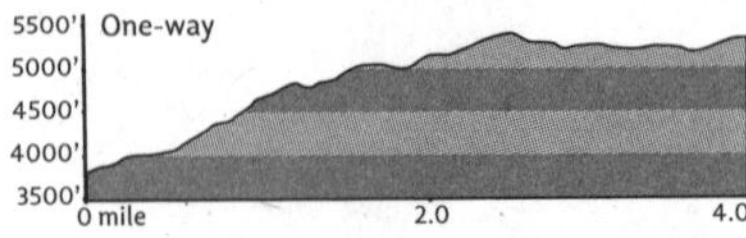

Maps: Green Trails Mount Rainier East, No. 270; **Contact:** Sunrise Ranger Station, (360) 663-2425; **GPS:** N46 53.431, W121 35.807

The local wildlife love the Owyhigh Lakes. This pair of shallow forest lakes provides good water, lots of forage in the shoreline meadows, and wonderful cover in the forests that press in around the lakes. Hikers find limited views from the trail—though there are nice views up to Cowlitz Chimneys and Tamanos Mountain. But the forest environment this trail explores is unmatched for those who appreciate a rich woodland ecosystem. Kids and adults appreciate the wildlife-viewing potential. Birds and beasts (large and small) thrive in this forest, and birds fill the lakes basin. Repeated visits to the lakes have let me spot grouse, pileated woodpeckers, mountain blue jays, cedar waxwings, ospreys, bald eagles, golden eagles, tanagers, and a host of birds I couldn't identify. There's also a fair amount of huckleberries along the route if you time your trip just right.

The Owyhigh Lakes trail passing by huge old-growth firs

GETTING THERE

From Enumclaw, drive east 43 miles on State Route 410 to the Mount Rainier National Park White River Entrance. Veer right onto the Sunrise Road and follow it 3 miles to the trailhead parking area about 1 mile after crossing Shaw Creek.

ON THE TRAIL

Running south through lush old forest, the trail climbs steadily from the get-go. The initial climb starts with a 0.25-mile-long ascending traverse before swinging into a series of switchbacks. The rush upward continues

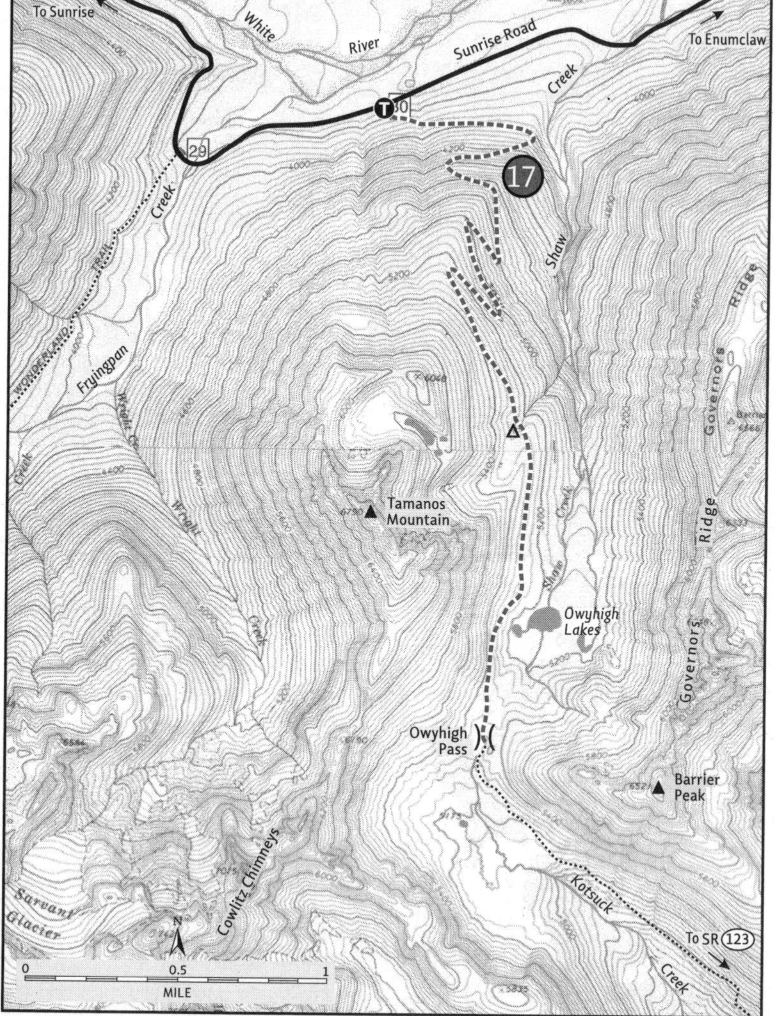

over the first 2.5 miles as the trail runs up the northern spine of Tamanos Mountain. Listen for birdsong along this stretch, and keep your eyes open for small critters in the forests along the trail.

At 2.5 miles, the trail sweeps out into a hillside traverse, reaching Tamanos Creek Camp at 3 miles. The small namesake creek is a seasonal feeder of Shaw Creek, which drains Owyhigh Lakes. Tamanos Creek usually dries up by early September, so don't plan on camping here late in the season.

From the camp, the trail drops to a nearly flat pitch for the final 0.5 mile to the lakes basin. The shallow lakes are wonderful for cooling your feet—but not great for swimming. As you approach the lakes, stay quiet and keep a keen eye out for a moment in the forests and meadows around the lakes. You might see deer, elk, or even mountain goats—the goats descend from the craggy heights above to drink here.

Enjoy the views of the Cowlitz Chimneys above the lakes, and maybe doze in the sun-dappled meadows, before pushing on the final 0.5 mile to the 5400-foot pass separating Governors Ridge from Tamanos Mountain. The pass provides good views of each peak, as well as the high spires of the Chimneys to the west. Turn back here. **Note:** This trail was severely damaged in the November 2006 floods. As this book went to press, this trail was relocated through rough terrain. Check with the park for the current status of this trail.

EXTENDING YOUR TRIP

If you have two vehicles for a shuttle, you can push on through the pass and descend about 4.5 miles to a junction with the Eastside Trail at Deer Creek Camp. From there, it's just 0.5 mile up to the Cayuse Pass Highway–State Route 123 (Hike 35). Check road conditions for SR 123 (see the next chapter for details).

18 Panhandle Gap

RATING/ DIFFICULTY	ROUND-TRIP	ELEV GAIN/ HIGH POINT	SEASON
*****/5	12 miles	2950 feet/ 6800 feet	June–Oct

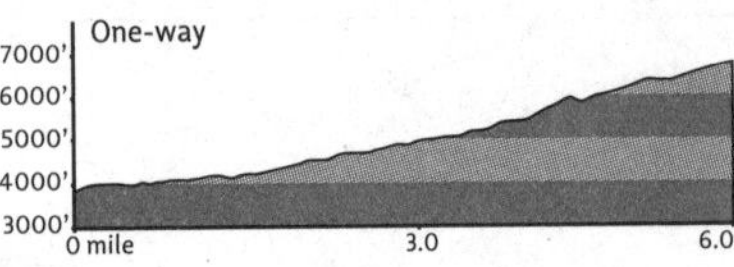

Maps: Green Trails Mount Rainier East, No. 270; **Contact:** Sunrise Ranger Station, (360) 663-2425; **GPS:** N46 53.302, W121 36.662

I'll admit it: I think this is the single most spectacular day hike in the entire park. It's also one of the toughest, but the workout is well worth the effort. This section of the Wonderland Trail is also the highest of that entire 94-mile loop route. The section of trail leading up the Fryingpan Creek basin isn't all that spectacular, but once you get high, the beauty stacks up like cordwood until the sheer splendor of the route nearly overwhelms you. The wildflower meadows of Summerland are staggeringly beautiful. The rock and ice basin below Fryingpan Glacier is wonderful. Then you crest the last rocky ridge at Panhandle Gap and see the vast alpine world of Ohanapecosh Park stretched out to the south, with the spires of the Cowlitz Chimneys punctuating the eastern skyline and massive Mount Rainier towering over it all to the west. Chances are also good you'll see one of the large local herds of mountain goats either browsing or napping in one of the meadows or snowfields.

GETTING THERE

From Enumclaw, drive east 43 miles on State Route 410 to the Mount Rainier National Park

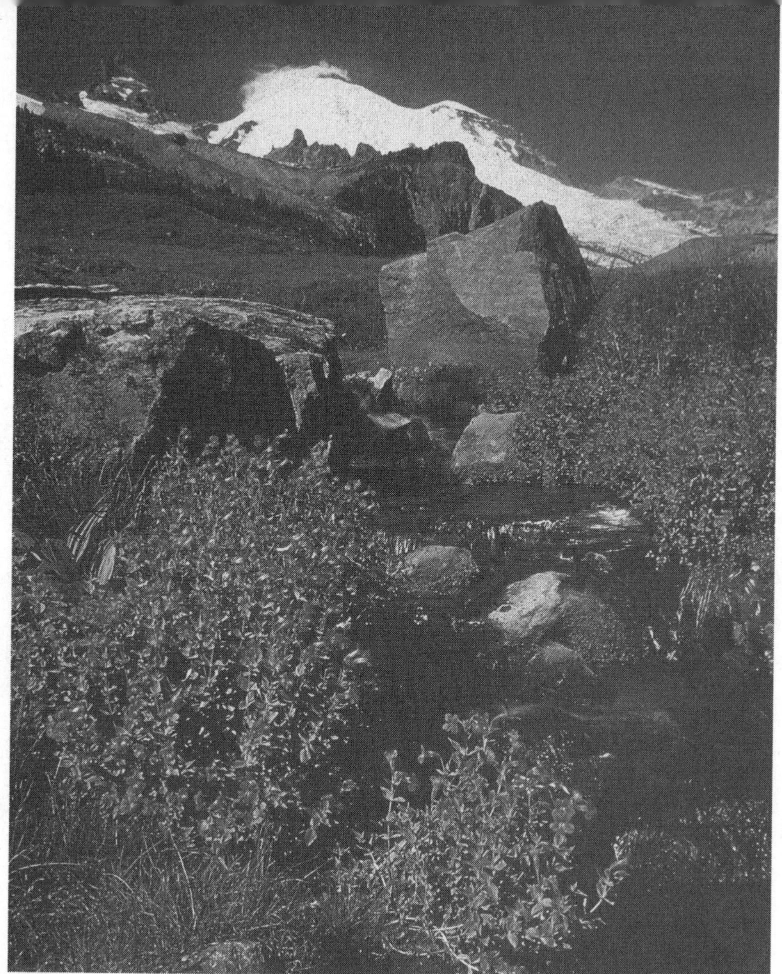

Pink monkey-flower lines a small stream along the Wonderland Trail between Summerland and Panhandle Gap.

White River Entrance. Veer right onto Sunrise Road and follow it 4 miles to the trailhead parking area near the bridge over Fryingpan Creek.

ON THE TRAIL

The trail climbs gradually for the first couple of miles, ascending the Fryingpan valley. Late in the season (late August and early September), you can find a few huckleberries in the sun-dappled forest along the first couple of miles of trail. At 2 miles out, the trail offers a view of the constricted waters of the creek as it pounds down a rocky chasm. The thundering waters can be near-deafening early in the year when snowmelt fills the river to near flood stage.

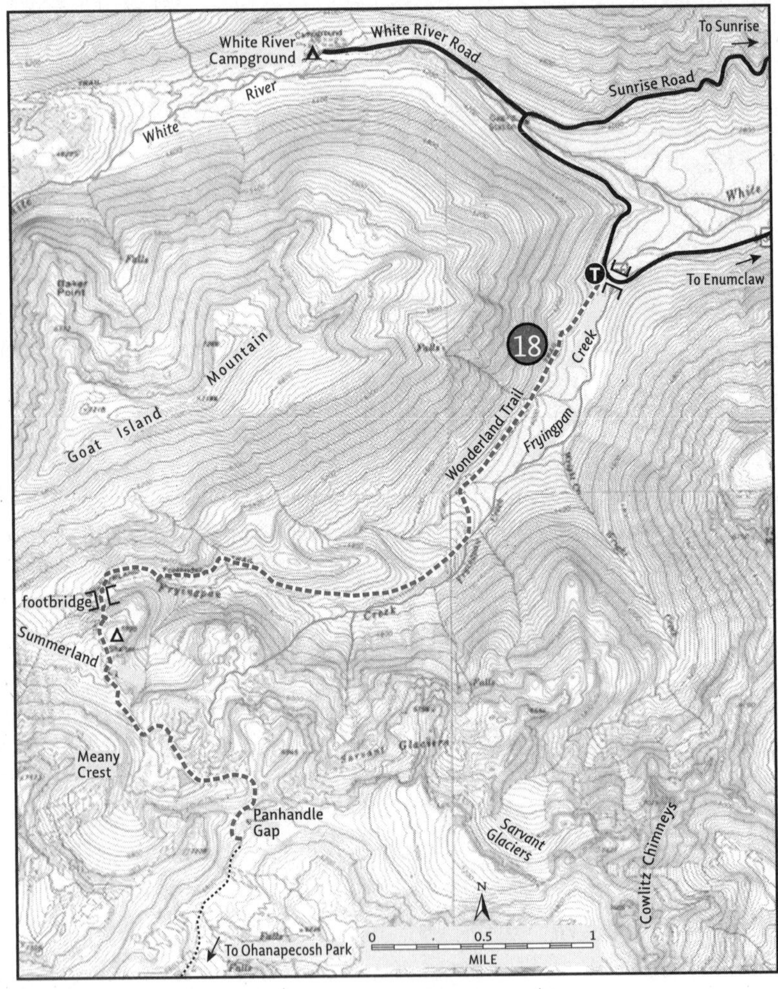

At 2.5 miles, the trail starts to traverse through a series of avalanche slopes. These avalanche chutes are largely full of slide alder, but the areas along their edges sport salmonberries and, at times, broad huckleberry brambles. At 3 miles, you find the largest avalanche chute. Here, the trail turns and crosses the creek before climbing steeply up the opposite valley wall. The creek crossing can be impossible early in the year—the long footlog typically has to be replaced each spring, and until crews get that done, there is no safe way across the churning water.

Once over the creek, the trail climbs steeply for 1 mile, then enters 0.25 mile of tight switchbacks before erupting out into the sprawling meadows of Summerland (5900 feet). A wonderful open backcountry camp is nestled on a small spine along the flank of Summerland meadows, and huge boulders provide plenty of warm places to lie out and rest in the sunshine. Hikers who have had their fill of scenic beauty (not to mention thigh-burning climbing) can turn back here for a wonderful 8.5-mile round trip.

The better option, though, is to push on. The next 2 miles ascend gradually. You climb the eastern wall of the Summerland basin and, at about 5 miles, enter a world of rock and ice (well, rock and compact snow). This basin below the Fryingpan Glacier is above the vegetation zone, so little grows here. Still, you'll see birds darting through the basin and possibly find mountain goats taking their leisure on the cool year-round snowfields.

Close-up of a yellow violet, an early spring wildflower of the damp forests

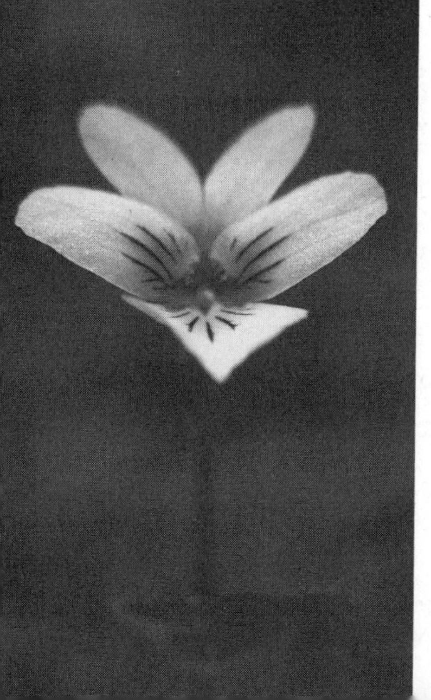

At 6 miles, you top out of the last climb to find yourself on the narrow ridge of Panhandle Gap. Behind you is Summerland and Mount Rainier. Before you is the vast Ohanapecosh valley and the broad meadows that circle the head of that valley—meadows that form Ohanapecosh Park.

EXTENDING YOUR TRIP

If you can arrange a shuttle vehicle, you can push on along the Wonderland Trail through Ohanapecosh Park to Indian Bar Camp, then down the Cowlitz Divide to Box Canyon trailhead on the Stevens Canyon Road, about 12 miles farther on. Plan on two days to complete this section, if only to ensure a night's stay at beautiful Indian Bar Camp.

19 Glacier Basin

RATING/ DIFFICULTY	ROUND-TRIP	ELEV GAIN/ HIGH POINT	SEASON
****/4	6 miles	1600 feet/ 5900 feet	July–Oct

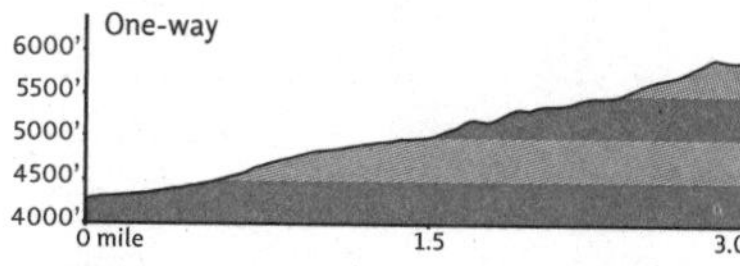

Maps: Green Trails Mount Rainier East, No. 270; **Contact:** Sunrise Ranger Station, (360) 663-2425; **GPS:** N46 54.129, W121 38.621

Your time is running out. Without radical changes in global practices, glaciers could disappear entirely in the Lower 48 states, and the ice rivers on Mount Rainier are already in full retreat. Fortunately, we can still see the mighty ice sheets

and even get up-close and personal with them. This trail ascends the upper reaches of the White River valley, crawling through scraggly forest and craggy moraines—ridges of rock pushed aside by the moving glaciers. If you have the skill and the time, you can scramble up the bottom section of a climbers trail to reach the ice of Inter Glacier.

GETTING THERE

From Enumclaw, drive east 43 miles on State Route 410 to the Mount Rainier National Park White River Entrance. Veer right onto the Sunrise Road and follow it 5 miles, cross the White River, and turn left onto the White River Road. Follow this road to its end at the White River Campground. Park in the hikers lot and find the trailhead at the upper end of the campground loop.

ON THE TRAIL

Head up the trail as it follows the frigid, churning waters of the White River upstream. The trail is broad and easy to walk. In fact, it's actually an old road, once used by miners and then by tourists until the late 1940s. The trail dips near the river periodically, and even on the hottest summer days, you can often feel a refreshingly cool breeze off the icy waters.

At 1 mile, the trail splits. Stay right to continue up the Inter Fork of the White River. This branch of the river is spawned by the melting waters of the Inter Glacier, the river of ice nestled in the rocky basin below the pointed crest of Steamboat Prow.

From the fork, the trail continues west, climbing along the river at the foot of Burroughs Mountain until reaching another trail junction at 2.5 miles (5500 feet). The trail on the right climbs steeply to the crest of Second Burroughs Mountain. You want to stay left and push upward toward The Wedge—the headwall of Glacier Basin.

At 3 miles, the official trail ends at Glacier Basin Camp (5900 feet). From here, you can look upward at the rocky notch of St. Elmo

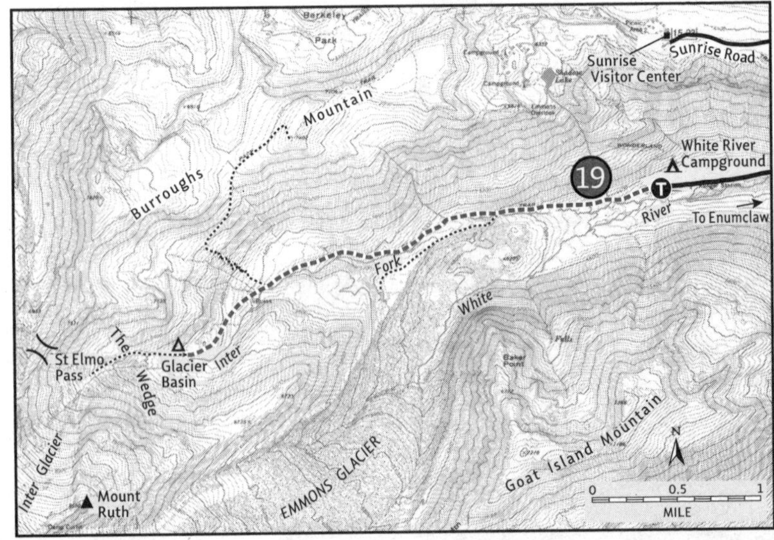

A small side-creek waterfall tumbles onto the Glacier Basin trail.

UNDERSTANDING ELK

Elk. Such a small, simple word for such a massive, majestic beast. I much prefer the Shawnee Indian name of *wapiti*, meaning "white rump." But a name is just a name and, whether you call them wapiti or elk, these animals earn the respect and appreciation of anyone fortunate enough to see them in the wild.

But not all elk are created equal. Indeed, Washington boasts two distinct subspecies of elk. Roosevelt elk, named for Theodore Roosevelt, are found on the Olympic Peninsula (hence their nickname, Olympic elk). In the Cascades—and points east—Rocky Mountain elk reign supreme. Elk can be found mostly around the northern and northeastern portions of Mount Rainier National Park. The White River drainage hosts the largest herds.

Rocky Mountain elk are somewhat smaller than their Roosevelt cousins (a big Roosevelt bull may weigh more than a half ton), but they generally sport broader, heavier antler sets. A large part of this antler difference stems from the different habitats of each subspecies. Roosevelt elk tend to be found in the foliage-rich rain forests of the Olympic Peninsula, where broad, heavy antlers would be more problematic. Rocky Mountain elk thrive in the drier, more open forests of the Cascades, but they also move out over the plains of the eastern Cascade foothills and even onto the desert steppes of the Columbia River basin. Indeed, Rocky Mountain elk once existed in vast herds on the Great Plains, alongside the mighty American bison.

Elk of both subspecies feed by browsing on a variety of vegetation, from grasses to berries to evergreen needles. The most impressive time to experience elk is autumn, when the herds are in rut—in other words, mating season. Like most ungulates, the elk males (bulls) fight among themselves to establish dominance and decide which bull gets to mate with the female elk (cows).

As part of the ritual, the bulls challenge each other by issuing ringing calls. Known as bugling, these calls can be an eerie trumpet tone that sends chills down your spine. Listening to the undulating, high-pitched calls as twilight falls over a forest glade will get even the most unimaginative hikers thinking that they're lost in the forest primeval.

Pass, through which flows the headwaters of the Inter Fork of White River. After enjoying the views, turn back at the camp and return the way you came. **Note:** This trail was severely damaged in the November 2006 floods. As this book went to press, this trail was relocated through rough terrain. Check with the park for the current status of this trail.

EXTENDING YOUR TRIP

For more rugged adventures, follow the climbers track as it ascends from the camp through the rocky rubble of The Wedge. In just under 1 mile you gain 1200 feet, crossing under St. Elmo Pass, to reach the foot of Inter Glacier. **Note:** This is a rough scramble route that deserves a great deal of respect and caution.

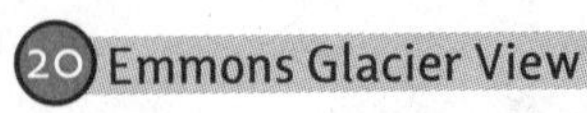

20 Emmons Glacier View

RATING/ DIFFICULTY	ROUND-TRIP	ELEV GAIN/ HIGH POINT	SEASON
***/2	3 miles	900 feet/ 5200 feet	July–Oct

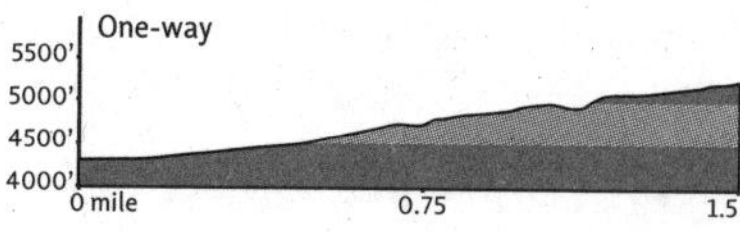

Maps: Green Trails Mount Rainier East, No. 270; **Contact:** Sunrise Ranger Station, (360) 663-2425; **GPS:** N46 54.129, W121 38.621

The rewards are grand views, wonderful lessons in geology, and easy hiking. The only drawback of the route is the potential for crowds—the hiking is relatively easy, leading out of a popular car campground, so the masses flock to this scenic trail. Fortunately, the broad trail can handle the pressure. In fact, it once handled hordes of tourists in Model Ts and Park Service buses, so a bit of foot traffic won't be a problem. The road-turned-trail offers easy walking for the most part, close to the river. Look up at the hulk of Rainier looming to the southwest as you hike, and you can enjoy the towering wall of Goat Island Mountain to the south.

GETTING THERE

From Enumclaw, drive east 43 miles on State Route 410 to the Mount Rainier National Park White River Entrance. Veer right onto the Sunrise Road and follow it 5 miles, cross the White River, and turn left onto the White River Road. Follow this road to its end at the White River Campground. Park in the hikers lot and find the trailhead at the upper end of the campground loop.

ON THE TRAIL

Start on the broad trail as it leaves the upper loop of the campground, following the White River upstream for 1 mile. The route stays away from the river most of the way but dips in close to the water frequently enough to bring you a refreshingly cool breeze off the ice-melt water.

At 1 mile, the trail splits. To the right is the Glacier Basin Trail (Hike 19). Turn left, crossing the Inter Fork of the White River on a broad footlog (or, depending on the river course, multiple footlogs across the braided river).

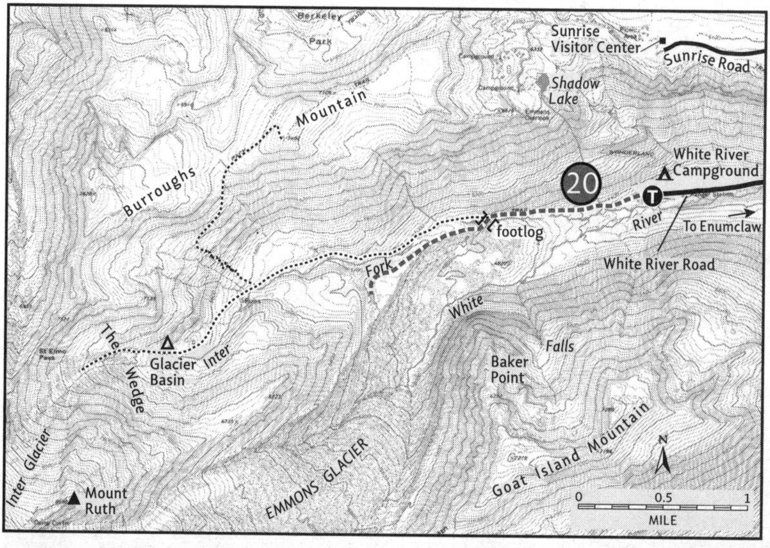

Once over the river, you follow the rough trail as it weaves through the long spines of rocky moraine—rubble left behind by the retreating glacier.

At 1.5 miles, the trail officially ends at a viewpoint offering panoramic views up the face of Emmons Glacier. Look up the length of the long finger of ice to the summit of mighty Mount Rainier. As tempting as it may be, avoid the urge to scramble around the moraine at trail's end—the braided headwaters of the White River are unpredictable, the footing in the area is marginal, and the waters of the river are deathly cold. Stay on the trail, and return as you came. **Note:** This trail was severely damaged in the November 2006 floods. As this book went to press, this trail was relocated through rough terrain. Check with the park for the current status of this trail.

EXTENDING YOUR TRIP

If you want more miles under your boots, return to the trail junction and turn left to push on up the main trail toward Glacier Basin (Hike 19).

21 White River to Sunrise

RATING/ DIFFICULTY	ROUND-TRIP	ELEV GAIN/ HIGH POINT	SEASON
***/4	6 miles	Shadow Lake 1900 feet; Sunrise 2100 feet/ Shadow Lake 6200 feet; Sunrise 6400 feet	July–Oct

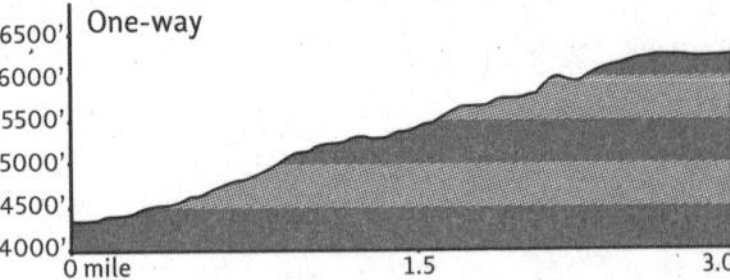

Maps: Green Trails Mount Rainier East, No. 270; **Contact:** Sunrise Ranger Station, (360) 663-2425; **GPS:** N46 54.129, W121 38.621

The birth of the White River exits the terminus of the Emmons Glacier.

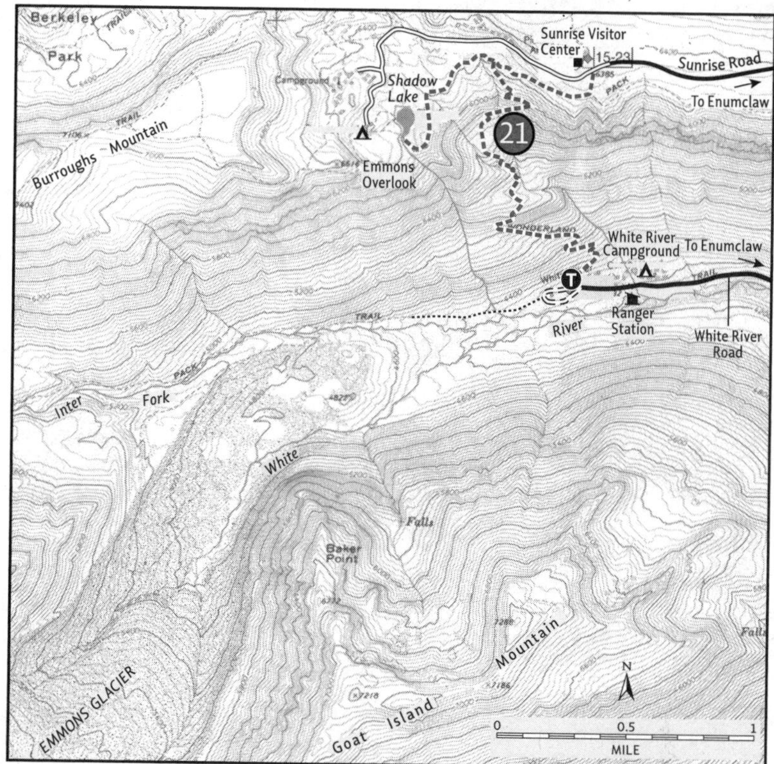

If you need a hike that stretches your legs, exercises your lungs, and offers a good dose of solitude in a very popular part of the park, check out this route. This section of the Wonderland Trail, recently renovated by volunteers, leads from the White River Campground straight up the valley wall to Sunrise, 3 miles above. The trail sticks strictly to forest until you reach the top, so don't expect sweeping views until you reach Sunrise. The combination of elevation gain, lack of views, and car-accessible destination means this trail is seldom visited and therefore perfect for the hiker who wants a wild-country workout in a cool forest.

GETTING THERE

From Enumclaw, drive east 43 miles on State Route 410 to the Mount Rainier National Park White River Entrance. Veer right onto the Sunrise Road and follow it 5 miles, cross the White River, and turn left onto the White River Road. Follow this road to its end at the White River Campground. Park in the hikers lot and find the trailhead on the north side of the campground.

ON THE TRAIL

The trail leaves the campground and starts climbing immediately. The first 0.1 mile is a gradual ascent as the trail traverses to the

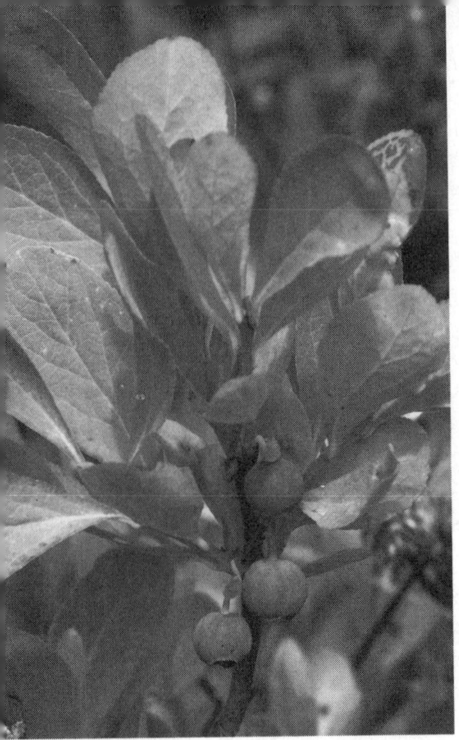

east before turning uphill into a series of steep switchbacks. You weave back and forth, climbing all the while, as the trail ascends through fragrant forests of fir and hemlock. Listen (and look) for grouse and small forest critters. Squirrels are common; weasels are less so, but still present.

At about 1.5 miles, the trail crosses a small creek, climbs straight up a small ridge face, then recrosses the creek around 2 miles. At 2.5 miles, you reach a trail junction and the first broken views.

Turn right to reach Sunrise Ranger Station in 0.5 mile, or turn left to reach Shadow Lake and its surrounding meadows in 0.5 mile. I recommend the lake option. Stop at the lake for a relaxing rest before descending back to your starting point. Or head into Sunrise and see if you can hitch a ride down the mountain (or arrange a vehicle shuttle) to save your legs the pounding descent.

There are never too many huckleberries to stop and admire . . . and eat!

Opposite: View down into Berkley Park from Skyscraper Mountain

sunrise

Aptly named Sunrise rises on the northeast side of Mount Rainier to grab the first morning light each day. The vast parklands that make up the Sunrise area truly capture the alpine spirit of the mountain. Long, rolling fields of green splashed with vibrantly colored wildflowers cover the long ridgelines, while high, craggy peaks push up past the green zone into the stark world of rock and ice. Sunrise offers an array of hiking opportunities, from short, nearly flat routes perfect for families and folk short of time, to long meadow and forest rambles that lead to some of the most picturesque places in this park known for its photogenic wonders. Sunrise is the highest elevation trailhead in the park, so many of the trails have the benefit of starting high and staying high, meaning you can generally enjoy more miles with less effort.

22 Sunrise Lake

RATING/ DIFFICULTY	ROUND-TRIP	ELEV GAIN/ HIGH POINT	SEASON
**/2	1.5 miles	425 feet/ 6150 feet	July–Oct

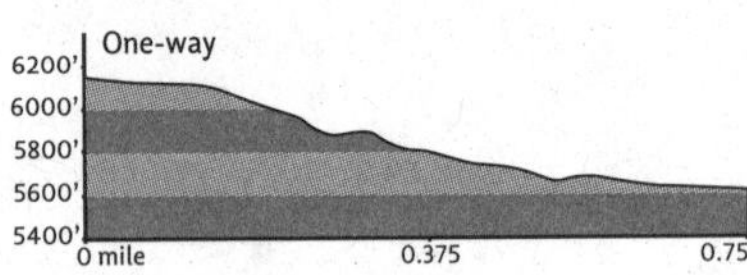

Maps: Green Trails Mount Rainier East, No. 270; **Contact:** Sunrise Ranger Station, (360) 663-2425; **GPS:** N46 55.053, W121 35.268

Kids, as well as parents, love this short hike since it's just long enough to tire out young legs without being too tiring—you can set aside your worries about having to tote your tot back to the trailhead. Kids appreciate the views and absolutely love the pikas and marmots that pop out of crevices in the rocky slope bisected by the trail. Of course, kids young and old have fun wading in the cold waters of Sunrise Lake, watching the mudskippers and tadpoles thrashing in the shallows.

GETTING THERE

From Enumclaw, drive east 43 miles on State Route 410 to the Mount Rainier National Park White River Entrance. Veer right onto the Sunrise Road and follow it 12 miles west to the

Huge buck grazing on autumn's dried wildflowers

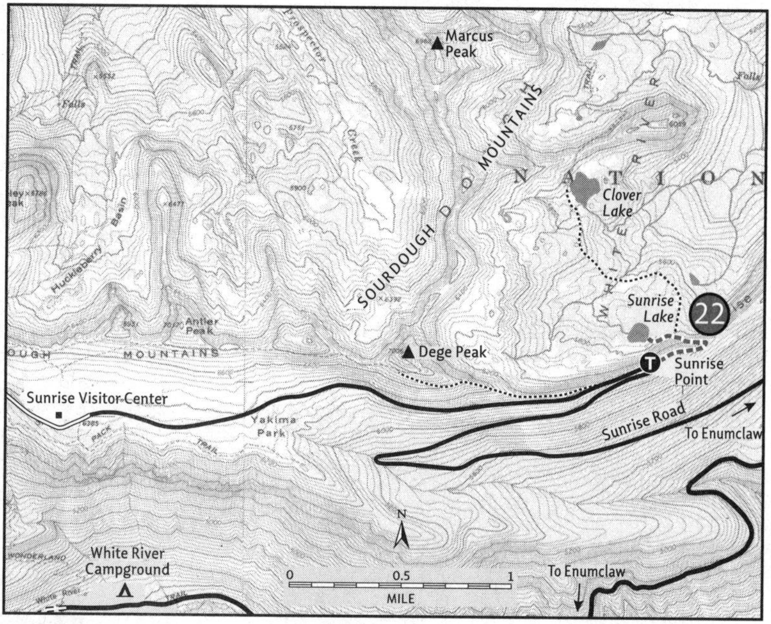

parking lot inside the hairpin turn at Sunrise Point. **Note:** Sunrise Road usually doesn't open until early July.

ON THE TRAIL

Cross to the north side of the road at the apex of the road curve and find the trail swinging around the rock wall and dropping down the north face of the ridge. The trail descends through a long talus slope, but trail crews have made the path smooth and safe for little legs. The broken rocks of the talus field have been stacked into retaining walls in the steepest sections and rearranged into paved walkways where necessary. Goofy-looking marmots galumph over the rocky slopes, and cute little pikas—rabbitlike rock dwellers with short, round ears and a high-pitched *eep* call—pop in and out of the rocky crevices.

At 0.5 mile, the trail forks. Go left and descend another 0.25 mile to reach the shoreline of Sunrise Lake (elevation 5725 feet). From the lake, look north along the flank of the Sourdough Mountains, and you might spot the snowy-fleeced mountain goats that call this range home.

23 Palisades Lakes

RATING/ DIFFICULTY	ROUND-TRIP	ELEV GAIN/ HIGH POINT	SEASON
****/3	7.5 miles	500 feet/ 6150 feet	July–Oct

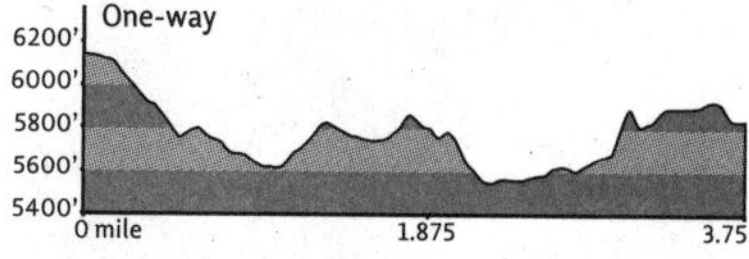

Maps: Green Trails Mount Rainier East, No. 270; **Contact:** Sunrise Ranger Station, (360) 663-2425; **GPS:** N46 55.053, W121 35.268

The combination of sprawling meadows, few trails, and virgin forest for cover makes the Palisades Lakes basin a haven for wildlife. This trail is the only one in the vast area between Huckleberry Creek and the White River, and it dead-ends at the lakes' basin. As a result, this wild high country gets relatively few human visitors. The broad wildflower meadows that blanket the upper flanks of the Sourdough Mountains (from Dege Peak to Slide Mountain) attract deer, elk, and mountain goats. During one late September visit, my intrepid hiking companion and I found ourselves enjoying a spectacular sunset with views of the alpenglow on the Palisades—a tall band of cliffs above Palisades Lakes. As the orange glow faded on the rock wall, the haunting

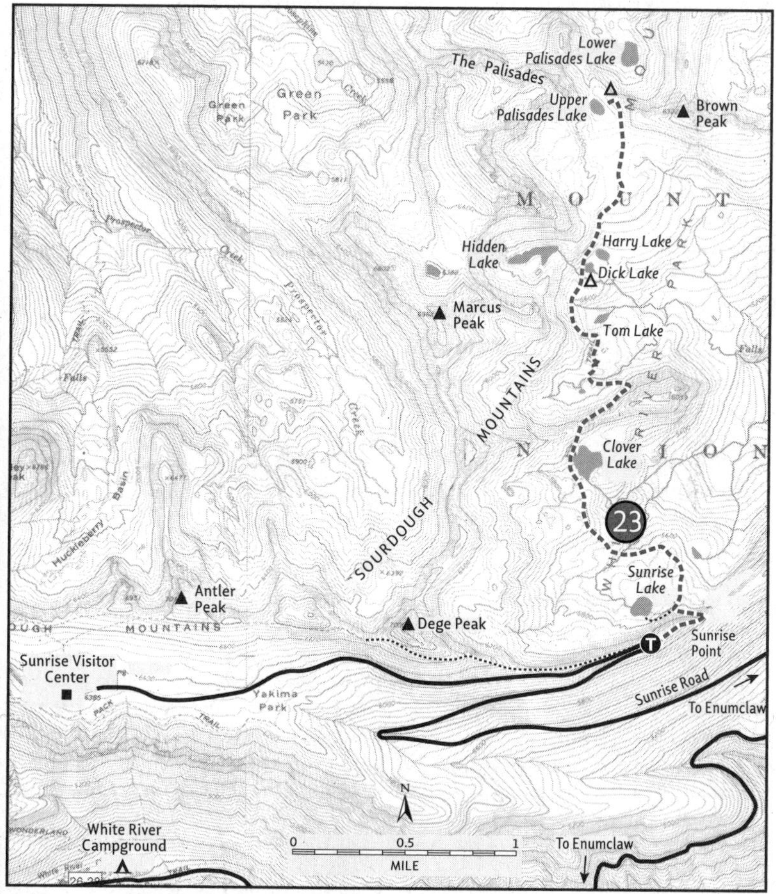

Opposite: Wildflower-filled meadows approaching Palisades Lakes

call of bull elk in the midst of their rut—mating season—echoed across the meadows. Soon, no fewer than six bulls were bugling their challenges, converging onto our evening retreat. Fortunately, the big males noticed that the band of cow elk had moved off to the west, and the amorous bulls veered that way before challenging each other in a clash of wills, each seeking the right to mate. Even without the elk encounter, however, the hike was memorable for the incredible scenery at the lakes.

GETTING THERE

From Enumclaw, drive east 43 miles on State Route 410 to the Mount Rainier National Park White River Entrance. Veer right onto the Sunrise Road and follow it 12 miles west to the parking lot inside the hairpin turn at Sunrise Point. **Note:** Sunrise Road usually doesn't open until early July.

ON THE TRAIL

From the parking lot, cross the road near the apex of the hairpin turn to find the trailhead on the north side of the roadway. The trail descends through some gentle switchbacks for 0.5 mile to a trail junction. Go right and follow the path as it meanders through stands of forests, small forest glades, and broad alpine meadows.

At 1.5 miles, the trail skirts the shore of Clover Lake (a fine place to turn back for those wanting a shorter hike). The trail continues north around a small rocky spine and rolls out into a wet hillside awash in wildflowers. The water that seeps out of the hillside keeps a wide variety of flowers in bloom much of the summer. At 2.5 miles, the trail runs between the trio of lakes known as Tom, Dick, and Harry. There's a small campsite on the shore of Dick Lake.

The trail climbs from Dick Lake Camp, entering thicker stands of forest but still offering plenty of sun breaks for the next mile, where the trail enters the cirque of Upper Palisades Lake. The trail descends in 0.25 mile to the shores of the lake. Camping is available at Palisades Lakes—permits are required. Broad meadows run along the south and east sides of the lake basin. The tall wall of the Palisades towers to the west.

EXTENDING YOUR TRIP

Hikers who want to go a little farther have the option of a nice, open scramble through heather meadows to the summit of Brown Peak, about 0.5 mile to the east.

24 Sourdough Ridge

RATING/ DIFFICULTY	LOOP	ELEV GAIN/ HIGH POINT	SEASON
****/2	2.5 miles	400 feet/ 6800 feet	July–Oct

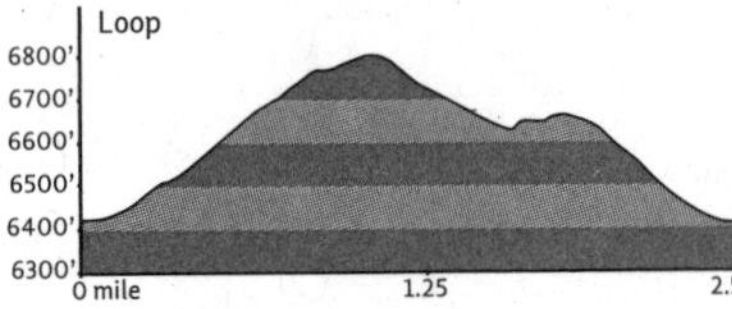

Maps: Green Trails Mount Rainier East, No. 270; **Contact:** Sunrise Ranger Station, (360) 663-2425; **GPS:** N46 54.877, W121 38.540

If you're looking for a quick way to get away from the car and into Mount Rainier's alpine splendor, this is your express lane to ecstasy. The Sourdough Ridge Trail, which begins in the thick of the tourist-choked Sunrise visitor center, leaves it all fairly quickly, climbing to a ridge top and turning east beneath Antler Peak. Kids love the open views and general abundance of marmots.

A hiker heading west along Sourdough Ridge with almost constant views of Mount Rainier

GETTING THERE

From Enumclaw, drive east 43 miles on State Route 410 to the Mount Rainier National Park White River Entrance. Veer right onto the Sunrise Road and follow it 17 miles west to the large parking lot and visitor center at the road's end. **Note:** Sunrise Road usually doesn't open until early July.

ON THE TRAIL

At the trailhead near the rest rooms on the north side of the parking lot, head north across meadows for 0.2 mile to reach a Y-junction. You'll start and end here, so you could go either way, though I recommend going right to do the loop counterclockwise. Follow the slanting trail about 0.5 mile to the top of Sourdough Ridge. The hard-packed trail climbs 400 feet to the crest of Sourdough Ridge and a junction with the ridge-top trail. If you go right (east), you'll wander 1.3 miles to Dege Peak (Hike 31). That's a trip for another day, however. Instead, go left and skirt under the summit of Antler Peak.

After about 0.2 mile, you'll get around Antler and find yourself on the edge of a sharp ridge line. From the ridge, you can look south to Mount Rainier and beyond. Little Tahoma Peak stands to the east of the mountain, and the deep green valleys of the William O. Douglas Wilderness push away to the east. To the north is the stunningly pretty valley of Huckleberry Creek, and the long line of the Sourdough Mountains stretches away to the northeast.

Continue west along this spine for another 0.3 mile, where you'll meet another trail fork (1.25 miles from the start). To the left is the trail forming the other branch of that Y you encountered at the start of your trek. Keep that in mind, but for now, continue straight ahead to follow Sourdough Ridge farther west—the best views are still ahead.

In just 0.25 mile, you come around a small

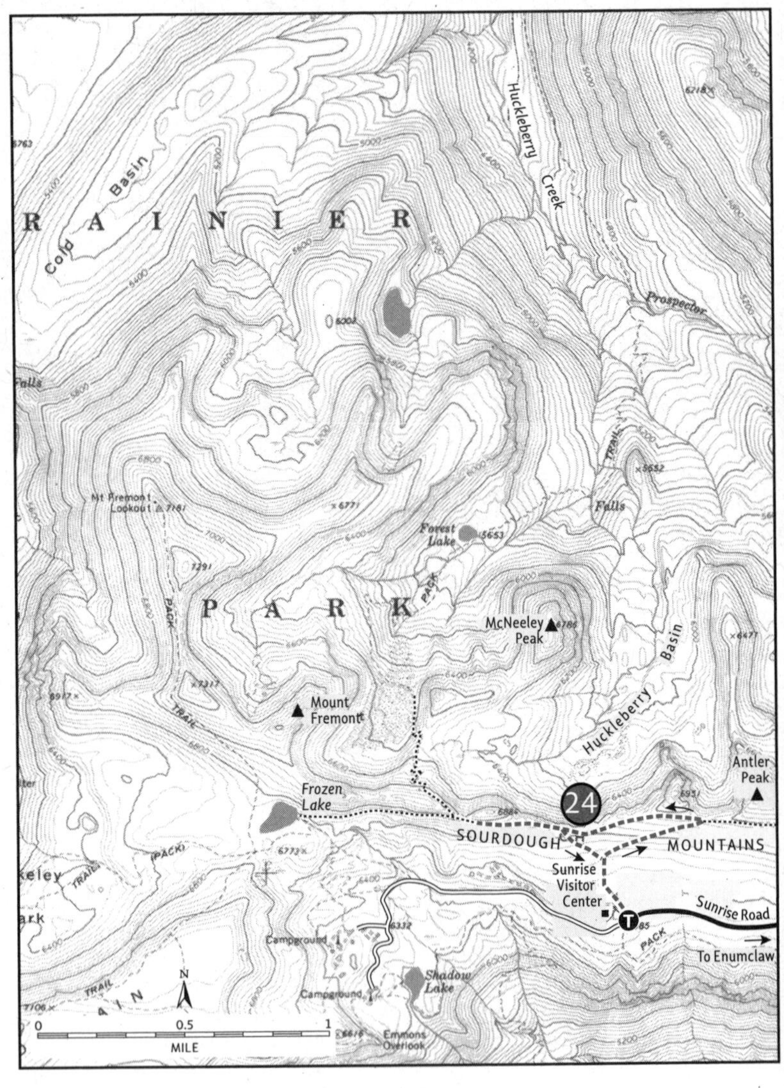

RAINIER
PARK
Cold Basin
Huckleberry Creek
Prospector
Mt Fremont Lookout
Forest Lake
Falls
McNeeley Peak
Huckleberry Basin
Mount Fremont
Frozen Lake
Antler Peak
24
SOURDOUGH
MOUNTAINS
Sunrise Visitor Center
Sunrise Road
To Enumclaw
Campground
Shadow Lake
Emmons Overlook
TRAIL
PACK
N
0
0.5
1
MILE

knoll to return to the precipitous edge of the ridge above Huckleberry Basin. This time, though, you'll be able to look down on a green parkland bench floating halfway down the valley wall. This green terrace frequently is graced by herds of mountain goats and, on occasion, elk.

This is a wonderful place to stop and rest before turning back to that just-past junction, where you turn right to descend 0.8 mile back to the trailhead, closing your stretched-out loop hike.

25 Fremont Lookout

RATING/ DIFFICULTY	ROUND-TRIP	ELEV GAIN/ HIGH POINT	SEASON
****/3	5.6 miles	800 feet/ 7200 feet	July–Oct

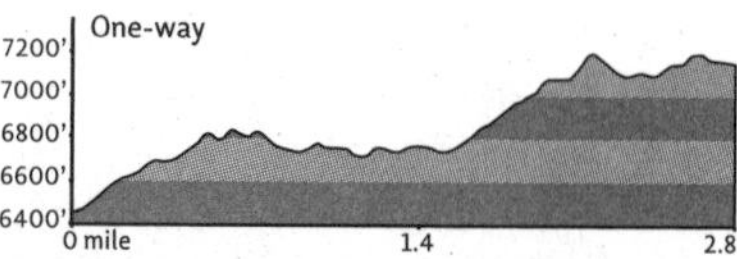

The table-flat appearance of Grand Park seen from the Mount Fremont lookout

Maps: Green Trails Mount Rainier East, No. 270; **Contact:** Sunrise Ranger Station, (360) 663-2425; **GPS:** N46 54.877, W121 38.540

The Mount Fremont Trail, an easy half-day hike from the popular (and spectacular) Sunrise area, is an extremely popular hike that can be combined with other Sunrise-area destinations for a full day of wandering among some of the most spectacular mountain and alpine parkland scenery in the United States. The old fire-watch tower at trail's end is dubbed the Fremont Lookout, but the stilted cabin actually sits on a secondary knoll, not the true summit, of Mount Fremont. That's okay, though, since the views from this historic structure are improved by its location at the more northern knob. On clear days, Glacier Peak, Mount Stuart, and even Mount Baker can be seen. If the air is too hazy for those distant views, watch the slopes around the north side of the ridge—mountain goats frequently rest on the slope as it drops off just past the trail's end.

A lone backpacker heading along the Wonderland Trail into Berkeley Park

GETTING THERE

From Enumclaw, drive east 43 miles on State Route 410 to the Mount Rainier National Park White River Entrance. Veer right onto the Sunrise Road and follow it 17 miles west to the large parking lot and visitor center at the road's end. **Note:** Sunrise Road usually doesn't open until early July.

ON THE TRAIL

The trail climbs to the top of Sourdough Ridge. At the Y-junction 0.2 mile out, go left and at the ridge-top junction at 0.3 mile, stay left again to hike west along the spine of Sourdough Ridge. At about 1 mile out, you pass a side trail on the right leading down to Forest Lake in Huckleberry Basin. Continue straight ahead (west) along the ridge top for 1.2 miles, passing small Frozen Lake. Watch for winking blond marmots in the rocks.

At lake's end is an intersection. Turn due north (right). It's an easy 1.3 miles through magnificent meadow and rugged rock-ridge terrain to the lookout, situated to keep watch on hundreds of miles of rolling green (or clear-cut) forest all the way to the central Cascades and Olympics.

If conditions are right, your binoculars might even find downtown Seattle. Look for the brown haze. Up closer, if your timing is right, you might see mountain goats. Excellent Rainier views, of course, tantalize you all along the route. Expect heavy traffic all summer long (many, many gapers) on this trail, which gains 800 feet one-way. It's a good family hike—even if you're here without a family.

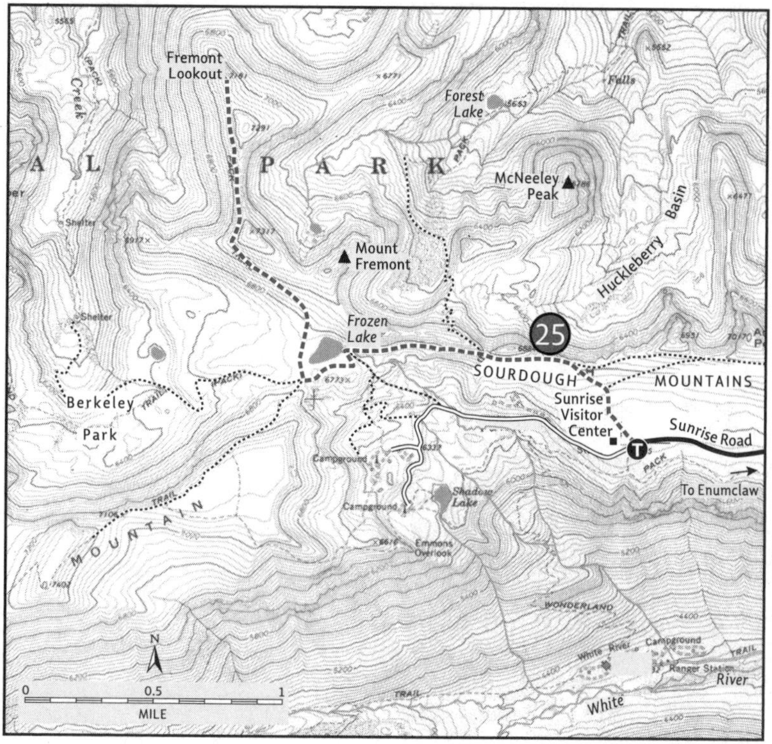

26 Berkeley Park

RATING/ DIFFICULTY	ROUND-TRIP	ELEV GAIN/ HIGH POINT	SEASON
****/3	7 miles	900 feet/ 6800 feet	July–Oct

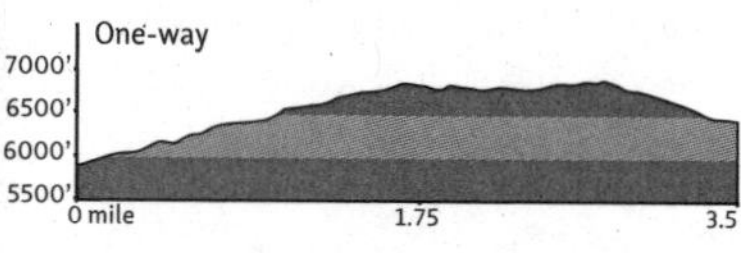

Maps: Green Trails Mount Rainier East, No. 270; **Contact:** Sunrise Ranger Station, (360) 663-2425; **GPS:** N46 54.877, W121 38.540

Berkeley Park may be the best place in the whole Sunrise area to throw yourself down on a patch of earth and simply sit and contemplate your good fortune. This is, after all, one of the richest wildflower gardens in the world. By late July, when the heavy mantle of snow has finally pulled away, Berkeley Park explodes in a rainbow of color. Other meadowlands around the mountain likewise boast of bright wildflower carpets, of course. But Berkeley, for some reason, seems special. Perhaps it's the

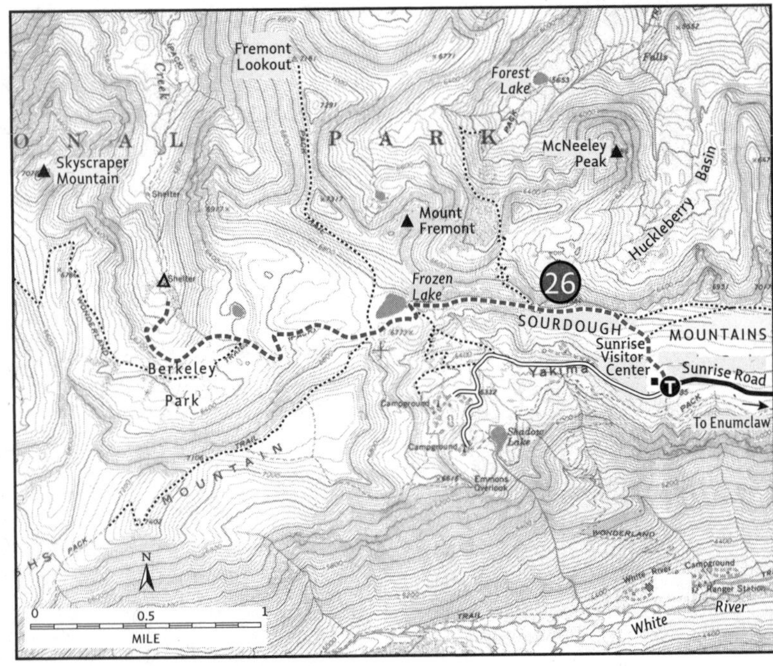

north-facing bowl of the park that keeps Mount Rainier largely out of the picture, forcing you to focus on the splendor underfoot. Or perhaps it's because this park gets fewer visitors than the other broad swathes of green in the area. Regardless, Berkeley Park is a special place that's easily reached by folks looking for a moderate day hike.

GETTING THERE

From Enumclaw, drive east 43 miles on State Route 410 to the Mount Rainier National Park White River Entrance. Veer right onto the Sunrise Road and follow it 17 miles west to the large parking lot and visitor center at the road's end. **Note:** Sunrise Road usually doesn't open until early July.

ON THE TRAIL

Head north from the parking lot to the crest of Sourdough Ridge. At the Y-junction 0.2 mile out, go left and at the ridge-top junction, stay left again to hike west along the spine of Sourdough Ridge. At about 1 mile out, you'll pass a side trail on the right leading down to Forest Lake in Huckleberry Basin. Continue straight ahead to reach the shores of Frozen Lake at 1.5 miles.

Trails fork off left, right, and straight ahead just past Frozen Lake. Follow the signs for the Wonderland Trail, or if signs aren't standing, stay straight, angling ever westward through most intersections to remain on the main trail. The path descends gradually just past Frozen Lake, looping around the wall of a shallow cirque that forms the head basin of Berkeley Park. At 2.5 miles, you come to yet another split.

Go right to leave the Wonderland Trail and descend into the heart of Berkeley Park. The trail curves around the valley wall, descending slowly for the next 1.3 miles to a backcountry camp in the forest nestled below the Berkeley meadows. Rather than roll all the way to that camp, stop when the trees begin to thicken and turn back here—about 1 mile after leaving the Wonderland (3.5 miles from the trailhead). Start back up the path to find a quiet corner to plop down in for some rest and reflection before finishing your return journey to Sunrise.

27 Skyscraper Mountain

RATING/ DIFFICULTY	ROUND-TRIP	ELEV GAIN/ HIGH POINT	SEASON
*****/4	8.5 miles	1078 feet/ 7078 feet	July–Oct

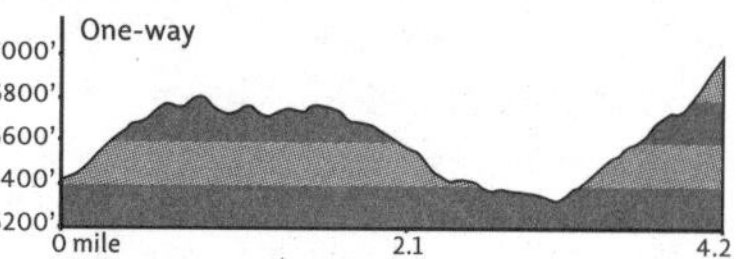

Maps: Green Trails Mount Rainier East, No. 270; **Contact:** Sunrise Ranger Station, (360) 663-2425; **GPS:** N46 54.877, W121 38.540

Gary contemplating the beauty seen from the summit of Skyscraper Mountain

HIKE WITH KIDS

School just let out for summer, and the kids are already bored and restless. What do you do? Take a hike!

This Day Hiking series features many scenic but gentle trails laced throughout our state lands and national forests and parks, offering wilderness adventures perfect for families with young kids. With the abundance of these easy to moderate hiking trails, there is no reason for anyone to miss out on the enjoyment of hiking. This pastime has grown to be truly a sport for people of all ages and all abilities.

The woods are full of things kids of all ages find fascinating. Besides bugs, birds, and animals, there are all sorts of relics of human history to discover and explore, from rusting railroad spikes and mining equipment to old fire lookouts and foresters' cabins, to Native American petroglyphs and rock art. There are fascinating geologic formations and countless forms of water bodies—streams, creeks, seeps, marshes, tarns, ponds, lakes, and bays.

Before heading out to discover your own great trail experiences, though, there are some things to consider. First and perhaps most important are the ages of the kids and their physical condition (not to mention your own). If you are new to hiking or have been away from it for a while (for instance, since the kids were born), or if your kids are under fourteen years old, stick to trails of less than 1 mile in length. Both you and the kids will find this to be long enough, and many of the trails in that range offer plenty to see and experience.

Once the trip is planned, parents can do a few things to make sure their kids have fun; for instance, never hike with just one child. Kids need companions to compete with, play with, and converse with. One child and a pair of adults make a hike seem too much like work for the poor kid. But let your child bring along a friend or two, and all will have the time of their lives.

When starting out on the trail, adults need to set goals and destinations that are attainable for everyone. Kids and adults alike are more likely to enjoy the hike if they know there is a specific destination rather than just an idea of "going until we feel like turning back."

Then, when hiking, make sure to take frequent breaks and offer the kids "energy food" consisting of a favorite cookie or tasty treat. These snacks serve two purposes. The kids will be motivated to make it to the next break site, knowing they will get a good-tasting treat, and the sugar will help keep the kids fueled up and energized on the trail. For maximum benefit, make the energy foods a special treat that the kids especially like but maybe don't get as often as they'd like. Pack plenty of water, too, to wash down the snacks and to replace what is lost as sweat.

Finally, let the kids explore and investigate the trail environment as much as they like. Patience is more than a virtue here—it's a necessity. Take the time to inspect the tadpoles in trailside bogs, to study the bugs on the bushes, and to try spotting the birds singing in the trees. Just let the kids be kids. If you can share in their excitement and enthusiasm, everyone will have a great time on the trail.

Never has sitting atop a Skyscraper been so enjoyable. Though no official trail leads to the mountaintop, this rounded peak is easily scaled by just about anyone. Indeed, summit seekers have beaten a boot track up the flank of the peak that rivals most established trails in the park. And from the summit, you'll enjoy views that stretch from the ever-present Rainier to the south, to Mount Baker to the north. Just don't expect complete solitude. Even if no other human hikers scale the Skyscraper, you'll find the local residents are typical nosy neighbors who have to check out any visitor. A small colony of marmots resides atop this peak, and I've yet to visit the top without having one of the big yellow-bellied beasts popping out to check on my lunch. Enjoy visiting with the big beggars, but don't share your food: the marmots don't need your granola, and feeding them just encourages unneighborly behaviors on their part.

GETTING THERE

From Enumclaw, drive east 43 miles on State Route 410 to the Mount Rainier National Park White River Entrance. Veer right onto the Sunrise Road and follow it 17 miles west to the large parking lot and visitor center at the road's end. **Note:** Sunrise Road usually doesn't open until early July.

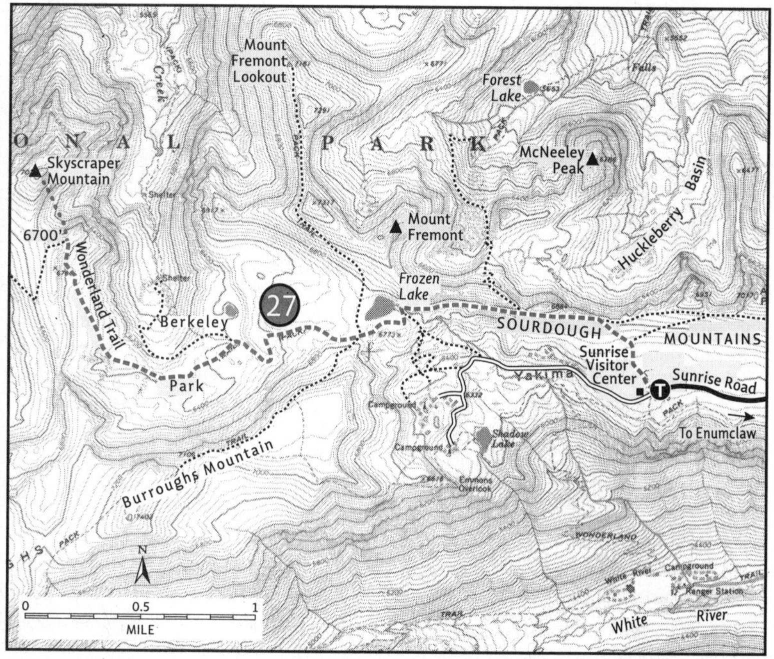

ON THE TRAIL

With the plethora of trails leading out of Sunrise, you have multiple options for getting onto this route, but the best bet is to scale Sourdough Ridge right off the bat. Head north from the parking lot to the crest of Sourdough Ridge. At the Y-junction 0.2 mile out, go left, and at the ridge-top junction, stay left again to hike west along the spine of Sourdough Ridge. At about 1 mile, pass a side trail on the right leading down to Forest Lake in Huckleberry Basin. Continue straight ahead to reach the shores of Frozen Lake at 1.5 miles. Within 0.1 mile of Frozen Lake, no less than four trails branch off the main Wonderland route.

For our journey, we want the Wonderland Trail, though, so follow its signs or simply keep moving west, avoiding trails leading north to Fremont Lookout (Hike 25) or south to First and Second Burroughs Mountain.

A descending mile past Frozen Lake, the Berkeley Park Trail (Hike 26) drops off to the right. Stay left to climb out of the shallow cirque you just dropped into. About 1.2 miles farther on, you have left Berkeley behind and have reached the top of the ridgeline at 6700 feet. The Wonderland bends sharply south here and descends once more. Our path, though, goes north less than 0.5 mile, up the face of Skyscraper Mountain. If you'd rather not make the hike up the boot path, simply rest at the 6700-foot ridgeline and enjoy the views from there.

Skyscraper Mountain (7078 feet) boasts a small, rounded, rocky top with plenty of perches for hikers to sit on and enjoy the 360-degree views. The green cirque of Berkeley Park lies to the east; the broad band of Winthrop Glacier fills the valley to the west. On the skyline stand Mount Fremont and Redstone Peak; the huge, table-flat meadow of Grand Park covers a good portion of the northern view; the stark face of Willis Wall on Mount Rainier dominates the south view.

28 Burroughs Mountain

RATING/ DIFFICULTY	ROUND-TRIP	ELEV GAIN/ HIGH POINT	SEASON
****/4	7.4 miles	1000 feet/ 7400 feet	July–Oct

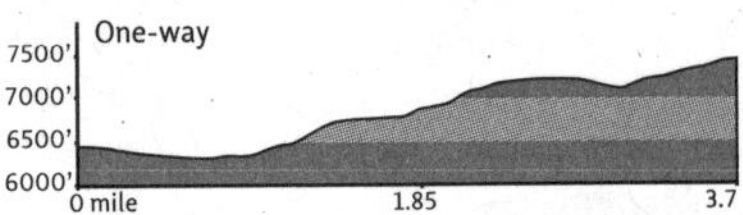

Maps: Green Trails Mount Rainier East, No. 270; **Contact:** Sunrise Ranger Station, (360) 663-2425; **GPS:** N46 54.877, W121 38.540

This route offers more than just wonderful wildlife viewing. The trail atop Burroughs Mountain provides hikers outstanding views of the northeast face of Mount Rainier. Little Tahoma can be seen flanking Rainier, and the tower-topped peak of Mount Fremont stands to the north. Closer at hand, marmots and pikas dash between the rocks along the trail. Mountain goats can be found showing off their agility on the sides of the local peaks. And raptors—from lightning-fast peregrines to massive golden eagles—soar overhead. All in all, the views and the local wildlife make this loop an unbeatable day hiking option for hikers young and old.

GETTING THERE

From Enumclaw, drive east 43 miles on State Route 410 to the Mount Rainier National Park White River Entrance. Veer right onto the

Opposite: Wildflowers dot the tundra-like landscape along Burroughs Mountain.

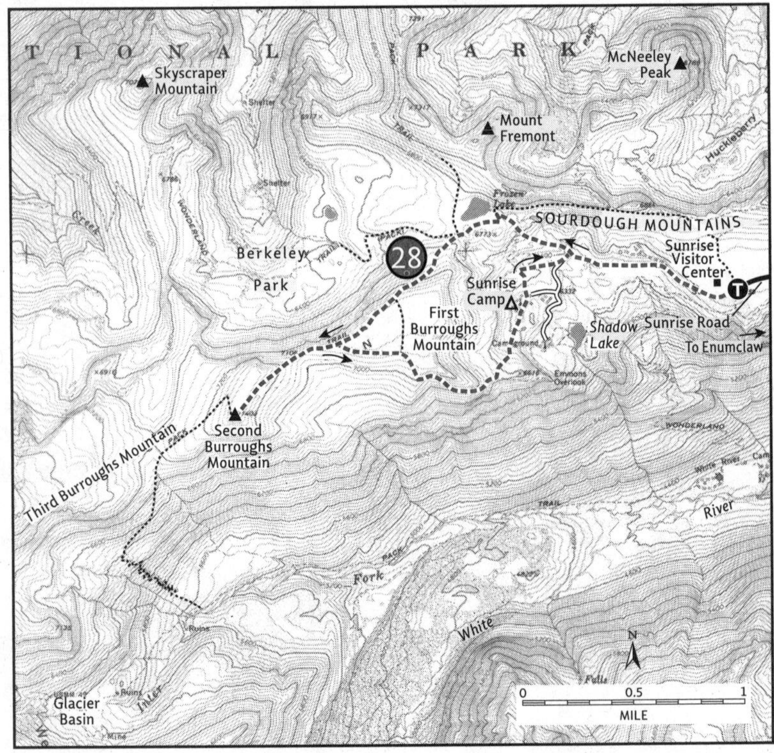

Sunrise Road and follow it 17 miles west to the large parking lot and visitor center at the road's end. **Note:** Sunrise Road usually doesn't open until early July.

ON THE TRAIL

From the Sunrise parking lot and visitor center, find the broad trail (an old road, actually) on the southwest side of the parking lot and follow it west toward Sunrise Camp. At 0.5 mile out, stay right rather than head toward the camp, however. This trail leads upward through meadowlands for another mile—stay straight ahead at the next junction (about 1 mile from the trailhead)—to reach Frozen Lake at 1.5 miles. Go left here to skirt around the lake, which serves as the source of all water for the Sunrise area facilities, and at the next junction (about 0.2 mile farther on) stay left again to climb the gentle, open slope leading up to the top of First Burroughs.

About 1 mile after leaving that last junction (2.7 miles from the trailhead), you will be on the western end of the broad top of First Burroughs (7200 feet). The trail then follows the ridge line about 1 mile across to Second Burroughs (7400 feet) before it angles southwest and descends around the side of Third Burroughs. Rather than drop off the top of Second, though, stop and enjoy the view. It is worth your time to relax here a long time not only to enjoy the views, but hopefully to be lucky enough to see some avalanche and rock-slide activity on the side of Mount Rainier. The sound of one of these events will stick in your memory forever. Turn around here.

If you want a little variety on the return trip, at the junction atop First Burroughs veer to the right and follow the steep trail down to Sunrise Camp and from there back to the trailhead parking lot. The mileage is about the same as the route you followed coming up.

29 Shadow Lake–Sunrise Camp Loop

RATING/ DIFFICULTY	LOOP	ELEV GAIN/ HIGH POINT	SEASON
****/2	3.5 miles	200 feet/ 6400 feet	July–Oct

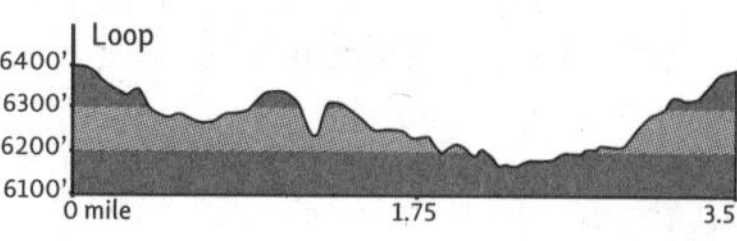

Maps: Green Trails Mount Rainier East, No. 270; **Contact:** Sunrise Ranger Station, (360) 663-2425; **GPS:** N46 54.877, W121 38.540

This is the perfect outing for families, or for anyone wanting an easy day in the glorious wildflower fields of the Sunrise area. Indeed, if you have out-of-town guests you want to impress, this gentle mountain stroll will have them thinking you live in heaven on earth. This little loop explores

A hoary marmot eating dried flowers in the meadows near Shadow Lake

wonderful alpine meadows and provides glorious views of Mount Rainier, with very little elevation gain.

GETTING THERE

From Enumclaw, drive east 43 miles on State Route 410 to the Mount Rainier National Park White River Entrance. Veer right onto the Sunrise Road and follow it 17 miles west to the large parking lot and visitor center at the road's end. **Note:** Sunrise Road usually doesn't open until early July.

ON THE TRAIL

Find the old road-turned-trail on the southwest side of the visitor center parking lot and follow it west toward Sunrise Camp, ignoring any faint side trails. At about 0.5 mile out, you'll notice a well-signed trail leading to the left—this is the Wonderland Trail, dropping down to White River. Continue straight ahead toward Shadow Lake and the Sunrise Camp.

Shadow Lake, 1.2 miles from the trailhead, is a shallow tarn nestled into the green meadows of the area. With its modest scattering of trees around its banks and open slopes between the wooded sections, the lake is a haven for wildlife. The trees provide perches and shelter for birds and good shade and cover for beasts. Deer frequent this pond, as do mountain goats, so approach it quietly if you want to see any visiting critters.

After passing a short spur to an Emmons Glacier overlook, you reach Sunrise Camp at about 1.8 miles. This was once a drive-up car-camping campground, but it is now a walk-in tent camp. At the junction on the far side of camp, turn right—the left fork leads to Frozen Lake and then steeply up the side of First Burroughs Mountain (Hike 28). The right fork leads you along the wildflower meadows

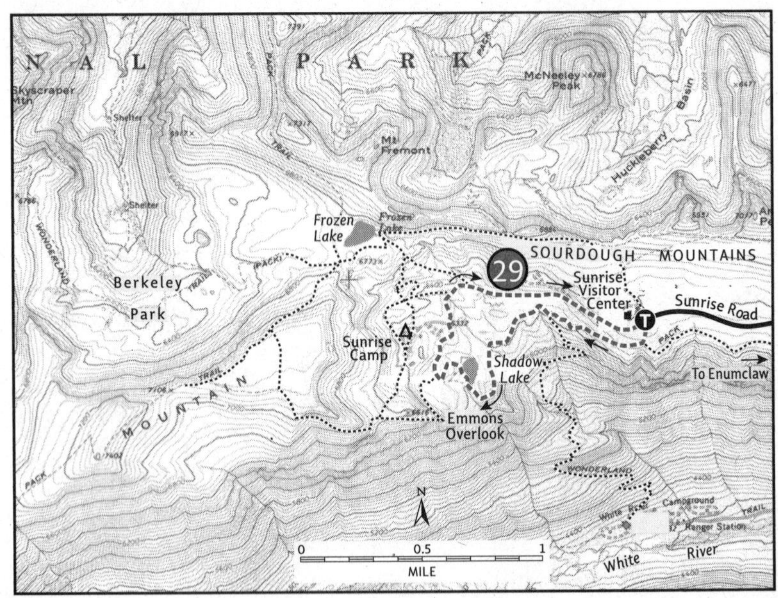

Bombs of fall color along the Huckleberry Creek trail dropping toward Forest Lake

below Burroughs for 0.6 mile to reach yet another trail junction. Go right here and follow this main path 1.4 miles back to the trailhead. **Note:** There are many old, decommissioned trails in the area. Stay on the main paths at all times.

30 Forest Lake

RATING/ DIFFICULTY	ROUND-TRIP	ELEV GAIN/ HIGH POINT	SEASON
***/3	5 miles	1000 feet/ 6800 feet	July–Oct

One-way

7000'
6500'
6000'
5500'
0 mile
1.25
2.5

Maps: Green Trails Mount Rainier East, No. 270; **Contact:** Sunrise Ranger Station, (360) 663-2425; **GPS:** N46 54.877, W121 38.540

Forest Lake may be the most underappreciated lake within Mount Rainier National Park. You won't find grand views. It's not in a broad, sun-filled meadow. There is minimal camping space available and not a lot of potential for extending the relatively short mileage. Many hikers see those as negatives. Perfect! Because that means there's a much higher likelihood that you and I can enjoy this wonderful route in relaxing solitude. What you will find is a gorgeous forest valley, a pristine woodland pond, lots of huckleberries

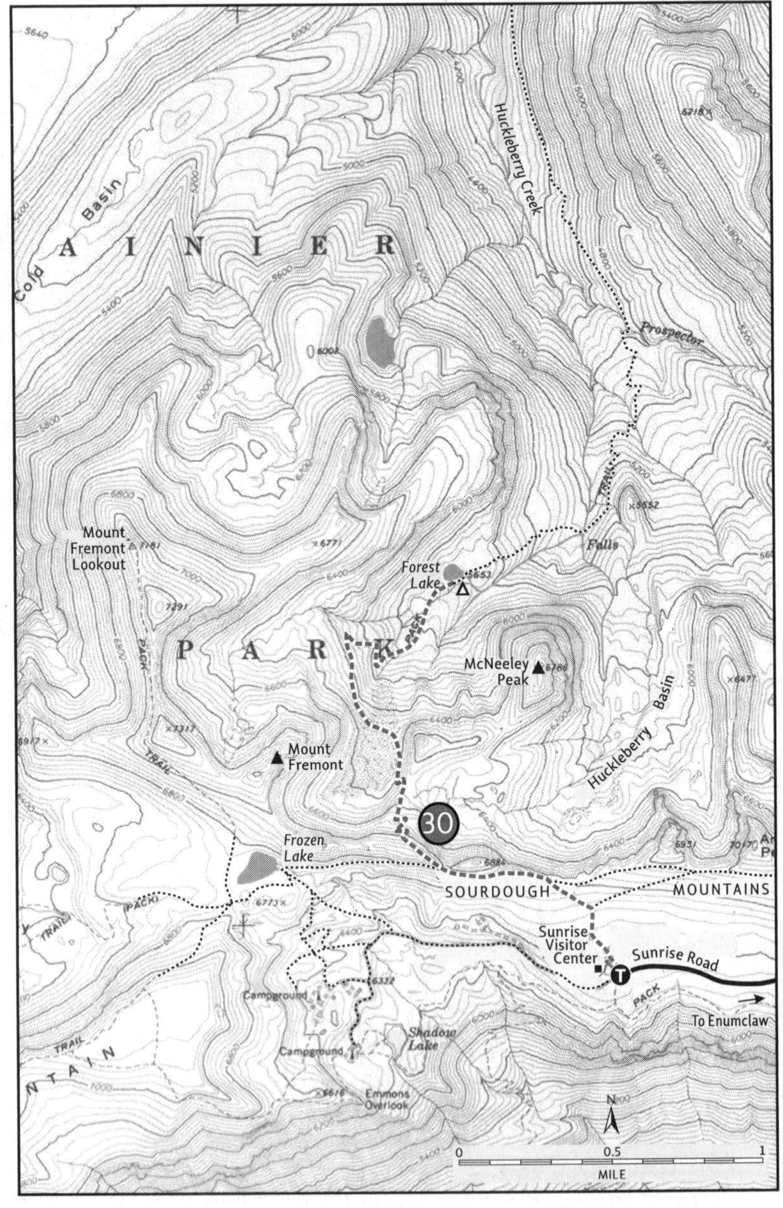
Cold Basin
RAINIER
PARK
Huckleberry Creek
Prospector
TRAIL
Falls
Mount Fremont Lookout
Forest Lake
McNeeley Peak
Huckleberry Basin
Mount Fremont
30
Frozen Lake
SOURDOUGH
MOUNTAINS
Sunrise Visitor Center
Sunrise Road
PACK
To Enumclaw
Campground
Shadow Lake
Campground
Emmons Overlook
0
0.5
1
MILE

(reason enough to visit!) and a wide assortment of wildlife.

GETTING THERE

From Enumclaw, drive east 43 miles on State Route 410 to the Mount Rainier National Park White River Entrance. Veer right onto the Sunrise Road and follow it 17 miles west to the large parking lot and visitor center at the road's end. **Note:** Sunrise Road usually doesn't open until early July.

ON THE TRAIL

Head north from the parking lot to the crest of Sourdough Ridge. At the Y-junction 0.2 mile out, go left and at the ridge-top junction, stay left again to hike west along the spine of Sourdough Ridge. At about 1 mile out, you'll find a side trail on the right. Take this path and climb over the ridge crest to descend steeply at first into upper Huckleberry Basin.

You reach a broad plateau on the valley wall in about 0.5 mile. Take a few minutes to leave the trail and amble off to the east, exploring this meadow. A number of small stands of trees provide excellent cover for animals, and I've frequently found mountain goats, elk, and black-tailed deer resting behind the trees. If you swing wide around the tree stand, you can often get into position to snap a picture or two without disturbing the majestic beasts.

From the meadowed plateau, continue to descend another mile, dropping gradually into forest as the trail rolls down to the headwaters of Huckleberry Creek. At 2.5 miles you reach Forest Lake, a large pond–small lake nestled into a sun-filled hemlock and fir forest. There are two campsites along the lake, but generally they have been empty on my visits. Odds are good, I've found, that you'll be able to enjoy a quiet, solitary swim in this shallow lake before returning the way you came.

31 Dege Peak

RATING/ DIFFICULTY	ROUND-TRIP	ELEV GAIN/ HIGH POINT	SEASON
***/2	4 miles	600 feet/ 7006 feet	July–Oct

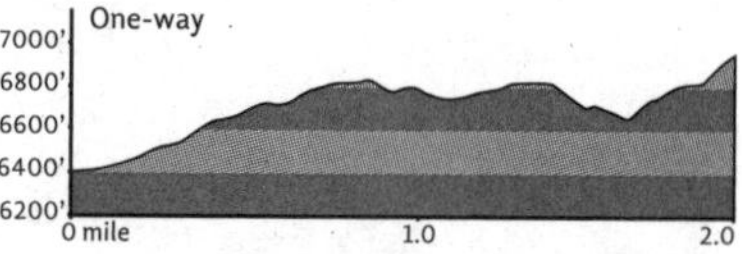

Maps: Green Trails Mount Rainier East, No. 270; **Contact:** Sunrise Ranger Station, (360) 663-2425; **GPS:** N46 54.877, W121 38.540

The good news is you'll have unmatched views nearly every step along this trail. The bad news is that the trail skirts high above the road for its entire length, so on busy days, you'll hear traffic noises. But if you simply tell yourself the sound of wheels on pavement is really just the humming of the wind in the trees, you'll soon forget the road is there and focus instead on the magnificence of your surroundings. Grand vistas to the north, east, south, and west await you here, so even if you can hear the tourist traffic on its way to and from Sunrise, you'll still have a great adventure—and you'll find your camera full of some of the best pictures of Mount Rainier you'll ever get.

GETTING THERE

From Enumclaw, drive east 43 miles on State Route 410 to the Mount Rainier National Park White River Entrance. Veer right onto the Sunrise Road and follow it 17 miles west to the large parking lot and visitor center at the road's end. **Note:** Sunrise Road usually doesn't open until early July.

ON THE TRAIL

Dege Peak can be tackled from east or west, but your best option is to start at the west end and climb eastward. Leave the Sunrise parking lot and start up the Sourdough Ridge trail. At the Y-junction found 0.2 mile from the parking lot, go right to angle east for 0.5 mile to the crest of Sourdough Ridge. There, you'll encounter a trail junction. Go right to continue your eastward heading, following the ridge that links Antler Peak, Sourdough Mountain, and Dege Peak. The trail stays on the south side of the ridge crest, but much of the time the trail is near the very top of the knife-edge ridge, so you'll have views north and south. Let the kids ramble out in front as they enjoy the views and look for marmots and mountain goats.

At about 1.9 miles out, a small side trail leads off to the left. This short spur (about 0.1 mile) climbs directly up to the 7006-foot summit of Dege Peak, on the crest of the Sourdough Mountains. Look for blobs of white on the rocky flanks below you—if the blobs move, they are mountain goats. If they don't move, they are probably mountain goats at rest. Bring a pair of binoculars to be sure.

Turn back after enjoying the 360-degree panoramic views from the summit. On the return hike, you'll enjoy nonstop views of Mount Rainier as you walk west.

EXTENDING YOUR TRIP

If you have two vehicles available, you can do this route as a one-way through-hike, linking

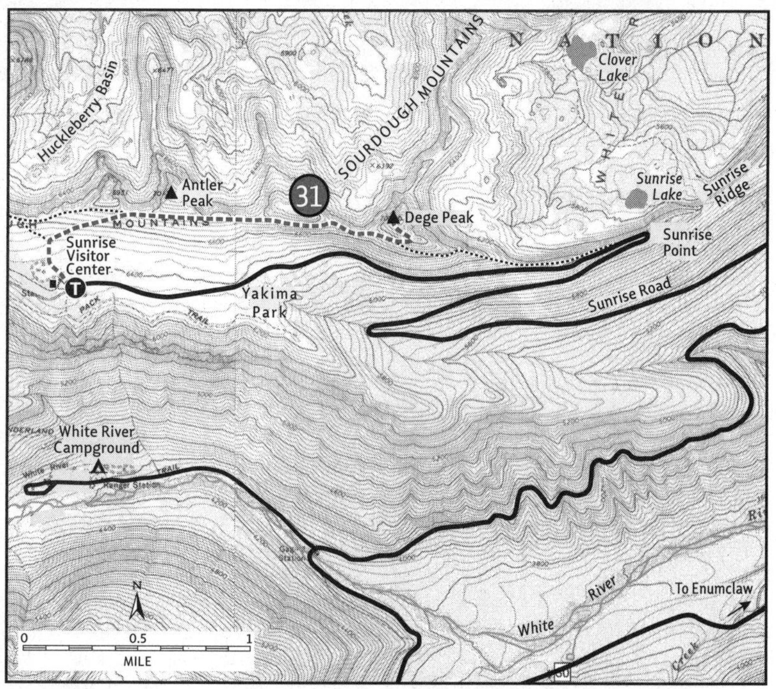

Opposite: Views overlooking the Sunrise area from the summit of Dege Peak

The Silver Forest trail passing through open meadows offering vast views of Mount Rainier

the trailheads at Sunrise and Sunrise Point. If this is your goal, start the hike at Sunrise Point (see "Getting There" for Hike 23) and hike west so you'll be able to enjoy that always-present view of Mount Rainier found on the westward walk. It's about 1 mile from Sunrise Point to Dege Peak summit, for a 3-mile one-way hike.

32 Silver Forest–Emmons Vista

RATING/ DIFFICULTY	ROUND-TRIP	ELEV GAIN/ HIGH POINT	SEASON
***/1	2.4 miles	200 feet/ 6400 feet	July–Oct

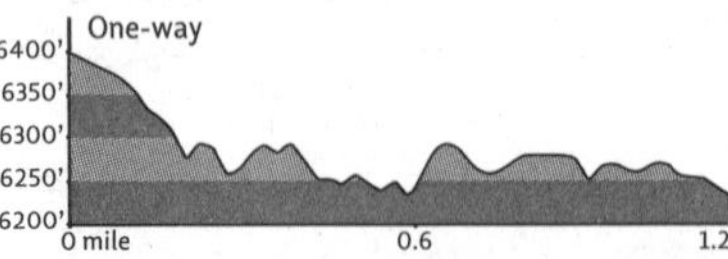

Maps: Green Trails Mount Rainier East, No. 270; **Contact:** Sunrise Ranger Station, (360) 663-2425; **GPS:** N46 54.877, W121 38.540

This route offers a perfect chance to see and experience a "silver forest" and to provide kids a learning experience as well. These stands of bright white trees can be found throughout the Pacific Northwest, thanks to the ever-present threat of wildfire. The silver forests are the standing skeletons of trees that were lashed by fast-moving, intensely hot forest fires. When the fires are hot enough and moving fast enough, they kill the trees and scorch many of the limbs and bark off but don't devour the entire trunk. As a result, entire forests are left standing, though they are dead and stripped of their "skin." Within a couple of years, the standing trunks are bleached white by exposure to the sun and

wind, resulting in a shadowy stand of gray ghosts: the silver forest. When one of these shining woods is seen against a backdrop of emerald green meadows, brilliant blue skies, and a massive white mountain, the effect is amazing. You'd never think a dead forest could look so beautiful and vibrant. But that's just what you'll find here.

GETTING THERE

From Enumclaw, drive east 43 miles on State Route 410 to the Mount Rainier National Park White River Entrance. Veer right onto the Sunrise Road and follow it 17 miles west to the large parking lot and visitor center at the road's end. **Note:** Sunrise Road usually doesn't open until early July.

ON THE TRAIL

From the trailhead, locate the trail on the south side of the parking area and head south. At the first junction, almost immediately after starting down, stay left to turn east toward the Emmons Vista viewpoint. Continue east along this path, staying left at the next trail split.

The first 0.5 mile is known as the Emmons Vista Nature Trail. Stroll along this broad path-

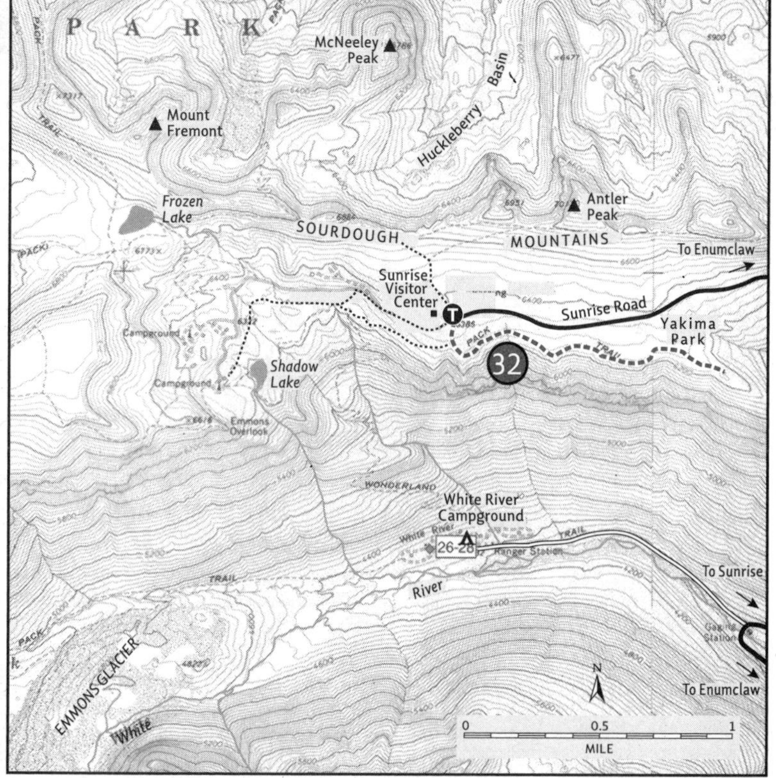

way, enjoying the stunning views back toward Mount Rainier and the long white river of the Emmons Glacier flowing off its northern face.

About 0.5 mile out, the trail extends into the silver forest. This glimmering wood is the remnant of the Sunrise wildfire that flashed through the area many years ago.

The trail ends at 1.2 miles on a knoll at the end of the Yakima Park ridge, high above the White River valley. Return the way you came.

Opposite: Springtime roar of water on the Ohanapecosh River going over Silver Falls

cayuse pass

Mount Rainier tries to reflect its glory in Tipsoo Lake.

The eastern portion of Mount Rainier National Park gets a great deal of vehicle traffic but fewer hikers than most other regions in the park. The traffic comes because of the north–south highway—State Route 123—that links the two most popular tourist destinations in the park: Paradise and Sunrise. That highway is likely the reason why hikers tend to stay away. The road runs through the heart of the eastern flank of the mountain, which discourages hikers. That's a shame, because some of the richest ecosystems in the park are found in this region. Ancient forests fairly dripping with life fill the lower valleys, while sprawling alpine meadows grace the highest peaks. The easternmost trails also offer access to the most bountiful berries in the park. The middle of SR 123 was reopened in late 2007 after repair of flood damage.

33 Tipsoo Lake–Naches Peak Loop

RATING/ DIFFICULTY	LOOP	ELEV GAIN/ HIGH POINT	SEASON
****/2	3 miles	600 feet/ 5849 feet	June–Oct

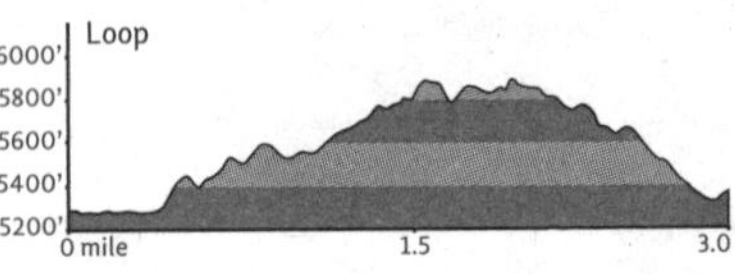

Maps: Green Trails Mount Rainier East, No. 270, and Bumping Lake, No. 271; **Contact:** Longmire Wilderness Information Center, (360) 569-4453; **GPS:** N46 52.041, W121 31.055

The loop trail leaving Tipsoo Lake meanders through meadows that offer some of the best views of Mount Rainier found anywhere. The route is relatively flat—it rolls up and down but has no ridiculously steep sections and only a few real climbs. The route takes advantage of the Pacific Crest Trail, as well as some of the heavily used tourist trails around Tipsoo Lake. Don't expect quiet solitude here, though the beauty of the terrain you pass through offsets any worries about crowds.

GETTING THERE

From Enumclaw, drive east about 47 miles on State Route 410 to the junction with SR 123. Stay left to continue east on SR 410 another 3 miles. Park in the Tipsoo Lake parking lot on your left just past the footbridge marking Chinook Pass. **Note:** SR 123 was severely damaged by the November 2006 floods. Although the road has been reopened, call to check on road conditions.

ON THE TRAIL

I recommend completing the loop in a clockwise direction in order to get the best views of Mount Rainier during the hike. Therefore, from the parking lot, follow the trail northeast around Tipsoo Lake and then descend through meadows to the Pacific Crest Trail parking lot on the east side of the pass. Cross to the south side of the highway and follow the PCT east, then south along the eastern flank of Naches Peak. As you stroll down the trail, enjoy masses of western anemone, beargrass, lupine, paintbrush, and more.

At 1.5 miles, stop for a rest or a leisurely lunch at the wide bench overlooking Dewey Lakes. The trail splits here. Our loop route goes right (west) around the southern flank of Naches Peak.

You'll soon see Mount Rainier thrusting skyward before you, while more meadows open up at your feet. In another 1.5 miles, you'll have looped back around the south and west side of Naches Peak and be back at the highway, opposite Tipsoo Lake. Cross the highway to return to your car.

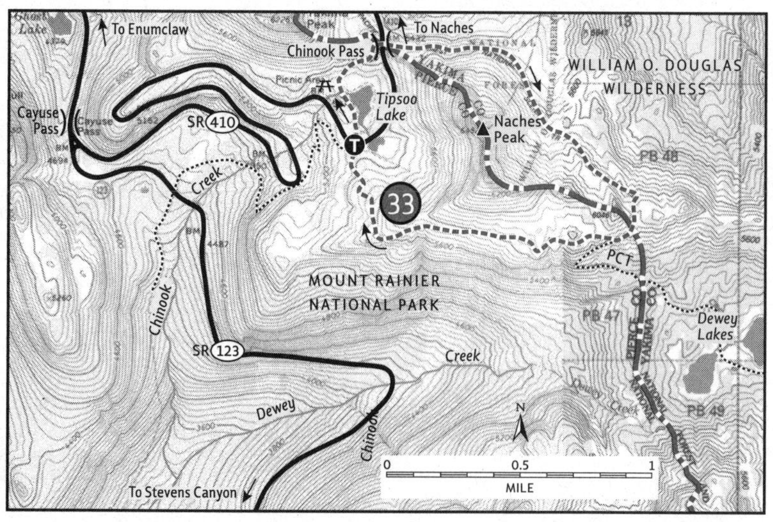

HOT UNDER THE SKIN: THE VOLCANIC HISTORY OF RAINIER

In geological terms, Mount Rainier is barely middle aged. The volcano we know and love today first erupted more than 500,000 years ago and most recently blew its top in the 1840s.

Though not the most active volcano in the Cascades, Mount Rainier has been called the most dangerous owing to its potential for eruption and the huge populations that reside within blast range of the peak. When—not if—the mountain next erupts, millions of people could be at risk from the pyroclastic blast, massive mudflows, and ash fallout that would follow an eruption.

The last few eruptions of Mount Rainier have been relatively minor—nothing like the spectacular explosion of Mount St. Helens in 1980. But even a minor eruption could cause enormous damage as lahars—volcanic mudflows fed by rapidly melting snow and glacial ice—race down heavily populated valleys.

Even without the force of a true eruption, the mountain can be deadly. The collapse of unstable parts of the northwest side of the volcano has created debris flows and lahars that pushed down as far as the shores of Puget Sound. Eons ago, one of these massive lahar events turned Puget Sound waterfront into what is today the location of the city of Puyallup.

Though the mountain isn't showing any signs of imminent eruption, the mountain is far from dormant. Volcanologists record hundreds of small earthquakes at Rainier annually, proving the mountain remains restless. Climbers, too, note the volcanic life of the mountain since steam vents can be found in the summit crater—these warm mountaintop caverns have been used periodically as emergency refuges by storm-stranded climbers.

Even hikers can experience the volcanic life of this mountain. The Ohanapecosh Hot Springs (Hike 39) and many small warm springs around the park—including those at Longmire (Hike 56) and some near Reflection Lakes in the Paradise Valley (Hike 63)—are indications of the volcanic furnace underfoot.

Mount Rainier stands as an indomitable landmark, seemingly unchanged and unchangeable when viewed through the brief lifespan of mere humans. But on a geological clock, the mountain is just taking a short break before its next fiery exhalation.

EXTENDING YOUR TRIP

For a longer hike, at the trail junction on the bench above Dewey Lakes, continue to your left down the Pacific Crest Trail to reach Dewey Lakes in 1.5 miles, descending gradually at first, then losing 650 feet in the last mile. At Dewey Lakes, bear to the left. Backcountry campsites are located on the north side of the lake.

34 Deer Creek Falls

RATING/ DIFFICULTY	ROUND-TRIP	ELEV GAIN/ HIGH POINT	SEASON
***/2	1 mile	300 feet/ 3200 feet	June–Oct

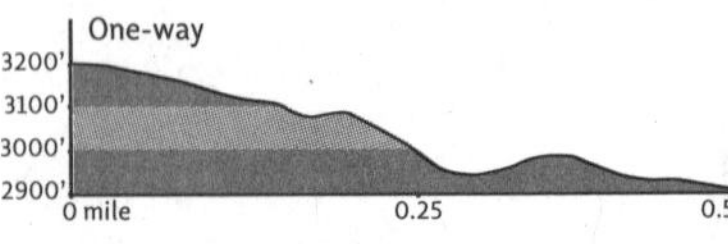

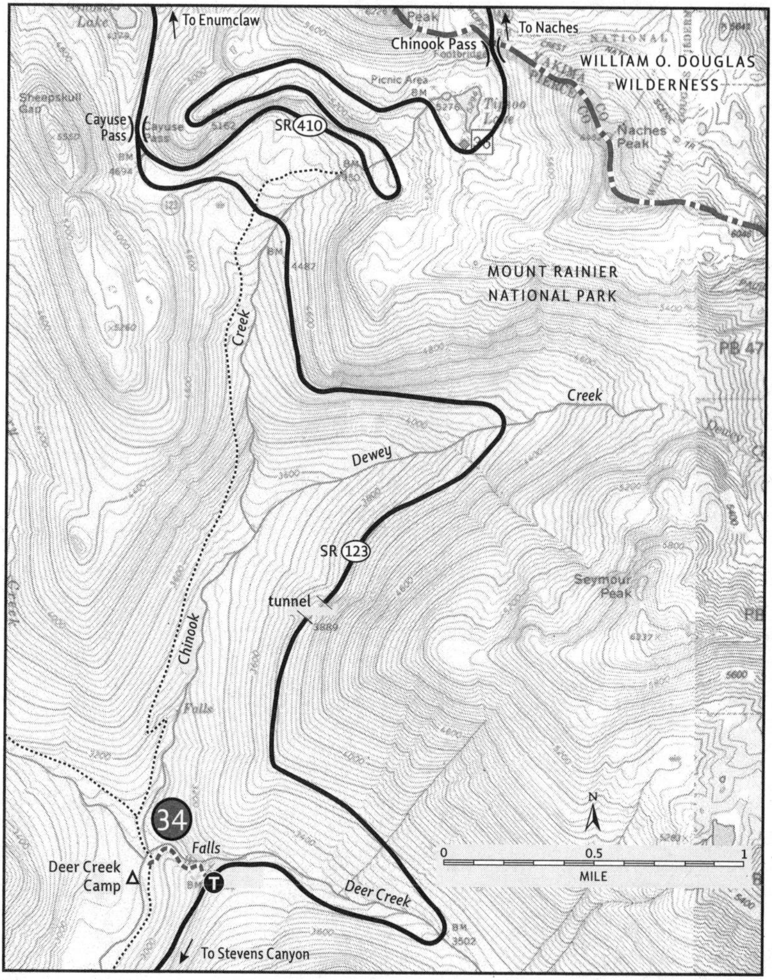

Maps: Green Trails Mount Rainier East, No. 270; **Contact:** Longmire Wilderness Information Center, (360) 569-4453; **GPS:** N46 50.012, W121 32.107

This short hike leads through lush old forest to a picturesque waterfall and a cool woodland camp along a pretty forest stream. The trail lacks the panoramic views and awesome alpine scenery you'll find along so many other Mount Rainier trails. Instead, this short walk offers you a look at a different aspect of this multifaceted park.

GETTING THERE

From Enumclaw, drive east about 47 miles on State Route 410 to the junction with SR 123. Stay right (straight ahead) to merge onto SR 123–Cayuse Pass Highway. Find the trailhead on the right about 4.5 miles farther south. **Note:** SR 123 was severely damaged by the November 2006 floods. Although the road has been reopened, call to check on road conditions.

ON THE TRAIL

The trail descends west, away from the roadway. The path drops along Deer Creek, and at just about 0.25 mile it slides over to an overlook point that provides great views of the small but pretty Deer Creek Waterfall. This simple woodland cascade tumbles down a rocky wall, with pretty forest wildflowers nearby. Look for trillium early in the year and Indian pipe by midsummer.

The trail continues down the Deer Creek valley for another 0.25 mile to Deer Creek Camp. Kids enjoy visiting the campsites along Chinook Creek before returning to the car. This route proves to be a fabulous leg-stretcher on the drive between Paradise and Sunrise.

EXTENDING YOUR TRIP

You can continue another 1.5 miles to another waterfall, on Kotsuck Creek (Hike 35).

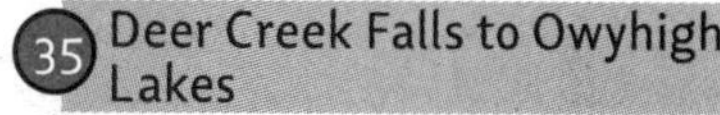

35 Deer Creek Falls to Owyhigh Lakes

RATING/ DIFFICULTY	ROUND-TRIP	ELEV GAIN/ HIGH POINT	SEASON
***/4	10 miles	2200 feet/ 5400 feet	June–Oct

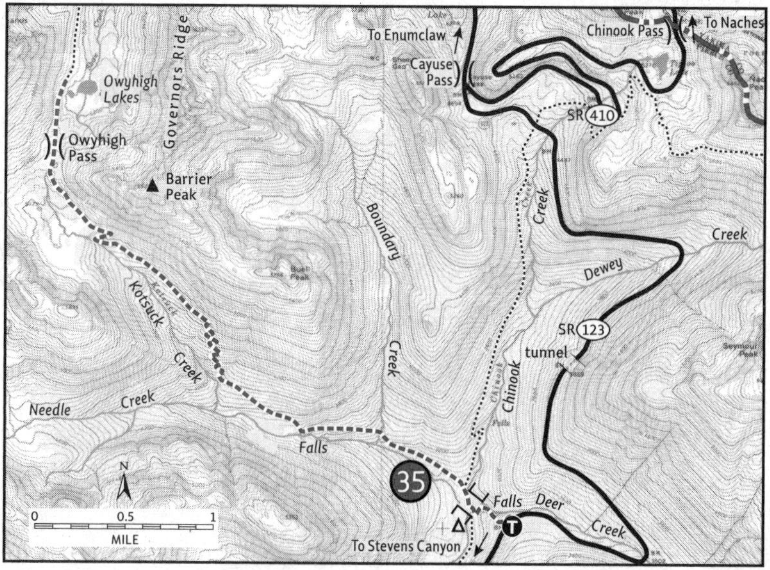

Opposite: An icy Deer Creek Falls during the cold of late autumn

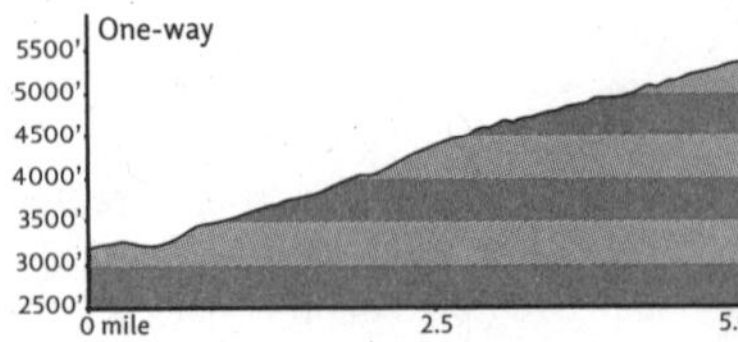

Maps: Green Trails Mount Rainier East, No. 270; **Contact:** Longmire Wilderness Information Center, (360) 569-4453; **GPS:** N46 50.012, W121 32.107

  *Seldom visited but deserving of more attention, this route rolls past a couple of sparkling waterfalls, climbs through lush old forest, and leads to moderate views from a wooded pass above a pretty wooded lake basin. The trail is on the maintenance logs, but the relatively light use leaves the route brushy and the trail tread rough at times. The best favor we can do for this sweet little forest route is to use it: the path needs people to use it and love it. It offers a great outing in a part of the park seldom visited by the hordes that descend on the big mountain each year.*

GETTING THERE

From Enumclaw, drive east about 47 miles on State Route 410 to the junction with SR 123. Stay right (straight ahead) to merge onto SR 123–Cayuse Pass Highway. Find the trailhead on the right about 4.5 miles farther south.

Chinook Creek tumbles down small falls through a collection of logs.

Note: SR 123 was severely damaged by the November 2006 floods. Although the road has been reopened, call to check on road conditions.

ON THE TRAIL

The trail runs west away from the highway, descending along Deer Creek. At 0.25 mile the trail passes the Deer Creek Falls—you'll want to have your camera out to capture this photogenic cascade. At 0.5 mile, find Deer Creek Camp where Deer Creek empties into Chinook Creek and where Kotsuck Creek flows in from the west.

Cross Chinook Creek on a footbridge and at a trail fork turn left to start up the Kotsuck valley (the right-hand trail heads north along Chinook Creek). Forests line the trail for most of its length, providing welcome relief from the scorching summer sun. At 1.5 miles, the trail provides grand views of another majestic waterfall.

At 2.5 miles, the trail enters a steep series of switchbacks on the flank of Barrier Peak, ascending high above the creek before entering a mile-long traverse of the slope. A few more switchbacks, and you're into the final ascent to the 5400-foot pass separating Governors Ridge and Tamanos Mountain.

Reach the pass at 4.5 miles, where you have views of Tamanos as well as Barrier Peak on the south end of Governors Ridge. Looking farther west, you'll see the two towers of the Cowlitz Chimneys. Press on another 0.5 mile to Owyhigh Lakes (Hike 17), about 5 miles from the trailhead, before turning back.

EXTENDING YOUR TRIP

If you have two vehicles for a shuttle, you can descend about 3.5 miles past Owyhigh Lakes to Sunrise Road (Hike 17). **Note:** Sunrise Road usually doesn't open until early July.

36 Deer Creek to Tipsoo Lake

RATING/ DIFFICULTY	ROUND-TRIP	ELEV GAIN/ HIGH POINT	SEASON
**/4	10 miles	2100 feet/ 5296 feet	June–Oct

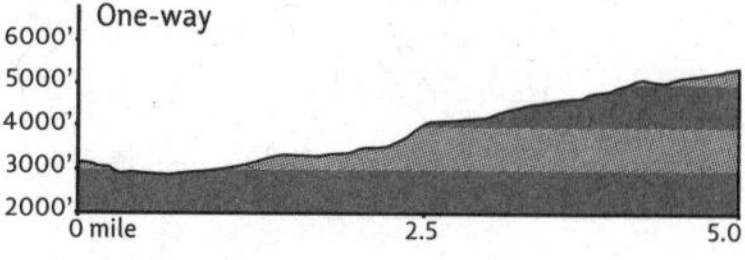

Maps: Green Trails Mount Rainier East, No. 270; **Contact:** Longmire Wilderness Information Center, (360) 569-4453; **GPS:** N46 50.012, W121 32.107

You start low, strolling up a deeply forested river valley, but end up in broad meadows with stellar views of Mount Rainier. The trail gets very little hiking pressure, so you're almost certain to have the route to yourself. The trail parallels the highway, but most of the way, the road is well out of both sight and hearing of the trail. Look for weasels and martens along the river—as well as dippers and other water-loving birds.

GETTING THERE

From Enumclaw, drive east about 47 miles on State Route 410 to the junction with SR 123. Stay right (straight ahead) to merge onto SR 123–Cayuse Pass Highway. Find the trailhead on the right about 4.5 miles farther south. **Note:** SR 123 was severely damaged by the November 2006 floods. Although the road has been reopened, call to check on road conditions.

ON THE TRAIL

Descend the Deer Creek Trail, passing the Deer Creek Falls at 0.25 mile, before reaching the Eastside Trail at Deer Creek Camp. Cross

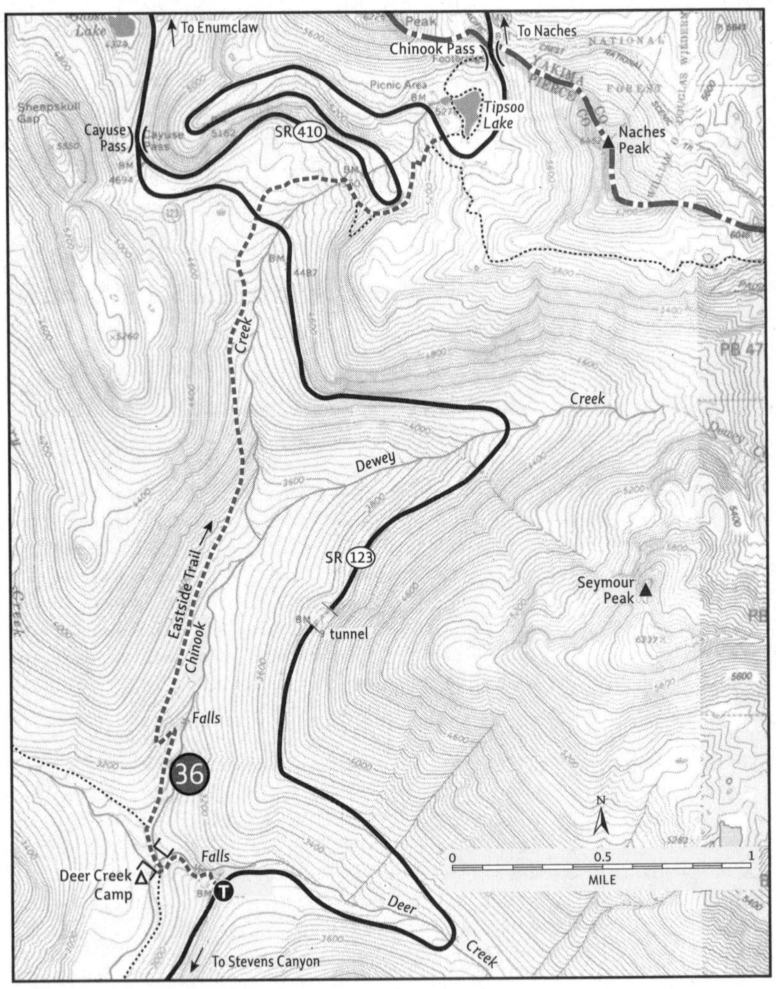

Chinook Creek on a footbridge and turn right onto the Eastside Trail; the left-hand trail goes up Kotsuck Creek (Hike 35) as it heads up the Chinook Creek valley.

The trail stays close to the creek for the first 0.5 mile past the camp before climbing the valley wall to ascend the valley well above the creek itself. At 3.3 miles, the trail approaches the head of the Chinook Creek valley and climbs out onto the Cayuse Pass Highway–State Route 123. Cross the road and immediately rejoin the trail on the north side of the road.

From here, the trail continues to climb as it swings east around the upper reaches of the

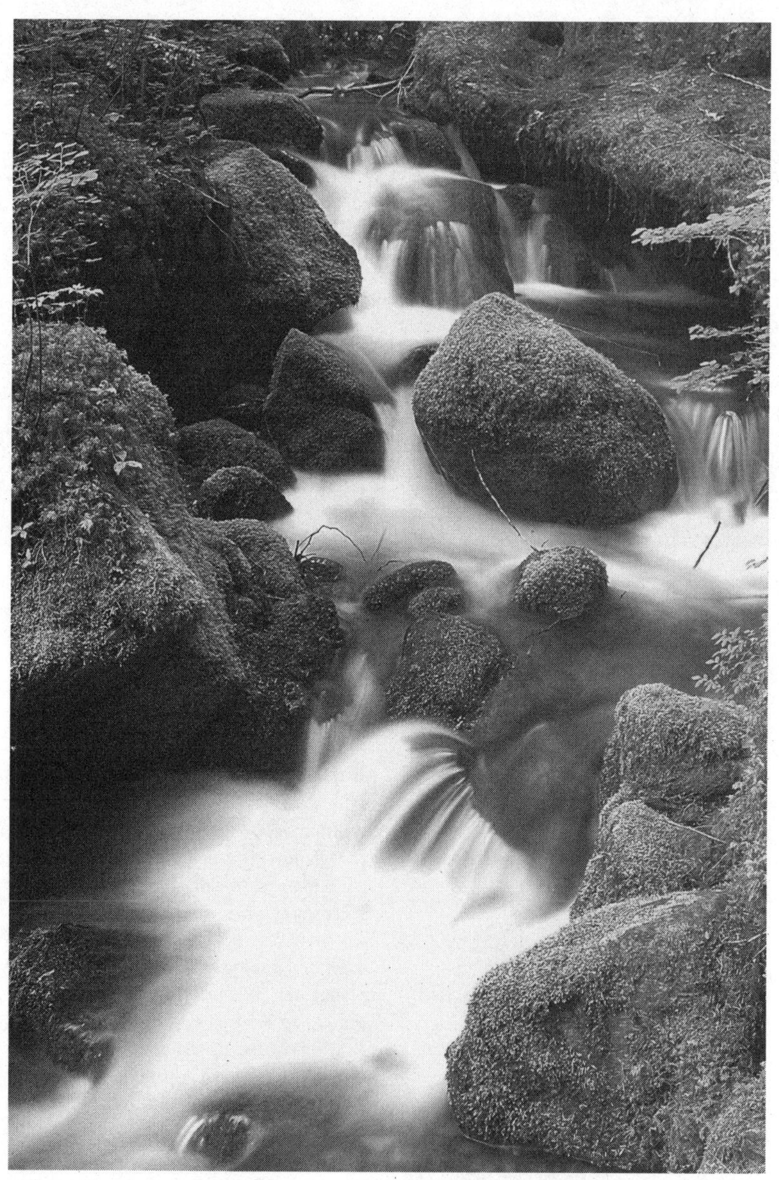

Mossy rocks outline a small stream along the Eastside Trail.

Autumn on the summit of Shriner Peak with the historic Shriner Peak lookout

headwall of the valley. The trail skirts around a loop of the Chinook Pass Highway–SR 410 before slicing up through heather meadows to the flank of Naches Peak. Here, you can cross SR 410 to rest and relax at Tipsoo Lake. You find grand flower meadows with stunning views of Rainier around the shores of the roadside lake. Return the way you came or, if you have two vehicles, set up a vehicle shuttle to this upper trailhead.

37 Shriner Peak

RATING/ DIFFICULTY	ROUND-TRIP	ELEV GAIN/ HIGH POINT	SEASON
*****/5	8.5 miles	3434 feet/ 5834 feet	June–Oct

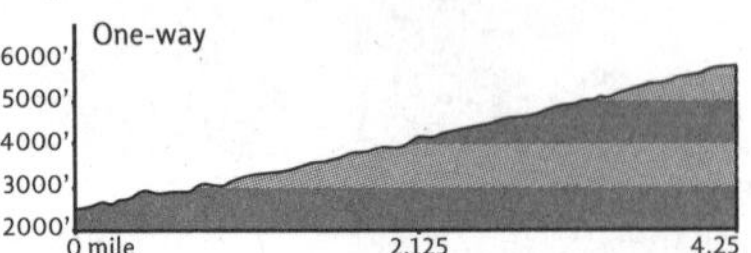

Maps: Green Trails Mount Rainier East, No. 270; **Contact:** Longmire Wilderness Information Center, (360) 569-4453; **GPS:** N46 48.106, W121 33.305

The old lookout cabin that served decades as guard against wildfires still stands atop Shiner Peak, though now it's a historic reminder of a bygone era. These cabins-on-stilts no longer serve as the first line of defense. Today's watch towers are much higher—satellites monitor lightning strikes, and if needed, airplanes do reconnaissance to check for smoke. So Shriner's summit tower serves only as a hikers' rest area with glorious views of the eastern reaches of Mount Rainier National Park, as well as the western peaks of the William O. Douglas Wilderness Area to the east. The trail is long and steep, but the views from the end are worth any effort to get there.

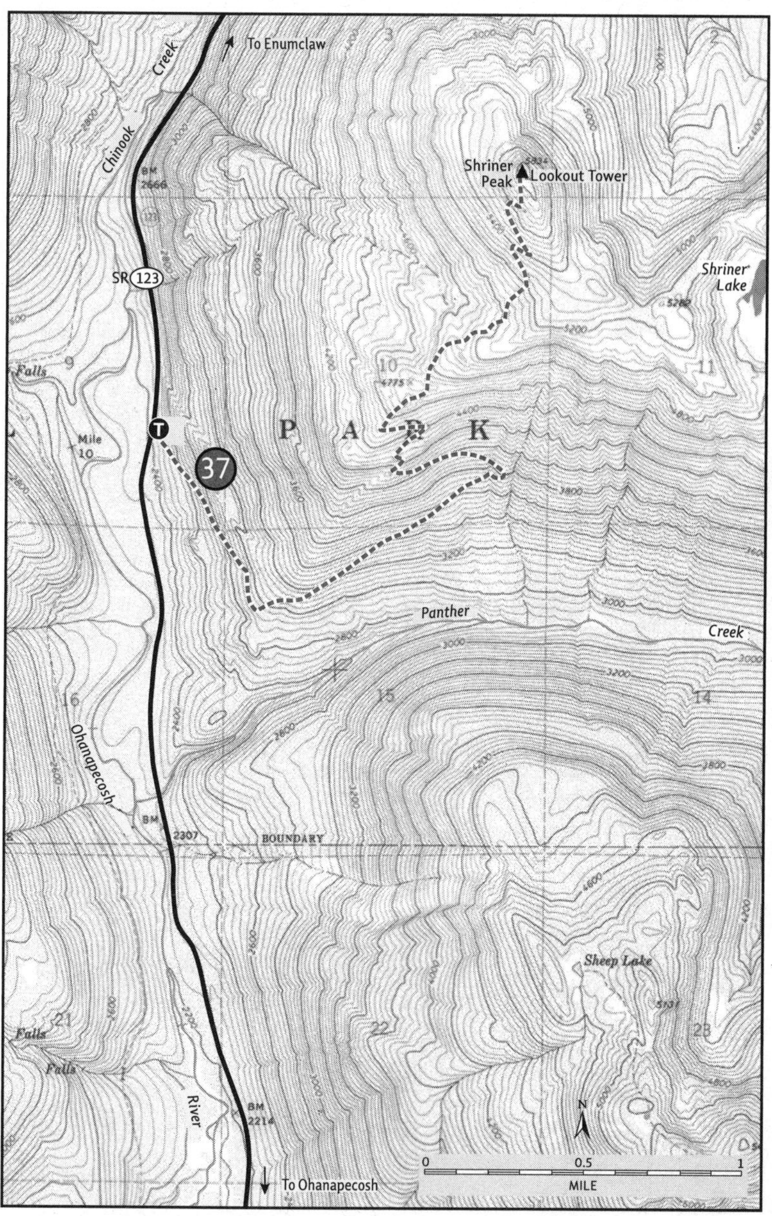
To Enumclaw
Chinook
Creek
BM
2666
SR 123
Shriner
Peak
Lookout Tower
Shriner
Lake
5282
10
4775
11
Falls
9
Mile
10
37
P A R K
Panther
Creek
16
15
14
Ohanapecosh
BM
2307
BOUNDARY
Sheep Lake
5131
21
Falls
Falls
22
23
River
BM
2214
To Ohanapecosh
N
0
0.5
1
MILE

GETTING THERE

From Enumclaw, drive east about 47 miles on State Route 410 to the junction with SR 123 at Cayuse Pass. Stay right (straight ahead) to merge onto SR 123–Cayuse Pass Highway. Find the trailhead parking area on the right about 7.5 miles south of that junction. Park on the right (west) side of the highway and find the trailhead on the east side of the road.

From Ohanapecosh, drive north about 11.5 miles on SR 123 to the parking area on the left (west) and the trailhead on the right (east). **Note:** SR 123 was severely damaged by the November 2006 floods. Although the road has been reopened, call to check on road conditions.

ON THE TRAIL

Much of this route is exposed, and since it faces south-southwest, it gets the full force of the solar heating. In other words, this hike can be a cooker during midsummer. Best bet is to start early, since the worst of the heating occurs in the afternoon.

The trail angles upward away from the road, cutting south along the lower flank of Shriner Peak before curving to the east at around 0.75 mile. Another mile-long climbing traverse leads to a short series of switchbacks. By this point, you've left the forest and entered first an old burned area—the silver snags and young new trees provide no shade—then venture up into the world of wildflower meadows.

At 2.5 miles, the trail crests a ridge leading up the south face of the peak. From here, you climb north into increasingly clear and spectacular views. Another 0.75 mile of climbing leads to a vantage point high above Shriner Lake. You can peer down into the blue pool far below before pushing on up the dusty trail for the final mile to the 5834-foot summit and its fantastic panoramas.

38 Laughingwater Creek to Three Lakes

RATING/ DIFFICULTY	ROUND-TRIP	ELEV GAIN/ HIGH POINT	SEASON
****/4	12 miles	2800 feet/ 4880 feet	July–Oct

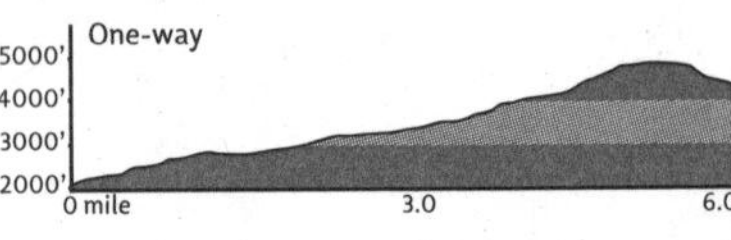

The vanilla-leaf-lined Laughingwater Creek trail in early spring

Maps: Green Trails Mount Rainier East and Bumping Lake, Nos. 270 and 271; **Contact:** Longmire Wilderness and Information Center, (360) 569-4453; **GPS:** N46 45.094, W121 33.429

Water tumbling over rocks creates a cheerful sound. Almost like a chuckle. Or a laugh. As though the water is laughing. Ah-haaaa! Tumbling water draining from a trio of lakes. It seems the namer of the features of this route started with a good creative streak and then got lazy. Laughingwater Creek is a beautiful stream tumbling through a moss-laden forest, and Three Lakes is a wonderful trio of tarns in a high alpine basin; they deserve a livelier name. This trail is a marvelous route to explore early—it's usually snow free by late June or early July. Visit while the waters are still running strong to hear the biggest chuckles.

GETTING THERE

From Enumclaw, drive east about 47 miles on State Route 410 to the junction with SR 123 at Cayuse Pass. Stay right (straight ahead) to merge onto SR 123–Cayuse Pass Highway. Drive south about 11.5 miles to the junction with the Stevens Canyon Road. Continue south on SR 123 past the Stevens Canyon Road for 0.2 mile, and find the trailhead parking area on the right (west) side of the road. The trailhead is on the east side of the highway.

From Ohanapecosh, drive north about 1.75 miles on SR 123 to the parking area on the left (west) and the trailhead on the right (east). **Note:** SR 123 was severely damaged by the November 2006 floods. Although the road has been reopened, call to check on road conditions.

ON THE TRAIL

You start parallel to the creek but well back from the water's edge. The trail climbs moderately before angling across the slope to intercept the creek at 1 mile. A small picnic area has been stomped out here, alongside the Laughingwater, and many casual hikers call it a day here.

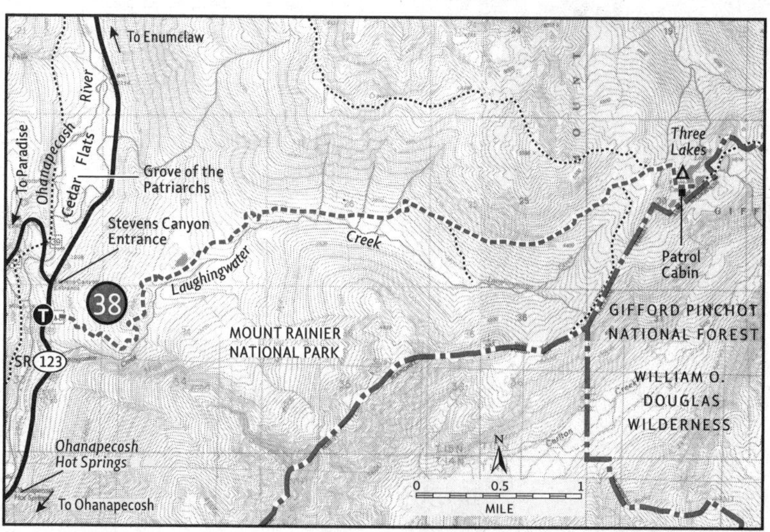

Push on, moving onward and upward—the best is yet to come. The trail continues its gradual ascent until it crosses a tributary to the Laughingwater at 3.5 miles. From this point, the trail gets more serious, turning steeply upward. The path climbs away from the creek as it ascends the headwall of the creek valley, passing faint way trails on either side in the upper basin.

You crest a small ridge at 4.5 miles and then drop slightly before running up into the Three Lakes Basin at 5.5 miles. The trail skirts around and between the lakes to a backcountry camp at 6 miles. Find a place to kick back and relax around the lakes before heading back down.

EXTENDING YOUR TRIP

You can push on another mile past the lakes basin to join the Pacific Crest Trail in the William O. Douglas Wilderness. Once there, you can turn south and hike about 2200 miles to Mexico or turn north and hike 350 miles to Canada. Or back at the trailhead, you can cross the highway and head north to the Grove of the Patriarchs (Hike 41) or south to Silver Falls (Hike 40).

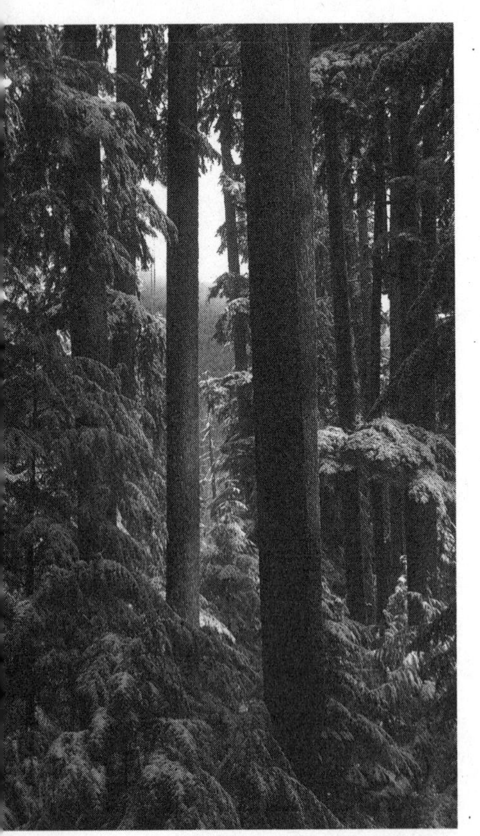

39 Ohanapecosh Hot Springs

RATING/ DIFFICULTY	LOOP	ELEV GAIN/ HIGH POINT	SEASON
**/1	1 mile	50 feet/ 1900 feet	May–Oct

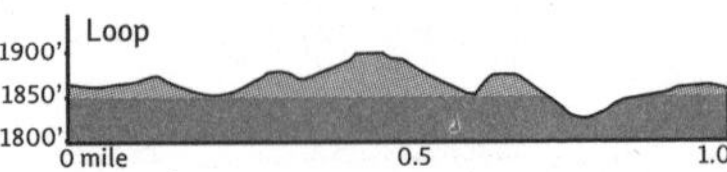

Maps: Green Trails Mount Rainier East, No. 270; **Contact:** Longmire Wilderness Information Center, (360) 569-4453; **GPS:** N46 43.983, W121 34.157

Early tourists flocked to Ohanapecosh not because it was so spectacularly pretty, but because of the water. More specifically, because of the hot water burbling out of the ground. Today, the lounging pools along the river are gone, but hot water still seeps out of the rocks before merging into the icy-cold waters of the Ohanapecosh River.

Towering frosty trees surround the Ohanapecosh Hot Springs loop scenery

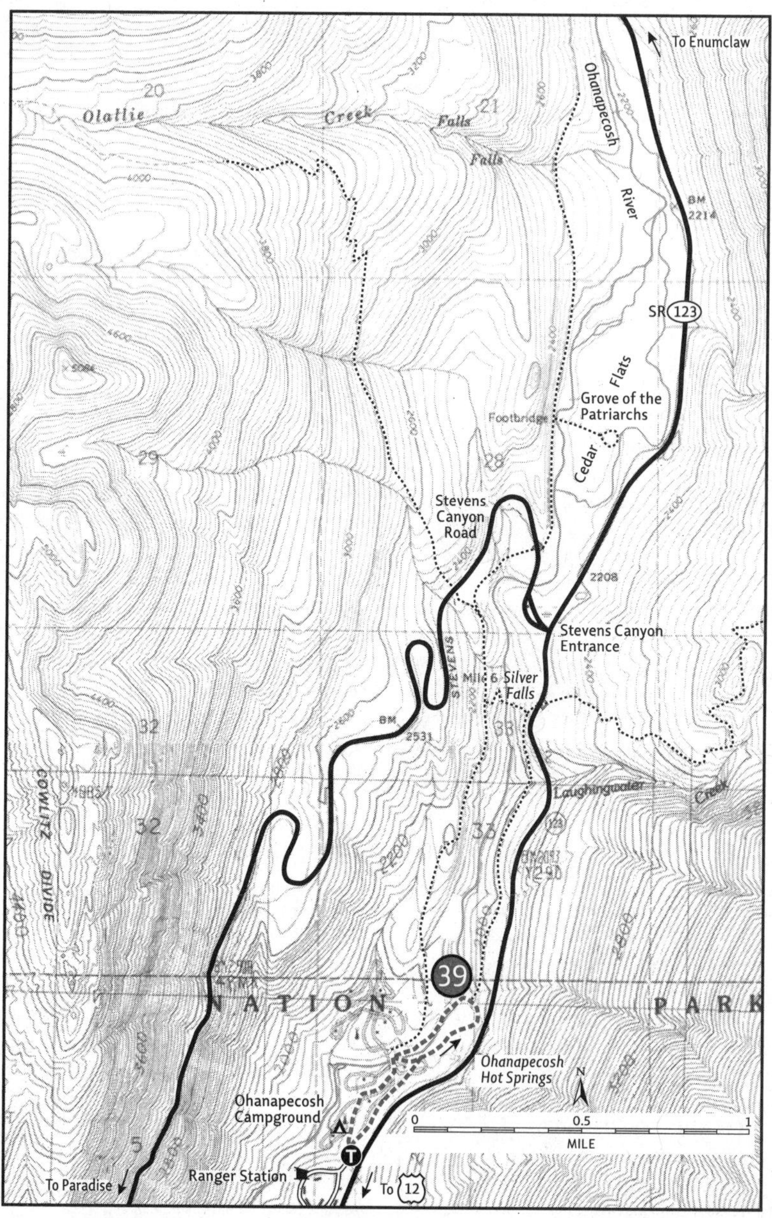
To Enumclaw
Olallie
Creek
Falls
Falls
Ohanapecosh
River
BM
2214
SR 123
Flats
Grove of the
Patriarchs
Footbridge
Cedar
Stevens
Canyon
Road
2208
Stevens Canyon
Entrance
STEVENS
Mile 6
Silver
Falls
BM
2531
Laughingwater
Creek
COWLITZ
DIVIDE
39
NATION
PARK
Ohanapecosh
Hot Springs
N
0
0.5
1
MILE
Ohanapecosh
Campground
Ranger Station
To Paradise
To 12

GETTING THERE

From Enumclaw, drive east about 47 miles on State Route 410 to the junction with SR 123 at Cayuse Pass. Stay right (straight ahead) to merge onto SR 123–Cayuse Pass Highway. Drive south about 11.5 miles to the junction with the Stevens Canyon Road. Continue south on SR 123 past the Stevens Canyon Road to the Ohanapecosh Campground on the right. Turn in to the campground and park in front of the visitor center. The trailhead is found behind the visitor center.

From the south, drive US 12 about 8 miles east of Packwood to the junction with SR 123. Turn north on SR 123 and continue 3.5 miles to Ohanapecosh Campground. Turn left (west) into the campground and park as described above. **Note:** SR 123 was severely damaged by the November 2006 floods. Although the road has been reopened, call to check on road conditions.

ON THE TRAIL

The trail takes off from the visitor center and wanders through the lush, moss-laden forests on the east bank of the Ohanapecosh River. The trail is well graded and easy to walk, even for kids with short legs and shorter attention spans. The route explores some wonderful forest environments, with a variety of plant life to examine.

At 0.5 mile, the trail splits. The right fork is the path to Silver Falls (Hike 40). For our purposes, we want to go left. The trail curves down near the river and the bubbling waters and burbling mud of the hot springs.

The trail continues another 0.3 mile back to the campground, coming out on one of the campground loops. Follow the road 0.25 mile back to the visitor center.

EXTENDING YOUR TRIP

At the junction with the Silver Falls Trail, you can continue north on that loop (Hike 40) and combine the two hikes.

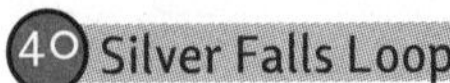

40 Silver Falls Loop

RATING/ DIFFICULTY	LOOP	ELEV GAIN/ HIGH POINT	SEASON
***/2	3 miles	200 feet/ 2100 feet	May–Oct

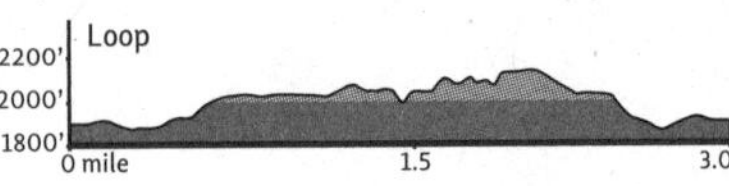

Maps: Green Trails Mount Rainier East, No. 270; **Contact:** Longmire Wilderness Information Center, (360) 569-4453; **GPS:** N46 43.983, W121 34.157

The Ohanapecosh River may be the most picturesque stream in the park, with its crystal-clear waters, moss-laden banks, and tall forests above. One of the prettiest sections of this most attractive river is Silver Falls. This sparkling cascade tumbles over a jagged, rocky ledge, creating a noisy splash full of silver streamers and frothy white water. The trail to the falls draws lots of hikers of all ages and abilities since it is relatively flat, well graded, and easily accessible. Don't let the masses get you down, though, since even on the busiest Saturday afternoons, this hike is well worth the effort.

GETTING THERE

From Enumclaw, drive east about 47 miles on State Route 410 to the junction with SR 123 at Cayuse Pass. Stay right (straight ahead) to merge onto SR 123–Cayuse Pass Highway. Drive south about 11.5 miles to the junction with the Stevens Canyon Road. Continue south on SR 123 past the Stevens Canyon Road to the Ohanapecosh Campground on the right in about 3 miles. Turn in to the campground and park in front of the visitor center. The trailhead is found behind the visitor center.

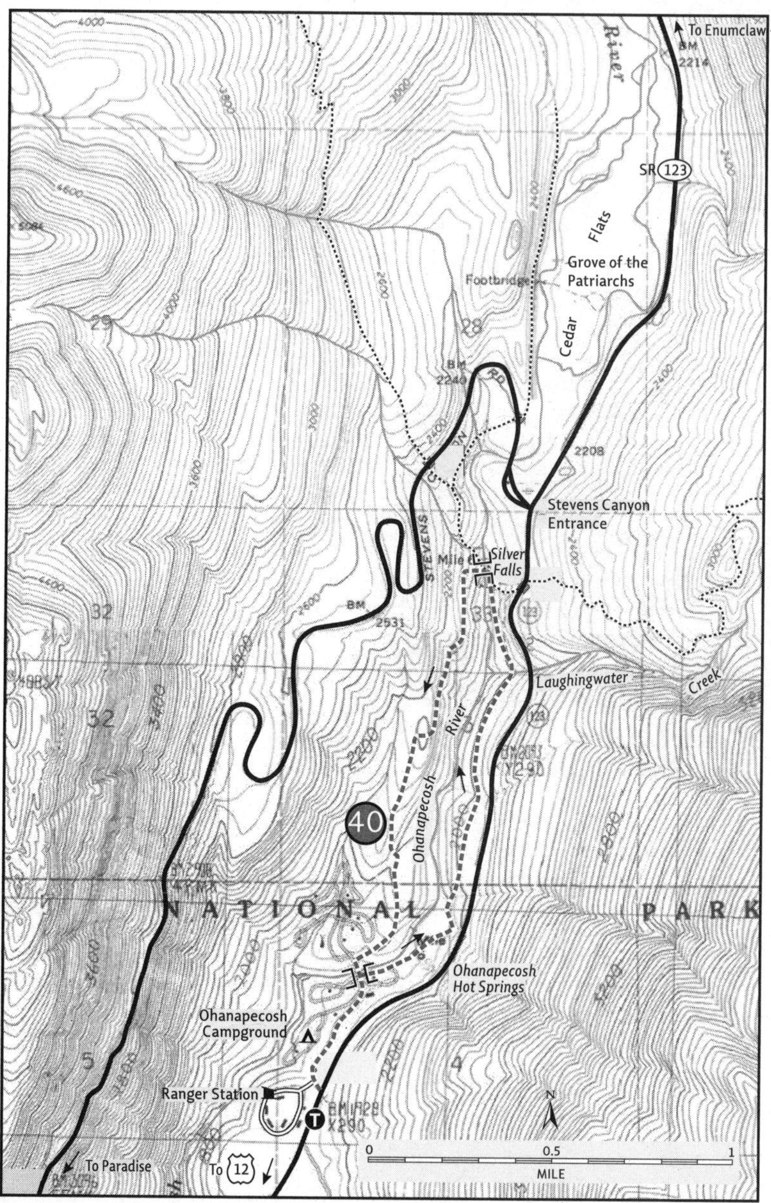
To Enumclaw
River
SR 123
Flats
Grove of the Patriarchs
Footbridge
Cedar
Stevens Canyon Entrance
Silver Falls
STEVENS
Laughingwater
Creek
Ohanapecosh
River
40
NATIONAL
PARK
Ohanapecosh Hot Springs
Ohanapecosh Campground
Ranger Station
To Paradise
To 12
N
0
0.5
1
MILE

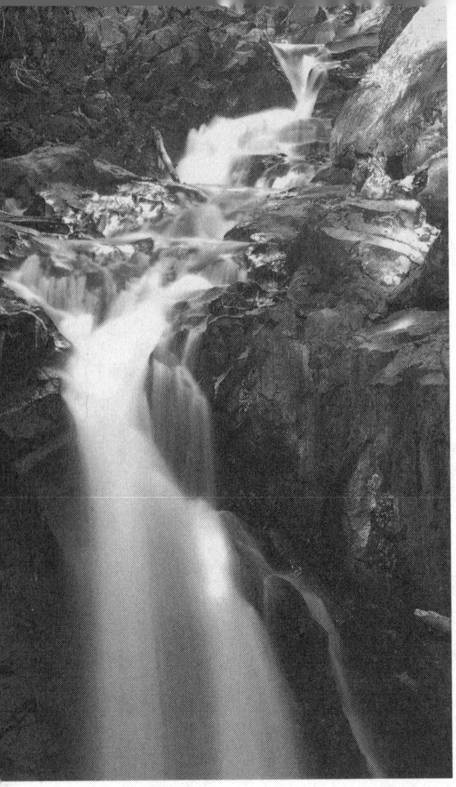

Silver Falls flowing at low autumn levels on the Ohanapecosh River

From the south, drive US 12 about 8 miles east of Packwood to the junction with SR 123. Turn north onto SR 123 and continue 3.5 miles to Ohanapecosh Campground. Turn left (west) into the campground and park as described above. **Note:** SR 123 was severely damaged by the November 2006 floods. Although the road has been reopened, call to check on road conditions.

ON THE TRAIL

The hike starts from the visitor center on an interpretive trail, but at 0.2 mile, you veer right onto the Silver Falls Trail to continue up the east side of the Ohanapecosh River. The trail is relatively flat and well maintained as it ambles north through the moss-laden forests flanking the river. The path stays above the river most of the way, with only occasional views of the pretty stream.

At about 1.7 miles, the trail reaches a junction with the Laughingwater Creek Trail (Hike 38). Stay left (straight) and in just a few moments the trail curves toward the river, dropping onto a sturdy footbridge that spans the narrow, rocky gorge of the river just below the falls. From the bridge deck, you have fantastic views of the cascade. Stop for pictures—then hold tight to your camera as you peer straight down into the depths of the clear pool below the falls.

After crossing the river, the trail climbs a few yards to join the Eastside Trail. Turn left to follow the river back downstream (to the right, the Eastside Trail reaches the Stevens Canyon Road trailhead in about 0.5 mile). In a mile, you pop out of the forest onto the back loop of Ohanapecosh Campground. Walk the road back across the river (the road bridge spans a beautiful, deep pool in a rocky bowl) to reach the visitor center parking lot after 3 miles of walking.

EXTENDING YOUR TRIP

At the footbridge above Silver Falls, you can continue north on the Eastside Trail about 0.5 mile to the Grove of the Patriarchs Loop (Hike 41).

Opposite: Mount Rainier from a grand lunch spot on the shore of Bench Lake

stevens canyon

Stevens Canyon provides access from the southeast corner of the park to Paradise. The long, deep cut of Stevens Canyon separates the wild alpine parklands on the flank of Mount Rainier proper from the craggy peaks and crystal lakes of the Tatoosh Range. Hikers can explore the best of both sides of the canyon, as well as the rich forest ecosystems of the lower valley. Finally, the section of the Wonderland Trail that runs up the floor of the canyon leads past a stunning collection of waterfalls and riparian environments.

Note: The Stevens Canyon area sustained heavy damage during the winter 2006 storms. Several bridges washed out, as did sections of the Wonderland Trail and even parts of the Stevens Canyon Road. At the time of this writing, the timetable for repairs stretched out indefinitely, though most routes were expected to be opened by 2008. Be sure to call ahead to confirm accessibility of any route.

41 Grove of the Patriarchs Loop

RATING/ DIFFICULTY	LOOP	ELEV GAIN/ HIGH POINT	SEASON
***/1	1.5 miles	50 feet/ 2200 feet	May–Oct

Maps: Green Trails Mount Rainier East, No. 270; **Contact:** Longmire Wilderness Information Center, (360) 569-4453; **GPS:** N46 45.478, W121 33.454

Some of the biggest, oldest trees in the Washington Cascades stand tall in the Grove of the Patriarchs. These silent old men of moss tower overhead, with a few lying down to show us just how massive the trunks really are. The Grove resides in a low, boggy area across the Ohanapecosh River, so you'll need to cross a sweet little suspension bridge to get there, offering you a chance to enjoy a bit of adventure on this simple little trail. Youngsters typically love the bridge, and kids of all ages marvel at the massive trees. Note: The floods of 2006 severely damaged the footbridge leading to the Grove. Call ahead to find out if it's been repaired before you visit.

GETTING THERE

From Enumclaw, drive east about 47 miles on State Route 410 to the junction with SR 123 at Cayuse Pass. Stay right (straight ahead) to merge onto SR 123–Cayuse Pass Highway. Drive south about 11.5 miles to the junction with the Stevens Canyon Road. Turn right (west) and pass through the Stevens Canyon Entrance to the park. About 0.25 mile from SR 123, park in the lot on the north side of the road.

From Ohanapecosh, drive north 2 miles on SR 123 to the Stevens Canyon Road. Turn left (west) and pass through the Stevens Canyon Entrance to the park. About 0.25 mile from SR 123, park in the lot on the north side of the road.

Note: SR 123 was severely damaged by the November 2006 floods. Although the road has been reopened, call to check on road conditions.

ON THE TRAIL

Head north on the trail as it parallels the Ohanapecosh River. You'll find yourself amid fine old forest along the first 0.5 mile, but then at a trail junction you turn right to cross the river on the bouncy bridge and enter the Grove.

A loop of nearly 0.5 mile weaves through the massive old trees. These ancient hemlocks, cedars, and Douglas firs make the rest of the region's forests appear as mere weeks old. Some of these ancient entities measure nearly 40 feet in circumference and tower nearly 300 feet tall.

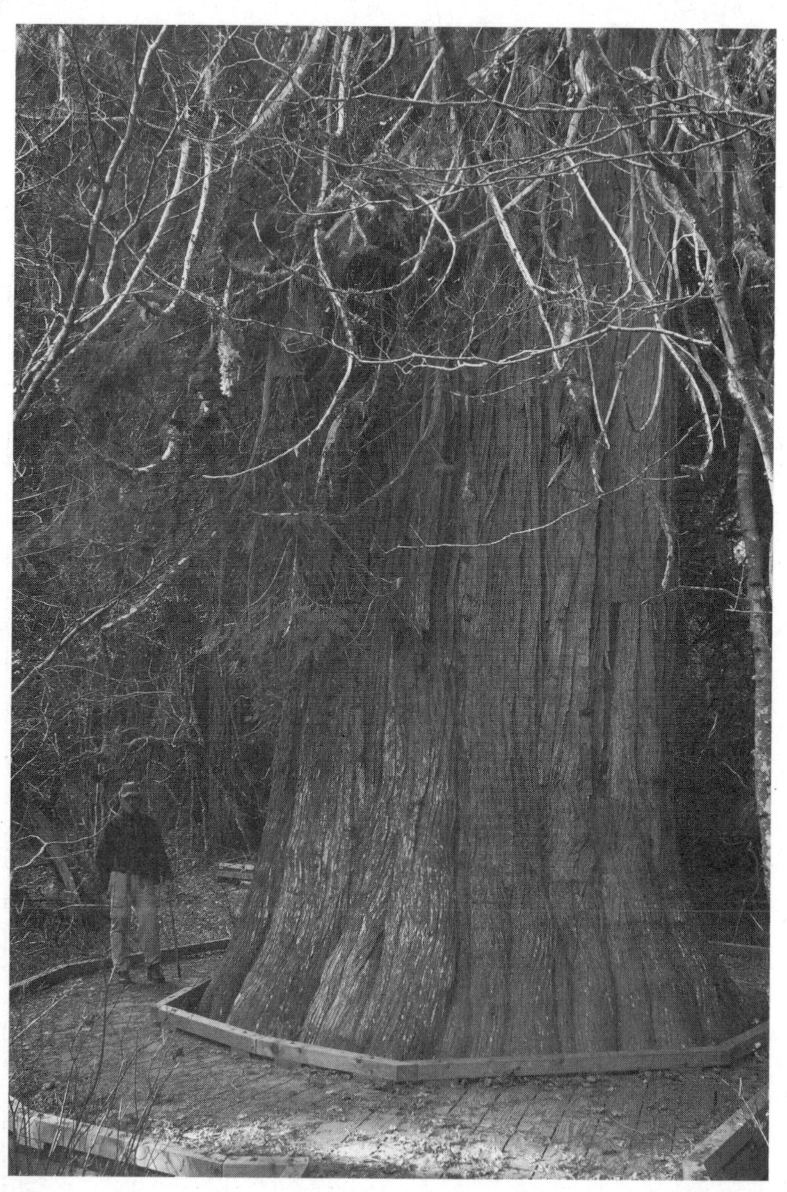

Massive western red cedar tree in the Grove of the Patriarchs

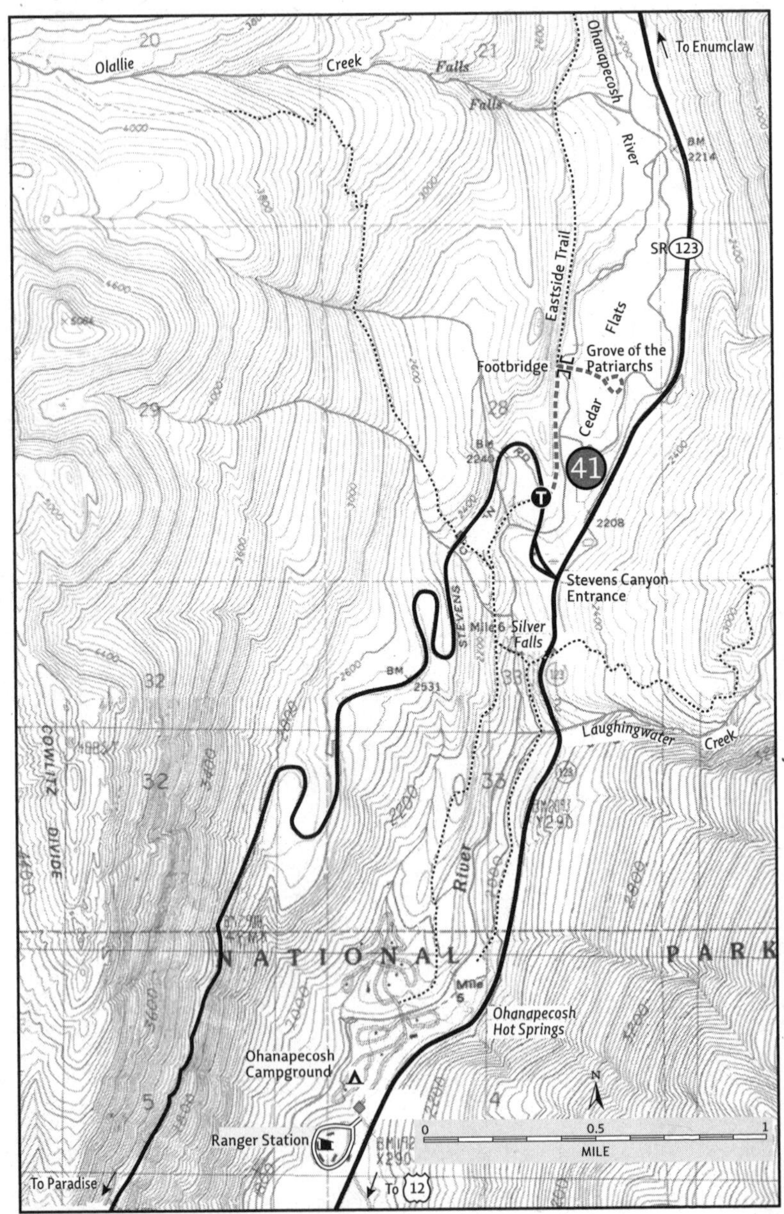

To Enumclaw
Olallie
Creek
Falls
Falls
Ohanapecosh
River
Eastside Trail
SR 123
Flats
Grove of the Patriarchs
Footbridge
Cedar
41
Stevens Canyon Entrance
Silver Falls
Mile 6
Laughingwater
Creek
COWLITZ DIVIDE
River
NATIONAL PARK
Mile 5
Ohanapecosh Hot Springs
Ohanapecosh Campground
Ranger Station
To Paradise
To 12
0
0.5
1
MILE

After following the winding loop through the Grove, recross the suspension bridge to return the way you came.

EXTENDING YOUR TRIP

After completing the loop and returning to the footbridge, you can continue north on the Eastside Trail, or you can head south from the trailhead, connecting to the Silver Falls loop trail (Hike 40) in about 0.5 mile.

42 Olallie Creek Camp

RATING/ DIFFICULTY	ROUND-TRIP	ELEV GAIN/ HIGH POINT	SEASON
***/3	5.6 miles	1600 feet/ 3900 feet	May–Oct

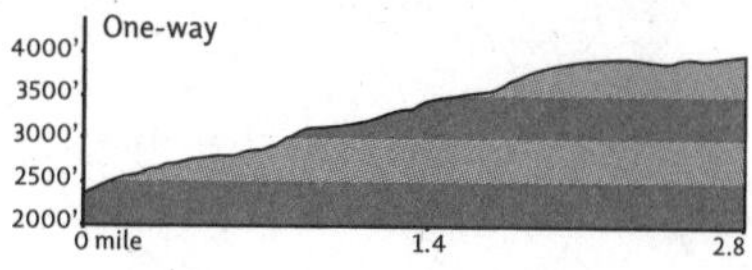

Maps: Green Trails Mount Rainier East, No. 270; **Contact:** Longmire Wilderness Information Center, (360) 569-4453; **GPS:** N46 45.373, W121 33.765

Few casual hikers venture out on this forest hike. After all, there are no grand vistas to enjoy, no thundering waterfalls, no vast fields of wildflowers. But you will find virgin forest ecosystems to explore, a pretty river valley to enjoy, and a quiet camp to relax in before turning home.

GETTING THERE

From Enumclaw, drive east about 47 miles on State Route 410 to the junction with SR 123 at Cayuse Pass. Stay right (straight ahead) to merge onto SR 123–Cayuse Pass Highway. Drive south about 11.5 miles to the junction with the Stevens Canyon Road. Turn right (west) and pass through the Stevens Canyon Entrance to the park. About 0.75 mile from SR 123, park in the small trailhead parking area on the north side of the road.

From the south, drive US 12 about 8 miles east of Packwood, to the junction with SR 123. Turn north on SR 123 and continue about 6 miles, passing Ohanapecosh Campground, to the Stevens Canyon Road. Turn left (west) and pass through the Stevens Canyon entrance to the park and find the trailhead as described above.

Note: Both SR 123 and Stevens Canyon Road have had closures due to washouts in the November 2006 flood. Although SR 123 has been reopened, call ahead for current road conditions.

Dennis pauses along the Olallie Creek trail, dwarfed by an old-growth Douglas fir tree.

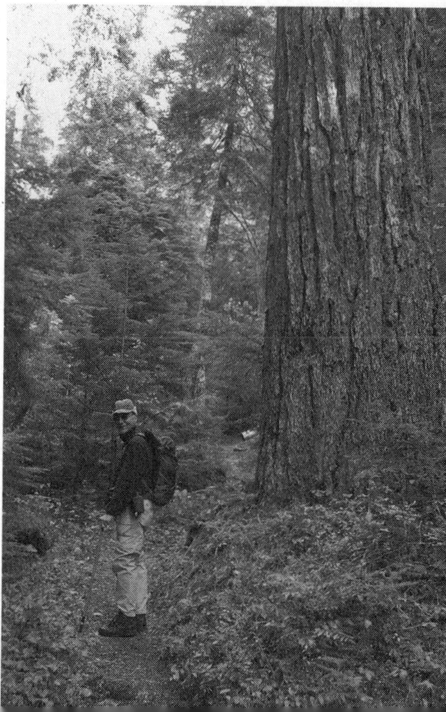

ON THE TRAIL

The trail leaves the Stevens Canyon Road and climbs steeply to the north, angling across the heavily forested flank of Cowlitz Divide for the first mile before hooking into a short series of switchbacks. That initial climb provides a good workout, but you can't relax yet.

The trail leaves the switchbacks behind at about 1.5 miles but goes into a steeply ascending traverse into the Olallie River valley. The trail stays well above the river, but the Olallie is close enough that you'll

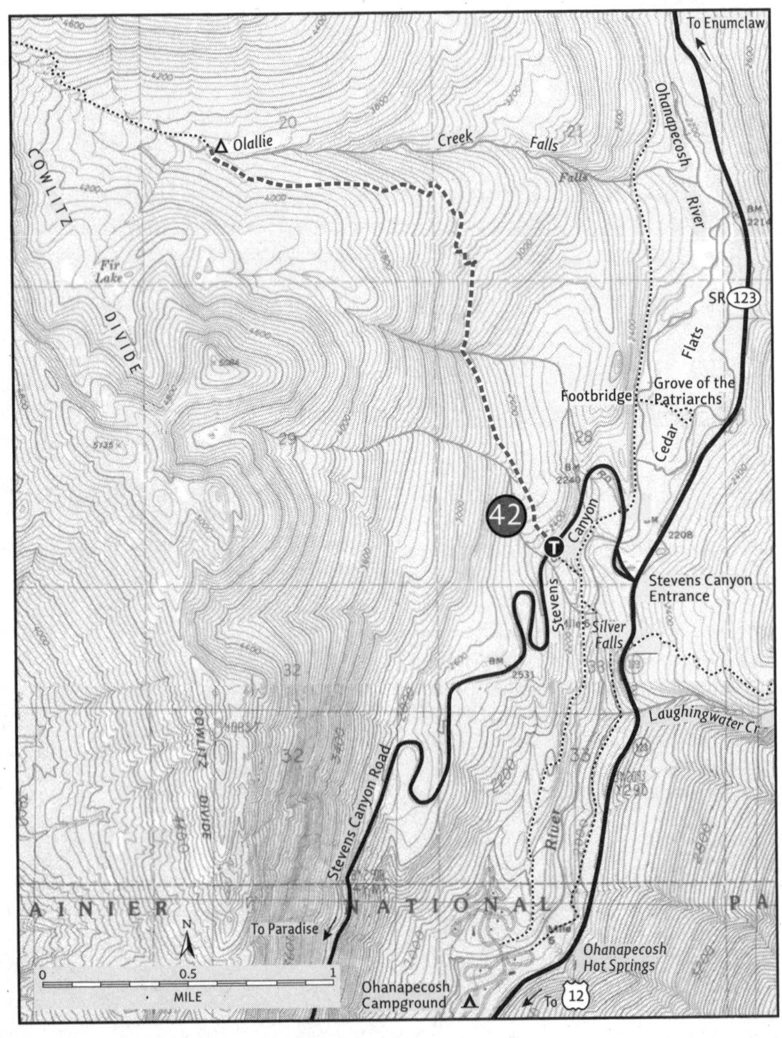

Nickel Creek Camp along the Wonderland Trail

be able to experience the birds and beasts that call the valley home. A variety of birds and small critters live here, from juncos to alligator lizards.

At 2.5 miles, the trail pitch moderates and you enjoy a relaxing final 0.3-mile stroll to the backcountry camp situated just above the creek. Stop at the camp if you want to stretch out, or drop down to where the trail crosses the creek for a rest before returning the way you came.

EXTENDING YOUR TRIP

You can climb beyond the camp for another 1.5 miles to reach the crest of Cowlitz Divide and a junction with the Wonderland Trail.

43 Box Canyon and Nickel Creek

RATING/ DIFFICULTY	ROUND-TRIP	ELEV GAIN/ HIGH POINT	SEASON
***/2	2 miles	400 feet/ 3400 feet	June–Oct

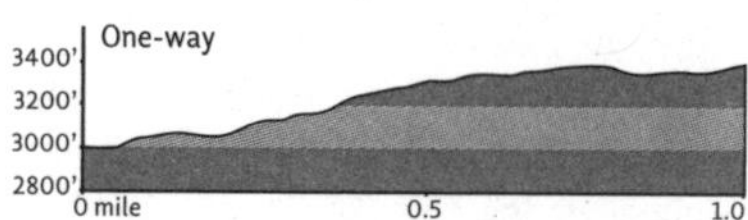

Maps: Green Trails Mount Rainier East, No. 270; **Contact:** Longmire Wilderness

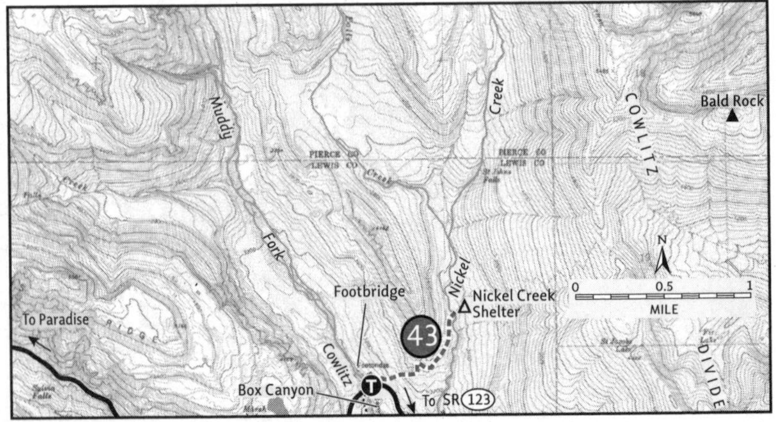

Information Center, (360) 569-4453; **GPS:** N46 45.918, W121 38.169

Box Canyon is one of the most unusual features in the park, and Nickel Creek Camp is a rustic backcountry retreat perfect for kids' first backpacking adventure. The trail explores the rim of the deep chasm of Box Canyon before swinging out through the forest for a woodland ramble into the Nickel Creek valley along this short section of the Wonderland Trail.

GETTING THERE

From Enumclaw, drive east about 47 miles on State Rout 410 to the junction with SR 123 at Cayuse Pass. Stay right (straight ahead) to merge onto SR 123–Cayuse Pass Highway. Drive south about 11.5 miles to the junction with the Stevens Canyon Road. Turn right (west) and pass through the Stevens Canyon Entrance to the park. About 10 miles from SR 123, park in the small trailhead parking area on the south side of the road.

From the south, drive US 12 about 8 miles east of Packwood to the junction with SR 123. Turn north on SR 123 and continue about 6 miles, passing Ohanapecosh Campground, to the Stevens Canyon Road. Turn left (west) and pass through the Stevens Canyon Entrance to the park and find the trailhead as described above.

From the west, via Paradise, drive SR 706 through the Nisqually Entrance and continue approximately 23 miles east to the trailhead on the south side of Stevens Canyon Road.

Note: Both SR 123 and Stevens Canyon Road have had closures due to washouts in the November 2006 flood. Although SR 123 has been reopened, call ahead for current road conditions.

ON THE TRAIL

Cross over to the north side of the road and, after strolling out to the middle of the road bridge to peer down into the deep cut of Box Canyon, find the trail on the east side of the canyon and start walking northeast. The first 0.1 mile stays near the canyon rim, offering great views into the gorge—which is more than 100 feet deep and only 13 feet wide at its narrowest point!

After leaving the gorge the trail angles east, and for the next 0.9 mile you climb the gentle slope through large, old trees to Nickel Creek. Look for raccoons along the creek and gray jays around the backcountry campsite, located just across the creek. An old three-sided backcountry shelter sits at the campsite, but I don't recommend you sleep in it—it's home to a hearty community of mice! Enjoy your time at the camp before heading back the way you came.

EXTENDING YOUR TRIP

You can continue on the trail beyond Nickel Camp, climbing to Indian Bar (Hike 44).

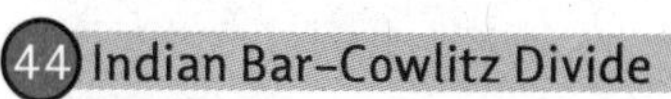

44 Indian Bar–Cowlitz Divide

RATING/ DIFFICULTY	ROUND-TRIP	ELEV GAIN/ HIGH POINT	SEASON
*****/5	15 miles	2900 feet/ 5914 feet	June–Oct

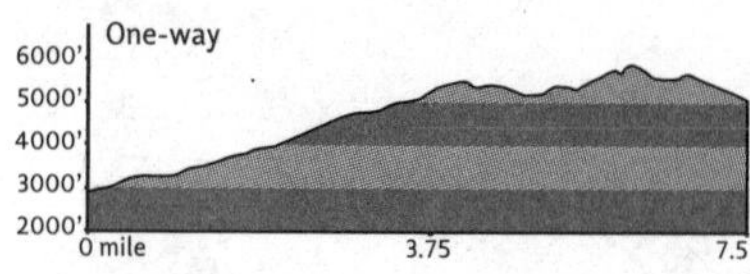

Maps: Green Trails Mount Rainier East, No. 270; **Contact:** Longmire Wilderness Information Center, (360) 569-4453; **GPS:** N46 45.918, W121 38.169

The trip to Indian Bar will test your trail stamina, but the payoff is an adventure in wildflowers. The basin that cradles Indian Bar Camp may well be the home of the best wildflower fields in the park. The main camp is on a small ridge above the meadows, though an old stone shelter in the heart of the meadow marks the location of the group camp. It's also worth noting that the single most spectacular backcountry toilet in the state is found here. Rather, the toilet itself is nothing fancy—just a lidded box, really—but the views from this "throne" include the whole of the wildflower meadows, the cascades tumbling down the cliffs at the head of the basin, and the crown of Mount Rainier above it all.

GETTING THERE

From Enumclaw, drive east about 47 miles on State Route 410 to the junction with SR 123 at Cayuse Pass. Stay right (straight ahead) to merge onto SR 123–Cayuse Pass Highway. Drive south about 11.5 miles to the junction with the Stevens Canyon Road. Turn right (west) and pass through the Stevens Canyon Entrance to the park. About 10 miles from SR 123, park in the small trailhead parking area on the south side of the road.

From the south, drive US 12 about 8 miles east of Packwood to the junction with SR 123. Turn north on SR 123 and continue about 6 miles, passing Ohanapecosh Campground, to the Stevens Canyon Road. Turn left (west) and pass through the Stevens Canyon Entrance to the park and find the trailhead as described above.

From the west, via Paradise, drive SR 706 through the Nisqually Entrance and continue approximately 23 miles east to the trailhead on the south side of Stevens Canyon Road.

Note: Both SR 123 and Stevens Canyon Road have had closures due to washouts in the November 2006 flood. Although SR 123 has reopened, call ahead for current road conditions.

ON THE TRAIL

The trail, a section of the Wonderland, leaves Box Canyon and provides a nice warm-up over the first mile, climbing only a few hundred feet to reach Nickel Creek Camp. Here, though, the trail gets serious about its climbing. You ascend steeply for the next 2 miles to reach the crest of the Cowlitz Divide ridgeline and a junction with the Olallie Creek trail (Hike 42). Stay left and follow the ridge crest north as it climbs toward Mount Rainier.

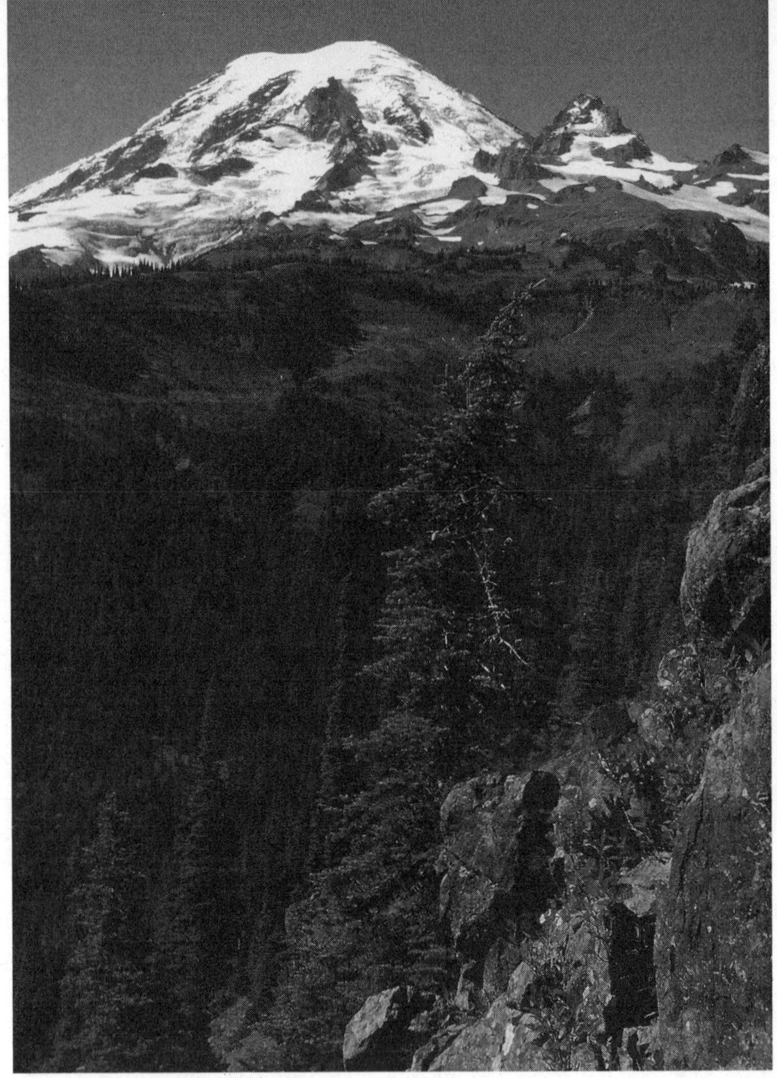

Mount Rainier from along the Cowlitz Divide dropping into Indian Bar

For nearly 4 miles you follow this ridgeline, staying atop the crest as it rolls through forests and broad meadows. You'll find glorious views of Mount Rainier at times, as well as looks east across the Ohanapecosh Valley to Double Peak and Shriner Peak.

At about 6.5 miles, the trail climbs above timberline and crosses an area of rock and permanent snowfield on the flank of Cowlitz Park before a final 800-foot descent into the

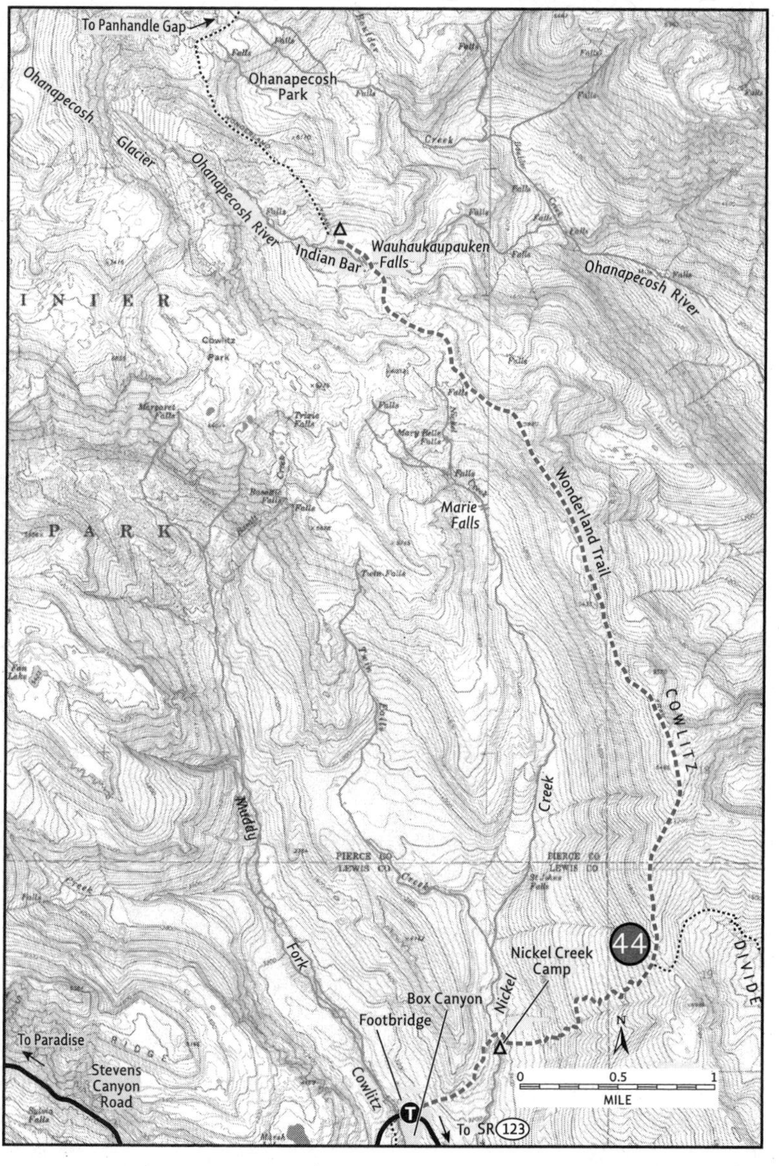

To Panhandle Gap
Ohanapecosh Park
Ohanapecosh Glacier
Ohanapecosh River
Indian Bar
Wauhaukaupauken Falls
Ohanapecosh River
Marie Falls
Wonderland Trail
COWLITZ
Creek
Muddy
Fork
44
DIVIDE
Nickel Creek Camp
Nickel
Box Canyon
Footbridge
To Paradise
Stevens Canyon Road
Cowlitz
To SR 123
N
0
0.5
1
MILE

Yes, the golden-mantled squirrels are that cute!

basin of Indian Bar. The Ohanapecosh River flows through the heart of this meadow, and you can see this remarkable river being born out of the waterfalls tumbling down the rocky walls surrounding the basin. As you walk into the basin, you pass the pretty cascade of Wauhaukaupauken Falls before reaching the impressive stone shelter at the group site in the heart of the meadow (7.5 miles from the trailhead). Enjoy the views, but give yourself plenty of time for the return trip.

EXTENDING YOUR TRIP

You can continue north on the Wonderland Trail beyond Indian Bar Camp, reaching Panhandle Gap (Hike 18) in about 12 miles.

45 Stevens Canyon Waterfalls

RATING/ DIFFICULTY	ROUND-TRIP	ELEV GAIN/ HIGH POINT	SEASON
****/4	7 miles	700 feet/ 3750 feet	June–Oct

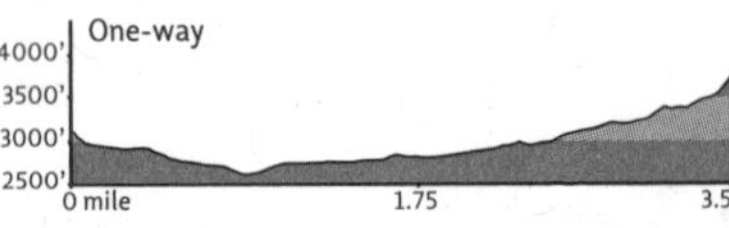

Maps: Green Trails Mount Rainier East, No. 270; **Contact:** Longmire Wilderness Information Center, (360) 569-4453 ; **GPS:** N46 45.610, W121 38.344

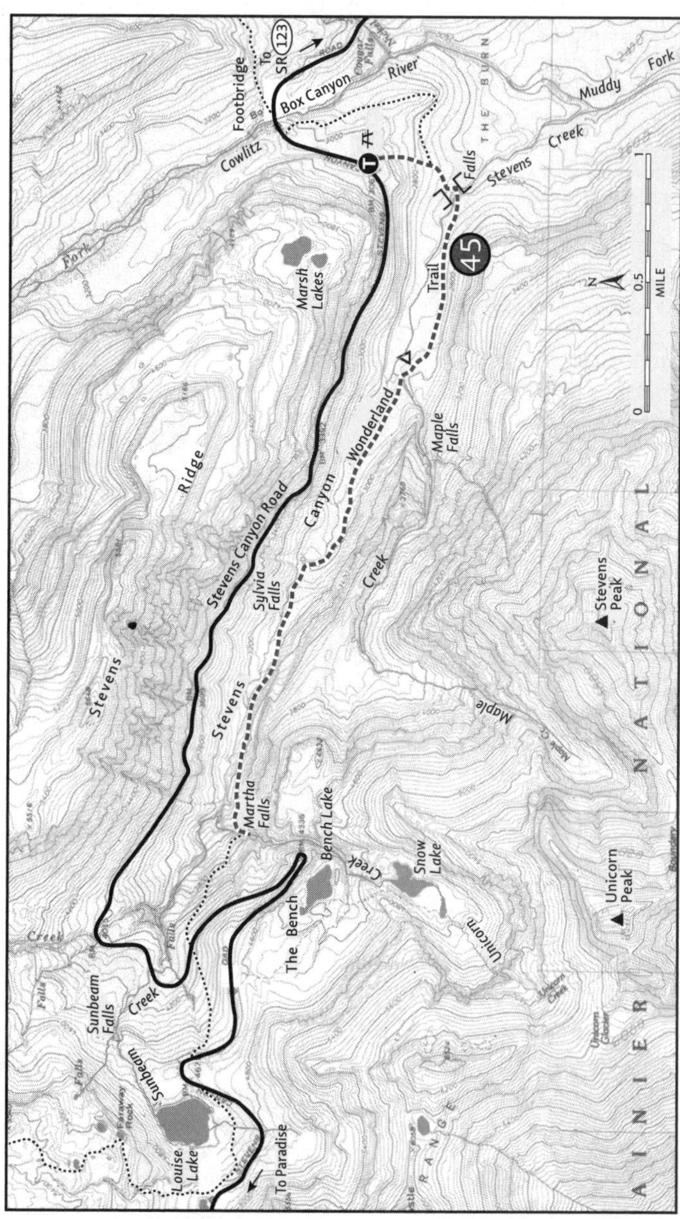
To SR 123
Footbridge
Box Canyon
Cowlitz
River
Muddy Fork
Stevens Creek
Falls
45
Trail
Marsh Lakes
Wonderland
Maple Falls
Ridge
Stevens Canyon Road
Canyon
Creek
Sylvia Falls
Stevens
Stevens
Stevens Peak
Maple
Martha Falls
Bench Lake
Snow Lake
The Bench
Unicorn Peak
Unicorn
Sunbeam Falls
Creek
Sunbeam
Louise Lake
To Paradise
N
0
0.5
1
MILE

Following the Wonderland Trail, this route explores the floor of Stevens Canyon, and along the way, you'll find a number of waterfalls along Stevens Creek and its tributaries. The trail is broad and generally well maintained, though the 2006 storms took out some of the bridges and washed out one section of trail. As of this writing, this section of the Wonderland Trail is closed, though repairs are underway. Hikers should contact the park before venturing out.

GETTING THERE

From Enumclaw, drive east about 47 miles on State Route 410 to the junction with SR 123 at Cayuse Pass. Stay right (straight ahead) to merge onto SR 123–Cayuse Pass Highway. Drive south about 11.5 miles to the junction with the Stevens Canyon Road. Turn right (west) and pass through the Stevens Canyon Entrance to the park. About 10.5 miles from SR 123, park in the Box Canyon Picnic Area (about 0.5 mile west of Box Canyon).

From the south, drive US 12 about 8 miles east of Packwood to the junction with SR 123. Turn north on SR 123 and continue about 6 miles, passing Ohanapecosh Campground, to the Stevens Canyon Road. Turn left (west) and pass through the Stevens Canyon Entrance to the park and find the trailhead as described above.

From the west, via Paradise, drive SR 706 through the Nisqually Entrance and continue approximately 23 miles east to the trailhead on the south side of Stevens Canyon Road.

Note: Both SR 123 and Stevens Canyon Road have had closures due to washouts in the November 2006 flood. Although SR 123 has reopened, call ahead for current road conditions.

ON THE TRAIL

Find the trail on the south side of the parking area and descend through open forest for about 0.75 mile to reach a bridge over Stevens Creek near the first small waterfall of the journey. Just before crossing the bridge, you'll find a junction with the Wonderland Trail. Turn right and start up the gentle climb along the floor of the canyon. Lush, moss-laden forests surround you on this lower section of the canyon.

At 1.5 miles, you reach Maple Creek Camp alongside the small tributary stream (yup, you guessed it: Maple Creek). A small waterfall crashes over a rocky ledge just above camp—a small boot track leads through the brushy forest to the cascade.

The Wonderland Trail continues upcanyon from Maple Creek, and at around 2.5 miles, you pass a vantage point offering good views of Sylvia Falls on Stevens Creek. Just 1 mile above this, the trail angles steeply away from the main creek to cross Unicorn Creek just below Martha Falls. Stop and enjoy this largest of the route's falls before turning back the way you came.

EXTENDING YOUR TRIP

You can continue west on the Wonderland Trail beyond Martha Falls to Louise Lake (Hike 47) in about 1.2 miles.

46 Bench and Snow Lakes

RATING/ DIFFICULTY	ROUND-TRIP	ELEV GAIN/ HIGH POINT	SEASON
***/2	2.6 miles	300 feet/ 4679 feet	June–Oct

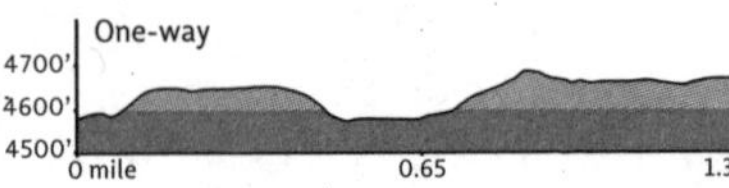

Maps: Green Trails Paradise, No. 270s; **Contact:** Longmire Wilderness Information Center, (360) 569-4453; **GPS:** N46 45.610, W121 38.344

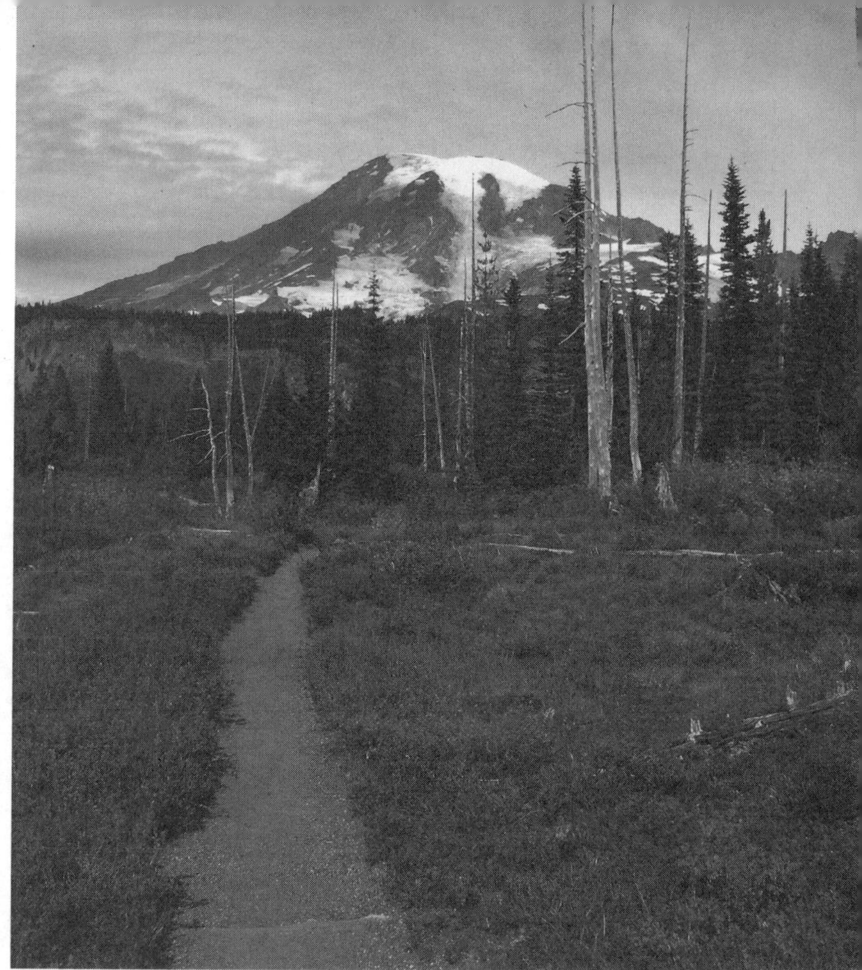

Silver snags in the meadows along the trail to Bench and Snow Lakes

Bench and Snow lakes are found just above the head of the Stevens Canyon Road, but you'll feel like you're deep in the backcountry once you immerse yourself in the cool lakes basin. The lakes are clear and pristine, and the upper lake, Snow, is nestled in a snow-filled cirque with fabulous views up to Unicorn Peak. Bench Lake boasts a great view of Mount Rainier.

GETTING THERE

From Enumclaw, drive east about 47 miles on State Route 410 to the junction with SR 123 at Cayuse Pass. Stay right (straight ahead) to merge onto SR 123–Cayuse Pass Highway. Drive south about 11.5 miles to the junction with the Stevens Canyon Road. Turn right (west) and pass through the Stevens Canyon Entrance to the park. About 16 miles from

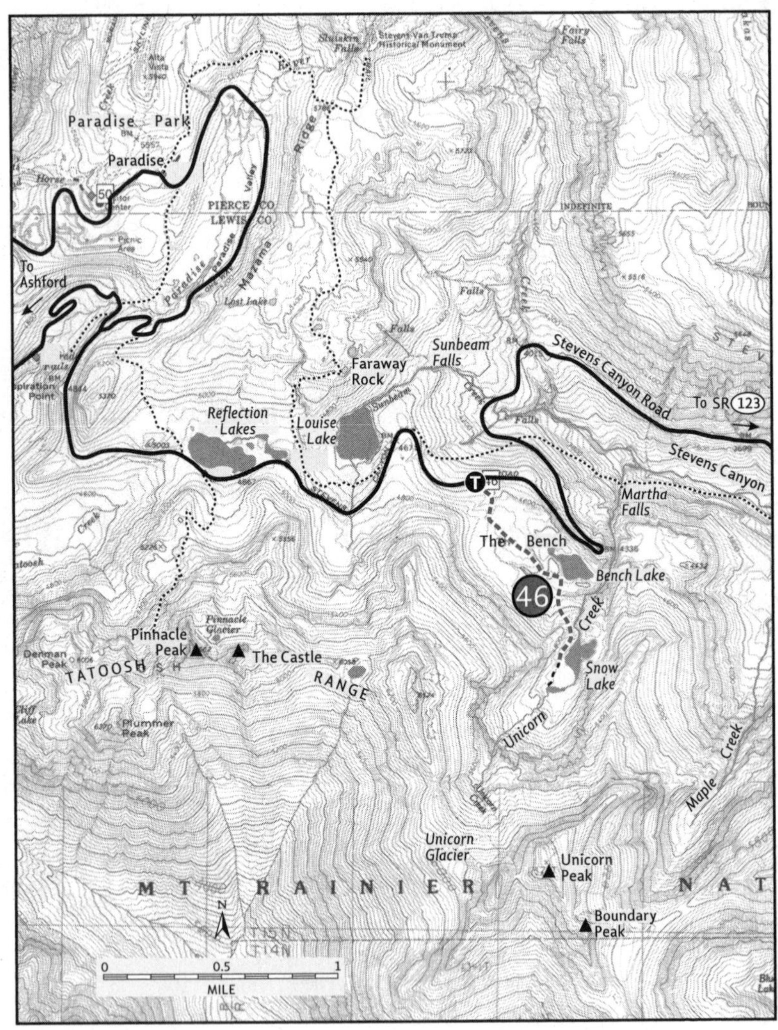

SR 123, park in the long parking area on the south side of the road.

From the south, drive US 12 about 8 miles east of Packwood to the junction with SR 123. Turn north on SR 123 and continue about 6 miles, passing Ohanapecosh Campground, to the Stevens Canyon Road. Turn left (west) and pass through the Stevens Canyon Entrance to the park and find the trailhead as described above.

From the west, via Paradise, drive SR 706 through the Nisqually Entrance and continue approximately 17 miles east to the trailhead on the south side of Stevens Canyon Road.

Note: Both SR 123 and Stevens Canyon Road have had closures due to washouts in the November 2006 flood. Although SR 123 has reopened, call ahead for current road conditions.

ON THE TRAIL

Head south from the parking area as the trail weaves through the tree-studded meadows of the Bench—a flat plateau above the road. In about 0.8 mile, the meandering trail rolls along above the shoreline of Bench Lake. From where you stand, Bench Lake is meadow lined, but the opposite shore drops quickly away as a steep cliff, making the views across the lake unique, since there is no real obstacle to the vistas beyond the lake.

The trail continues past Bench and in 0.5 mile reaches the shore of Snow Lake. This long lake sits in the midst of Unicorn Creek. Icy snowmelt rushes off the rocky flank of Unicorn Peak and fills the basin of Snow Lake before draining out the far end to fall steeply away, tumbling over Martha Falls far below (see Hike 45) and merging into the waters of Stevens Creek. Because Snow Lake lies deep in a rocky cirque, it doesn't get the full brunt of the sun. As a result, Snow Lake frequently has blocks of ice floating in its chilly waters well into August, and sometimes all summer long. A climbers path leads up through talus to a small tarn above Snow Lake. Use caution, as the route is not well marked or developed.

47 Louise Lake

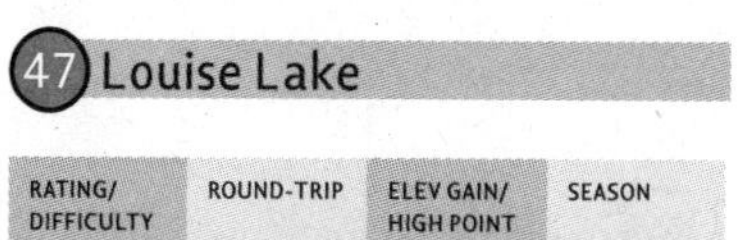

RATING/ DIFFICULTY	ROUND-TRIP	ELEV GAIN/ HIGH POINT	SEASON
**/2	2 miles	300 feet/ 4880 feet	June–Oct

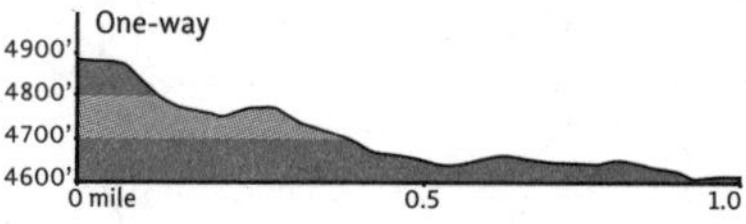

Maps: Green Trails Paradise, No. 270s; **Contact:** Longmire Wilderness Information Center, (360) 569-4453; **GPS:** N46 46.132, W121 43.442

From the shores of Reflection Lake, this trail leads down jumbled talus slopes to the cold blue waters of Louise Lake, a pretty pool beneath the rocky wall of lower Mazama Ridge. The trail is gentle and kid-friendly, and since access is so easy, it makes a great stroll on a hot summer day.

GETTING THERE

From Enumclaw, drive east about 47 miles on State Route 410 to the junction with SR 123 at Cayuse Pass. Stay right (straight ahead) to merge onto SR 123–Cayuse Pass Highway. Drive south about 11.5 miles to the junction with the Stevens Canyon Road. Turn right (west) and pass through the Stevens Canyon Entrance to the park. About 17 miles from SR 123, park at the Reflections Lake parking area (stay toward the east end for easiest access).

From the south, drive US 12 about 8 miles east of Packwood to the junction with SR 123. Turn north on SR 123 and continue about 6 miles, passing Ohanapecosh Campground, to the Stevens Canyon Road. Turn left (west) and pass through the Stevens Canyon Entrance to the park and find the trailhead as described above.

From the west, via Paradise, drive SR 706 through the Nisqually Entrance and continue approximately 16 miles east to the trailhead on the north side of Stevens Canyon Road.

Note: Both SR 123 and Stevens Canyon Road have had closures due to washouts in the November 2006 flood. Although SR 123 has reopened, call ahead for current road conditions.

ON THE TRAIL

The trail—a section of the Wonderland—leaves from the easternmost pools of the Reflection Lakes chain. Head north along the eastern shore trail and after just 0.25 mile, turn right at the junction with the Mazama Ridge Trail. You now start a slow, traversing descent around the circular wall above Louise Lake. Most of the trail is on open talus slope—the trail is well built across these rocky slopes, so you don't have to worry too much about footing. At about 0.5 mile, the trail reaches a brushy section, with a few huckleberries dangling near the trail.

At about 0.8 mile, the trail nears a loop of the Stevens Canyon Road. Just as you seem to be approaching the road, though, you find a spur trail on the left. Take this side track and in 0.1 mile reach the rocky lakeshore. Kick your feet in the icy waters before heading back up the gentle trail.

EXTENDING YOUR TRIP

From the spur trail, you can continue east on the Wonderland Trail to Martha Falls (see Hike 45) in about 1.5 miles. Or on the return, you could turn right (north) on the Mazama Ridge Trail up to Faraway Rock (Hike 48).

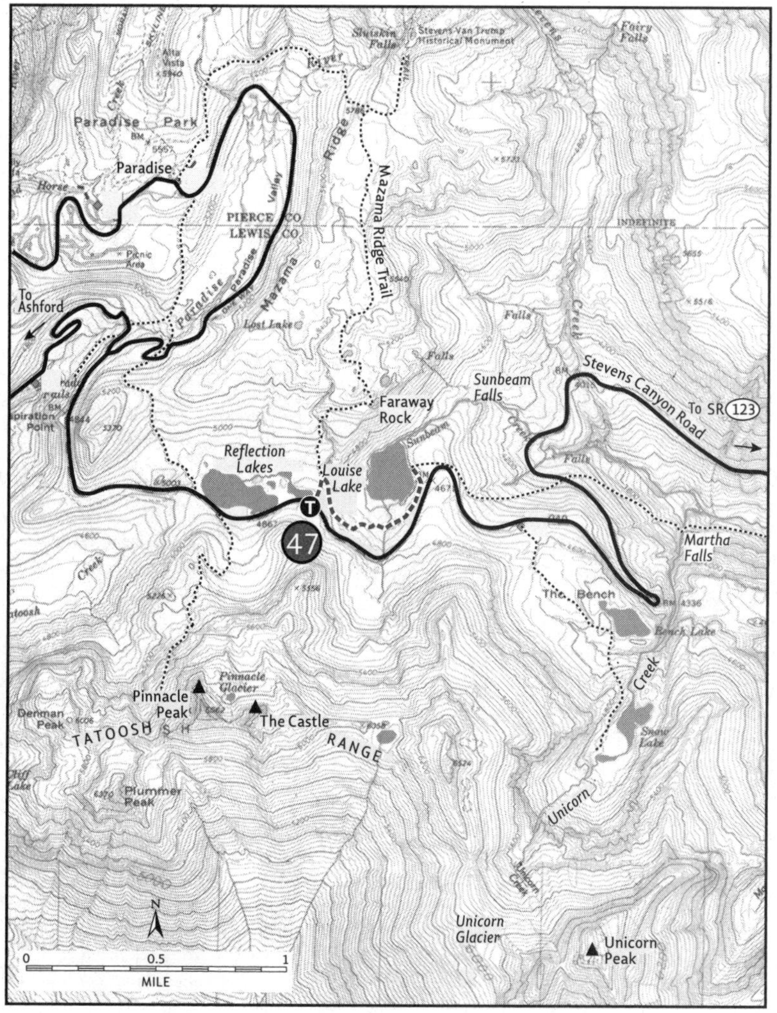

Opposite: A small tree seems ready for Louise Lake to finally thaw out during a late-spring visit.

WONDERS OF THE WONDERLAND TRAIL

Amazingly, this loop route encircling Mount Rainier has been done as a day hike—or, rather, a day run! According to the best available records, the fastest complete circuit of the 93.5-mile Wonderland Trail is 27 hours, 56 minutes, set in 1991 by a Colorado trail runner.

Most folks, though, take at least ten days (fourteen is more reasonable) to enjoy the rugged trail. Or they'll do it in stages, breaking the loop route into manageable day trips—some of which are in this guidebook—and short backpacks. Regardless, this granddaddy of Mount Rainier trails plays some role in virtually every hiking adventure in the park.

The 93.5-mile trail climbs—and loses—no less than 28,000 vertical feet as it winds up and down the many ridges that project out from the mountain like spokes on a wheel. The Wonderland runs through forests that stood before Columbus sailed and over ice fields holding snow that fell when the trees were saplings. The trail explores deep river valleys, crosses scores of rivers and streams, and skirts huge glaciers. Along the route are alpine meadows of unmatched beauty—and thundering waterfalls seldom seen up close.

The trail is dotted with seventeen backcountry camps. Many through-hikers start the trail at Longmire and do the loop clockwise. Looking at the trail from this perspective, you start with a trek from Longmire, traversing through the upper Kautz Creek valley (Hike 53), across the wide meadows and grass fields of Indian Henrys Hunting Ground (Hike 59), and over the narrow gorge of Tahoma River on a bouncy old suspension bridge. Above the gorge, the trail skirts the Tahoma Glacier, crosses the Puyallup River near its headwaters, and climbs into the scenic alpine meadows of Klapatche Park on the way to the Mowich Lake area.

After crossing the Mowich River (Hike 4), the route heads into the spectacular slopes of Spray Park (Hike 3)—a wonderland of grassy fields, heather meadows, and acres upon acres of wildflowers—only to drop via Seattle Park (Hike 12) to the Carbon River valley with its own bouncy suspension bridge and long ribbon of ice, the Carbon Glacier (Hike 8). Above the glacier, you'll find the magical waters of Mystic Lake (Hike 9) before strolling through endless fields of flowers via Grand Park (Hike 14) on the way to Berkeley Park (Hike 26) and Sunrise.

Dropping to the White River valley (Hike 21), the trail pierces ancient forests before climbing its high point (6800 feet) at Panhandle Gap (Hike 18). Keep a sharp eye out as you move through this area, as there is a large herd of resident mountain goats living around the gap, and they can usually be seen between Summerland and the gap.

The trail drops from Panhandle into the upper fields of Ohanapecosh Park (Hike 44), then down into Stevens Canyon (Hike 45). The trail turns west here, rolling upward along the southern wall of that canyon until it finally crests out near Reflection Lakes (Hike 47). The trail then drops past Narada Falls (Hike 63) and follows the river down to Longmire (Hike 60) to close this long, rambling loop.

48 Faraway Rock

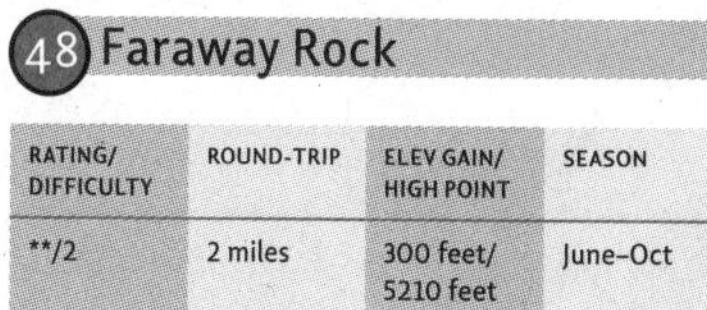

RATING/ DIFFICULTY	ROUND-TRIP	ELEV GAIN/ HIGH POINT	SEASON
**/2	2 miles	300 feet/ 5210 feet	June–Oct

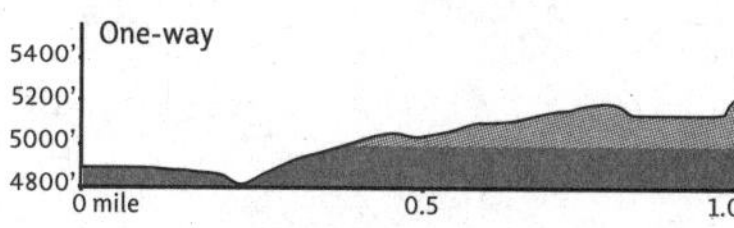

Maps: Green Trails Paradise, No. 270s; **Contact:** Longmire Wilderness Information Center, (360) 569-4453; **GPS:** N46 46.132, W121 43.442

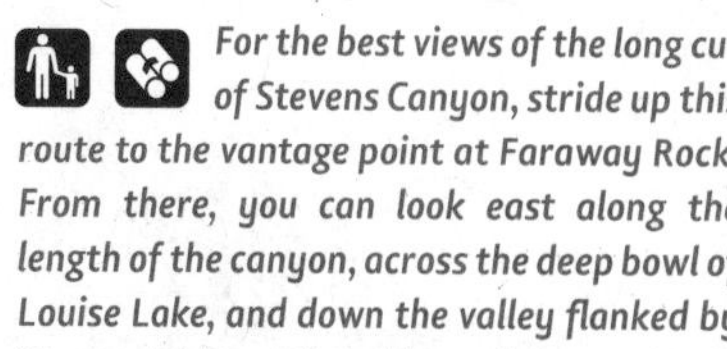

For the best views of the long cut of Stevens Canyon, stride up this route to the vantage point at Faraway Rock. From there, you can look east along the length of the canyon, across the deep bowl of Louise Lake, and down the valley flanked by Stevens Ridge and the Tatoosh Range. You'll also find wonderful views to the north.

GETTING THERE

From Enumclaw, drive east about 47 miles on State Route 410 to the junction with SR 123 at Cayuse Pass. Stay right (straight ahead) to merge onto SR 123–Cayuse Pass Highway. Drive south about 11.5 miles to the junction

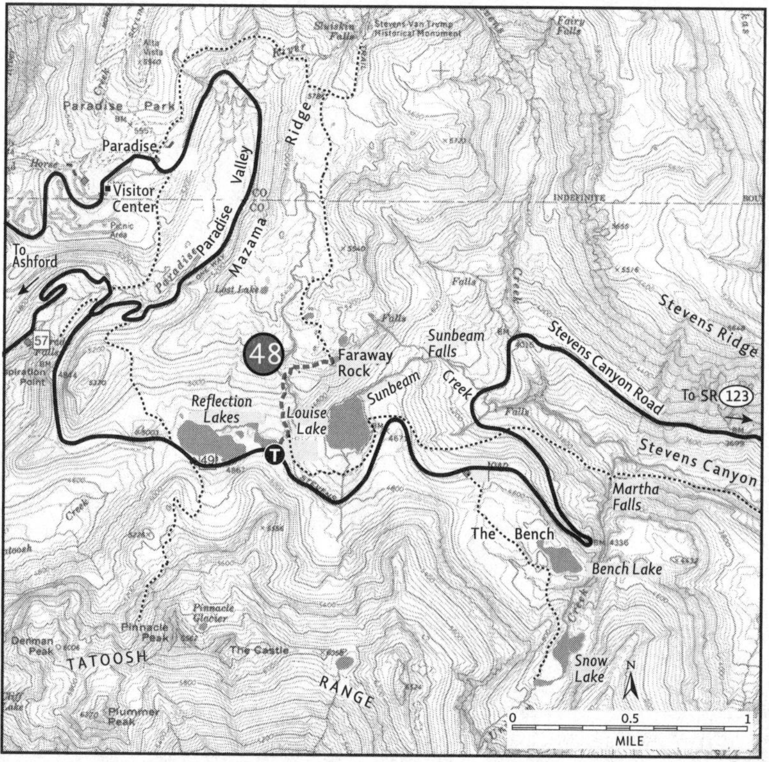

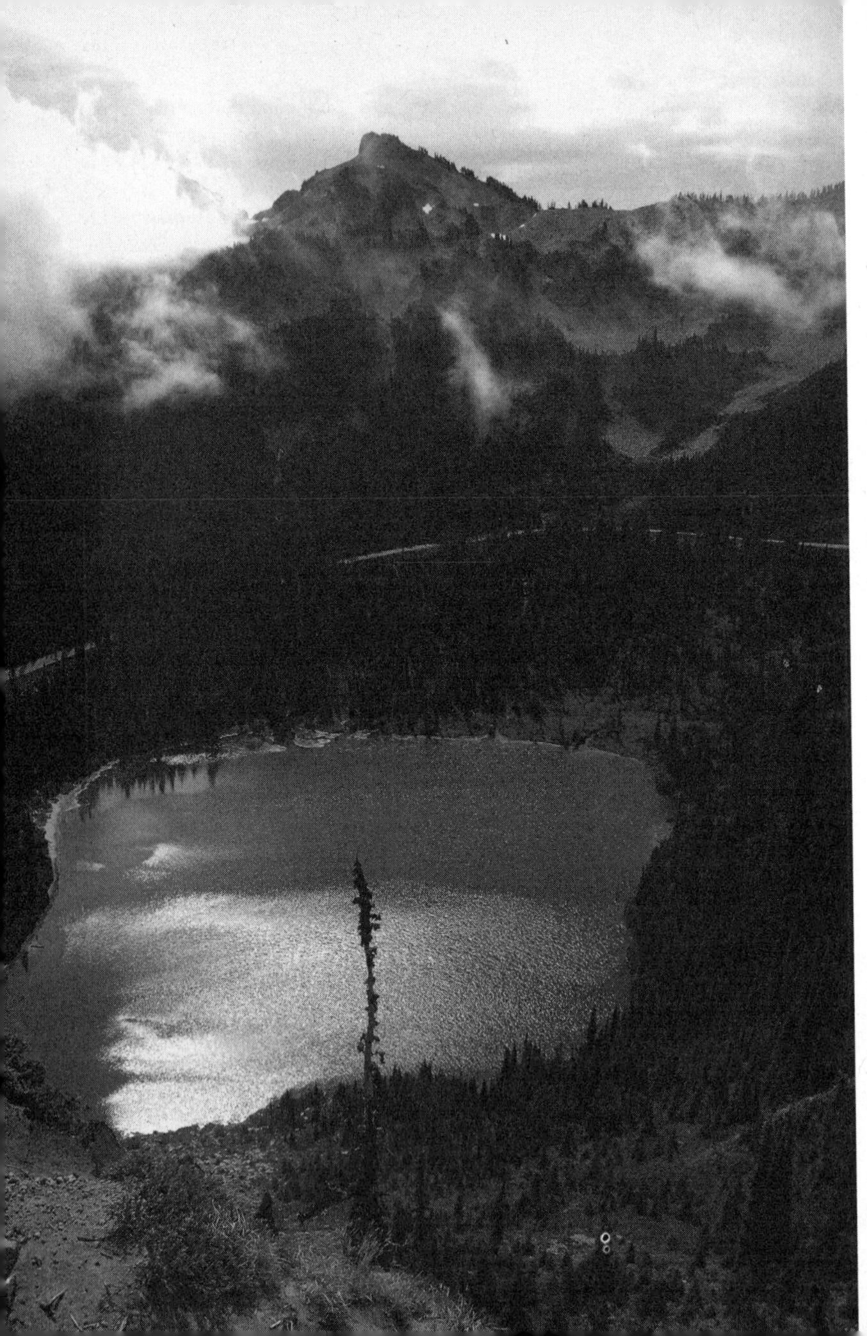

with the Stevens Canyon Road. Turn right (west) and pass through the Stevens Canyon Entrance to the park. About 17 miles from SR 123, park at the Reflections Lake parking area (stay toward the east end for easiest access).

From the south, drive US 12 about 8 miles east of Packwood to the junction with SR 123. Turn north on SR 123 and continue about 6 miles, passing Ohanapecosh Campground, to the Stevens Canyon Road. Turn left (west) and pass through the Stevens Canyon Entrance to the park and find the trailhead as described above.

From the west, via Paradise, drive SR 706 through the Nisqually Entrance and continue approximately 16 miles east to the trailhead on the north side of Stevens Canyon Road.

Note: Both SR 123 and Stevens Canyon Road have had closures due to washouts in the November 2006 flood. Call ahead for current road conditions.

ON THE TRAIL

Find the trail along the eastern edge of the Reflection Lakes basin, and start north along that path. In 0.25 mile, the trail intercepts the Mazama Ridge Trail. Turn left and start the gradual climb up the snout of Mazama Ridge. You dodge in and out of forest glades and small stands of timber before crossing a small creek at 0.7 mile.

At about 1 mile (5210 feet), the trail runs out alongside a small tarn nestled in a basin at the rim of a cliff. This high, rocky promontory is Faraway Rock, and the views here are truly far out! Enjoy the scenery here before heading back.

EXTENDING YOUR TRIP

To add miles to your hike, continue north along the Mazama Ridge Trail (Hike 67). You follow the crest of this long, meadow-capped ridge for another 3 miles to look around the end of the Paradise Valley and eventually reach the Paradise Visitor Center about 5 miles from your starting point.

49 Pinnacle Saddle

RATING/ DIFFICULTY	ROUND-TRIP	ELEV GAIN/ HIGH POINT	SEASON
*****/4	3.5 miles	1150 feet/ 6000 feet	June–Oct

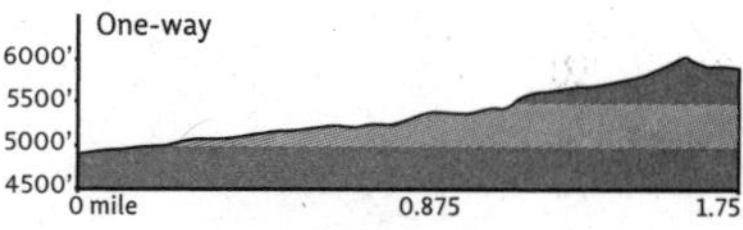

Maps: Green Trails Paradise, No. 270s; **Contact:** Longmire Wilderness Information Center, (360) 569-4453; **GPS:** N46 46.097, W121 43.885

Pinnacle Saddle resides in the Tatoosh Range, a craggy line of mountains due south of Rainier. This range sits well apart from Mount Rainier and its collection of smaller sibling summits nestled along its flank, but it offers one of the best "Mount Rainier experiences" you'll find. The climb is steep and rugged at times, but the payoff is the best views of the big mountain's south face you'll ever find.

GETTING THERE

From Enumclaw, drive east about 47 miles on State Route 410 to the junction with SR 123 at Cayuse Pass. Stay right (straight ahead) to merge onto SR 123–Cayuse Pass Highway. Drive south about 11.5 miles to the junction with the Stevens Canyon Road. Turn right (west) and pass through the Stevens Canyon Entrance to the park. About 17 miles from SR 123, park at the Reflections Lake parking area.

Opposite: Views down at Louise Lake from Faraway Rock

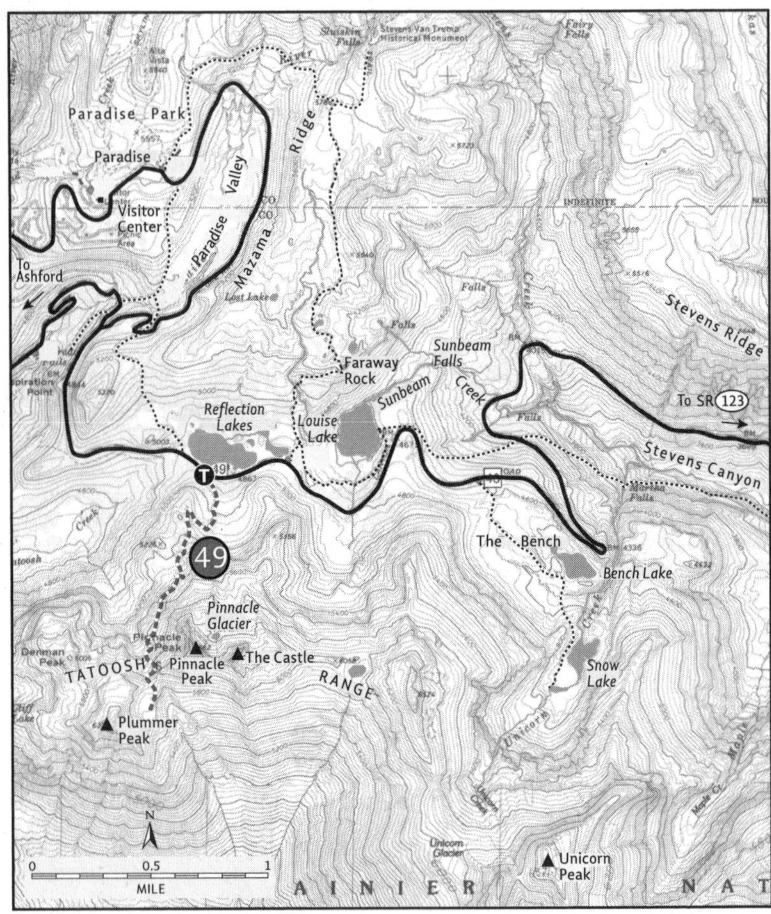

Look for the trail on the south side of the road near the western end of the parking area.

From the south, drive US 12 about 8 miles east of Packwood to the junction with SR 123. Turn north on SR 123 and continue about 6 miles, passing Ohanapecosh Campground, to the Stevens Canyon Road. Turn left (west) and pass through the Stevens Canyon Entrance to the park and find the trailhead as described above.

From the west, via Paradise, drive SR 706 through the Nisqually Entrance and continue a little less than 16 miles east to the trailhead on the south side of Stevens Canyon Road.

Note: Both SR 123 and Stevens Canyon Road have had closures due to washouts in the November 2006 flood. Although SR 123 has reopened, it's best to call ahead for current road conditions.

ON THE TRAIL

The trail climbs gently for the first 0.5 mile, sweeping through a dense alpine forest before entering a long climb up a rocky ridge. Many years, you'll encounter lingering snowfields well into July along the entire route, and at times, the snowfields are located on steep sections of hillside, making travel difficult and potentially dangerous. Use caution and exercise good common sense.

At around 0.7 mile the views start to open up, and over the next mile the views grow increasingly grand, with Mount Rainier ever present on the northern horizon. At 1.7 miles, the trail crests the ridge between Plummer Peak and Pinnacle Peak. The trail

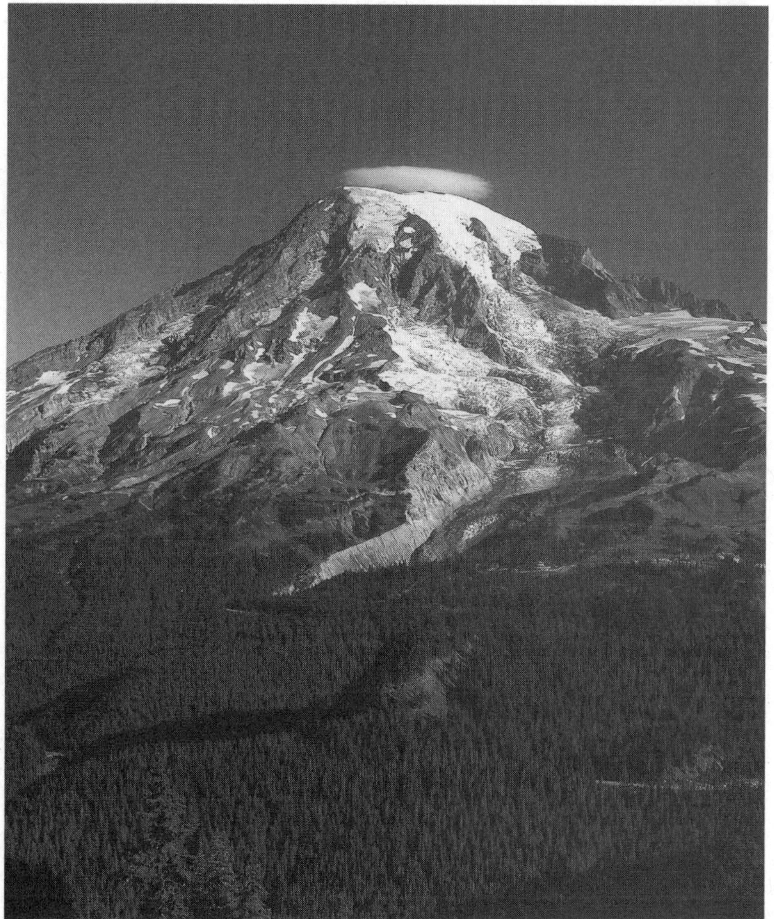

A lenticular cloud begins to form after sunrise, as seen from Pinnacle Saddle.

ends at this 6000-foot saddle, with incredible views north and south. To the north, Rainier looms large, but to the south, you can see the jagged teeth of the Goat Rocks Wilderness as well as the snowy cone of Mount Adams.

Climbers tracks lead onto the lower sections of the two flanking peaks, but both of these mountains require true rock climbing skills, so casual hikers must be content with the fabulous views from the saddle before returning the way they came.

Opposite: Eastward view from the summit of Gobblers Knob at Mount Rainier

longmire

James Longmire journeyed from his farm near Yelm to the base of Mount Rainier in 1861, finding himself in the broad meadows that today bear his name. Longmire summitted Mount Rainier in 1883 with P. B. Van Trump—it was Van Trump's second ascent, having achieved a first ascent with Hazard Stevens in 1870. Longmire had fallen in love with the mountain and its surroundings and, by 1890, had secured rights to 20 acres of what is today known as the Longmire Meadows. He quickly built a primitive road into the area and erected a small hotel and spa, which he advertised as the Longmire Medical Springs. The spa component of the resort is long gone, as is the original hotel. Today, though, the Park Service still operates a hotel at Longmire, and tourists still flock to the region to take advantage of the wonderful natural beauty of the area.

50 Mount Beljica

RATING/ DIFFICULTY	ROUND-TRIP	ELEV GAIN/ HIGH POINT	SEASON
***/3	4 miles	1100 feet/ 5478 feet	June–Oct

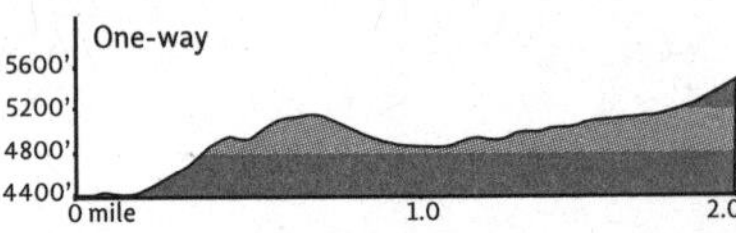

Maps: Green Trails Mount Rainier West, No. 269; **Contact:** Cowlitz Valley Ranger District,

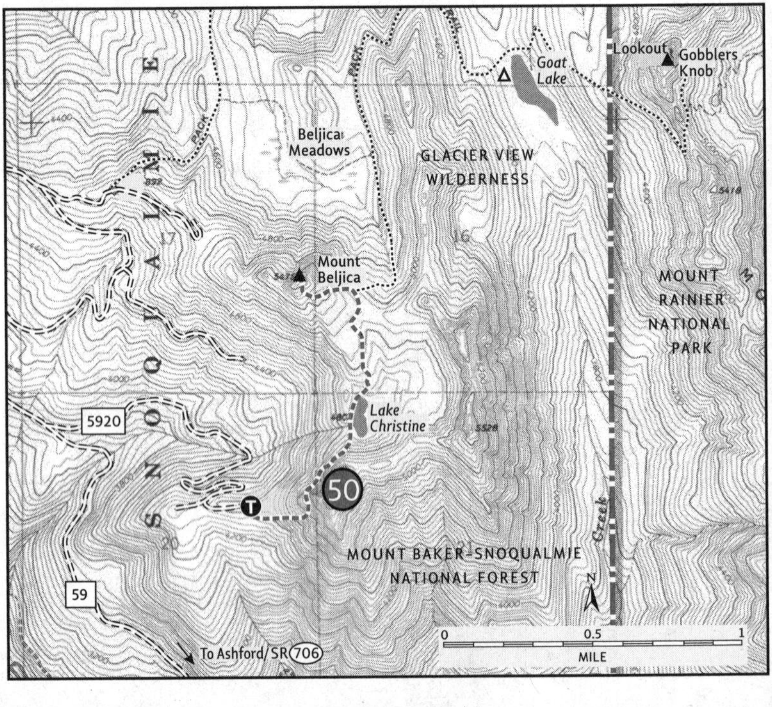

Mount Beljica seen from the Beljica Meadows area

(360) 494-5515; **GPS:** N46 46.405, W121 56.674

Too many people think you have to be in the national park to enjoy Mount Rainier. This quaint trail dispels that myth quite effectively. It ambles easily through forest and meadow, passing pretty woodland lakes and climbing to the high vantage point once utilized by professional fire watchers. Now, lest you ask, the unusual name is truly unique: the name is attributed to two families who climbed to the summit in 1897. The proud fathers of the Mesler and LaWall families pulled the first initial of each of their combined children and created the name: Burgon, Elizabeth, Lucy, Jessie, Isabel, Clara, and Alex. As the trail lies outside the national park, it is dog friendly.

GETTING THERE

From Tacoma, drive east on State Route 7 to Elbe, then veer left onto SR 706 to Ashford. Continue 3.8 miles east of Ashford and turn left (north) onto Forest Road 59 (Copper

Creek Road). Continue 3.4 miles up this road to a junction. Stay left, and in another 1.5 miles, turn right onto FR 5920. Continue 2.4 miles on this spur road to the Lake Christine trailhead (4400 feet).

ON THE TRAIL

The trail runs steeply up away from the trailhead, slicing upward on rough tread for about 100 yards, before moderating onto a boot-beaten trail along a high ridge. The path drops you at the shores of scenic Lake Christine in 1 mile. Pause here to enjoy the forest-lined lake and the views beyond. With luck, you might see bald eagles or ospreys fishing in this pool.

The trail curves around the west shore of the lake and then heads north to a trail junction. Go left here to scramble about 0.5 mile up a rough trail to the summit of Beljica (5478 feet). This old lookout site offers incredible views of Mount Rainier and the many peaks of the Longmire region.

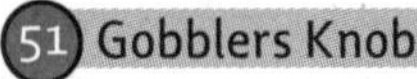

51 Gobblers Knob

RATING/ DIFFICULTY	ROUND-TRIP	ELEV GAIN/ HIGH POINT	SEASON
***/4	10 miles	1100 feet/ 5485 feet	July–Oct

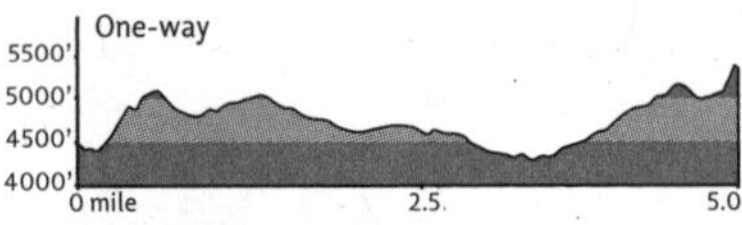

Maps: Green Trails Mount Rainier West, No. 269; **Contact:** Cowlitz Valley Ranger District, (360) 494-5515; **GPS:** N46 46.405, W121 56.674

Once upon a time, the easiest access to Gobblers Knob was via the Westside Road in Mount Rainier National Park. Unfortunately, that road washed out so frequently that it was permanently closed to public traffic a few years ago, though the Park Service did provide shuttle

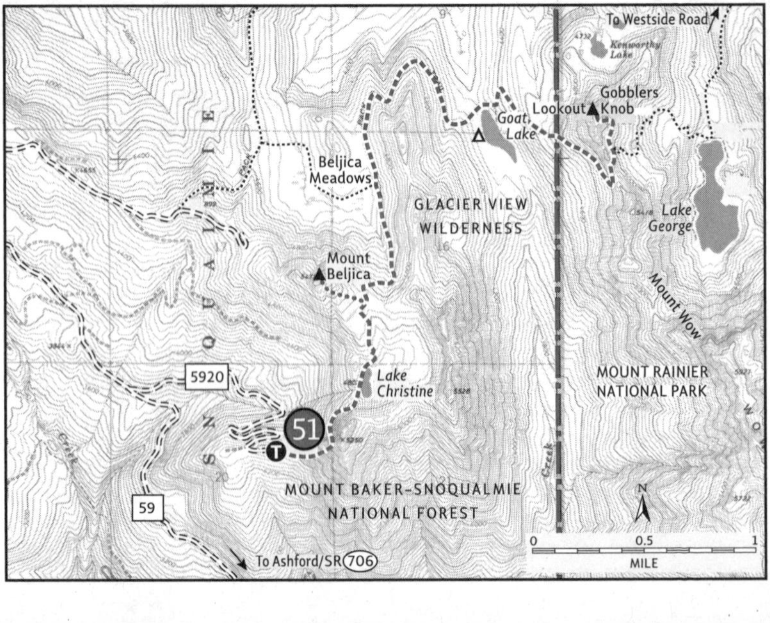

bus service for a time. Following the massive damage done by the winter 2006 floods, though, the road likely will remain closed to all vehicle traffic in the future. So we come into the old lookout side atop Gobblers Knob from the west.

GETTING THERE

From Tacoma, drive east on State Route 7 to Elbe, then veer left onto SR 706 to Ashford. Continue 3.8 miles east of Ashford and turn left (north) onto Forest Road 59 (Copper Creek Road). Continue 3.4 miles up this road to a junction. Stay left and in another 1.5 miles, turn right onto FR 5920. Continue 2.4 miles on this spur road to the Lake Christine trailhead (4400 feet).

ON THE TRAIL

Head up the steep trail to Lake Christine. The trail rolls through old forest and occasional meadows before reaching the junction with the trail to Mount Beljica at 1.5 miles (Hike 50). At this junction, stay right to follow the ridge north of Beljica. The trail hugs the west side of the ridge, staying mostly flat as it ambles north through open forests and meadows. At a little over 2 miles, reach a junction with a trail to the left into Beljica Meadows; continue straight ahead to reach Goat Lake at 4 miles from the trailhead.

Nice campsites are available at Goat Lake, which sits just outside the national park boundary. Our route curves around the north shore of Goat Lake and, in about 0.75 mile, reaches another junction, with a faint spur trail on the left. Take this spur and climb the 0.25 mile to the summit of Gobblers Knob (5485 feet). Outstanding views are found atop this remote Rainier peak. Look south along the length of Mount Wow and northeast to Mount Rainier itself.

Enjoy your time at the top before returning the way you came.

Mount Rainier seen from the decking around the Gobblers Knob lookout

Early fall snow on the summit of Glacier View

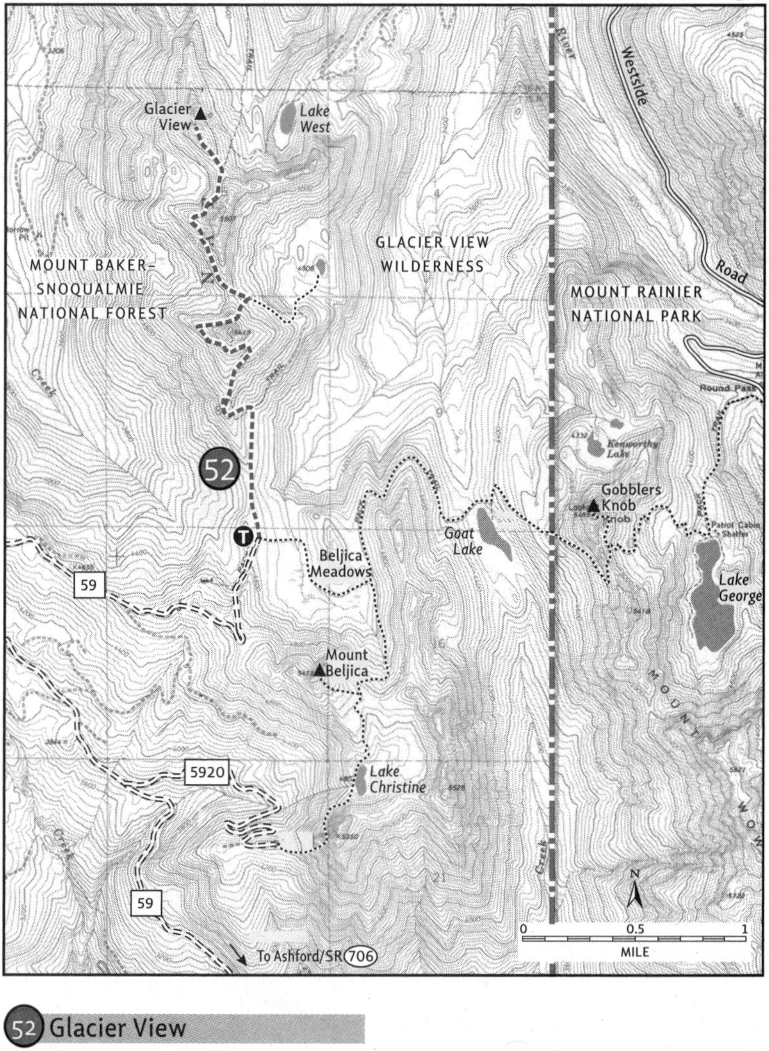

52 Glacier View

RATING/ DIFFICULTY	ROUND-TRIP	ELEV GAIN/ HIGH POINT	SEASON
***/3	4 miles	900 feet/ 5450 feet	July–Oct

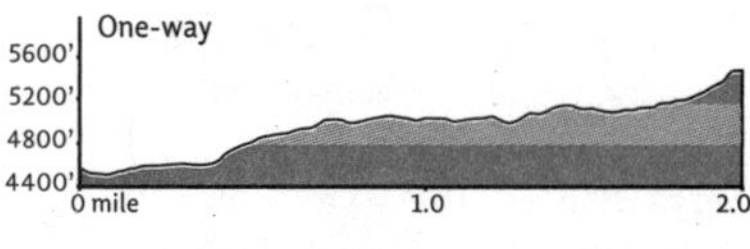

Views toward the Gobblers Knob lookout and the distant Tatoosh Range seen from the summit of Glacier View

Maps: Green Trails Mount Rainier West, No. 269; **Contact:** Cowlitz Valley Ranger District, (360) 494-5515; **GPS:** N46 46.405, W121 56.674

This trail stays just outside Mount Rainier National Park, but the highlights of the trek are the outstanding views east to the glaciers that cover the west flank of the big volcano. The trail is relatively flat and open, though at times the tread is rough and brushy—maintenance of the trail is a once-in-a-while occurrence. Fortunately, the path is easy to follow and offers a wonderfully unique view of Mount Rainier. Few people get to see the west face of the mountain from this close. Since the trail is completely outside the park, dogs are welcome on it.

GETTING THERE

From Tacoma, drive east on State Route 7 to Elbe, then veer left onto SR 706 to Ashford. Continue 3.8 miles east of Ashford and turn left (north) onto Forest Road 59 (Copper Creek Road). Continue 9 miles up this road to the trailhead on the right (elevation 4750 feet).

ON THE TRAIL

From the trailhead, head east on a short way trail to intercept the main Glacier View Trail in just 0.1 mile, just after entering the Glacier View Wilderness Area. Veer left (north) onto the Glacier View Trail and follow it along a low ridgeline, skirting along the boundary of the wilderness area.

The trail meanders north with gradual change in elevation over the next 1.6 miles. The terrain around the trail includes cool stands of forest and open, sun-drenched hillside meadows. Great huckleberry brambles can be found along the first mile of trail, bringing out berry pickers of both the two-legged variety (humans and birds) and those going on four legs (bears and small mammals).

At about 1 mile, the trail swings west around a knoll before curving back to the east to climb through a low gap for brief views of Mount Rainier. Continue bearing generally north and, at about 1.6 miles, reach a junction with the Lake Helen Trail to the right; stay straight. A rough trail leads left another 0.3 mile to a ridge top. Climb another hundred feet to the 5,450-foot summit of Glacier View—yet another former lookout site. The views stretch out in all directions, but for your own peace of mind, you'll want to stick with the north-, east-, and south-facing views. Look to the west, and the splendor of this hike is lost as you look out over endless acres of clear-cut scars.

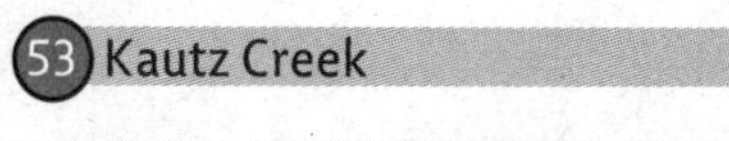

53 Kautz Creek

RATING/ DIFFICULTY	ROUND-TRIP	ELEV GAIN/ HIGH POINT	SEASON
***/5	12 miles	3100 feet/ 5600 feet	July–Oct

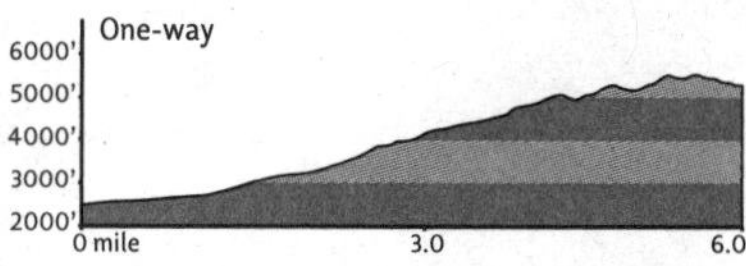

Maps: Green Trails Mount Rainier West, No. 269 and Green Trails Randle, No. 301; **Contact:** Longmire Wilderness Information Center, (360) 569-4453; **GPS:** N46 44.181, W121 51.333

  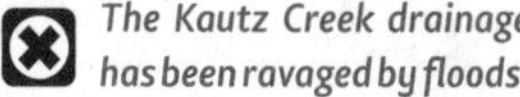

The Kautz Creek drainage has been ravaged by floods, decimated by fires, and rearranged by mud slides. This area offers a great lesson in the dynamic nature of a Cascades volcano. The biggest threat facing this trail is the fact that the Kautz Creek valley has been flushed by floods repeatedly over the years, with the most recent scouring being the winter 2006 flood that not only rearranged the trail but took out a section of the road. Repairs were expected but weren't begun at the time of this writing, so before heading out for this hike, be sure to contact the ranger to ensure the route has been rebuilt and reopened.

GETTING THERE

From Tacoma, drive east on State Route 7 to Elbe, then veer left onto SR 706 to enter the park at the Nisqually Entrance near Ashford. Continue east toward Longmire. Park at the Kautz Creek parking area on the south side the road, just after crossing a bridge and culvert.

ON THE TRAIL

The trail leaves from the north side of the road and weaves up the Kautz Creek valley, cutting through a forest killed by the Kautz Mudflow in 1947. The trail crosses to the west side of the creek at 1 mile (be sure to check with the ranger to make sure the bridge has been rebuilt), then climbs into virgin forests on the flank of the ridge between Tumtum Peak and Mount Ararat.

The route climbs steadily from this point on, approaching the summit ridge of Mount Ararat. At about 4 miles out, the trail crosses a section of hillside meadows that provide great views northeast to Mount Rainier and south to Satulick Mountain.

The trail climbs past the view-laden meadows to start a long traverse across the upper flank of Mount Ararat. Once on the northern flank of the mountain, the trail descends for about 1 mile to a junction with the Wonderland Trail in Indian Henrys Hunting Ground, 6 miles from the trailhead. Enjoy a snack at the ranger cabin's picnic table, then turn around to return the way you came.

EXTENDING YOUR TRIP

If you have a vehicle shuttle, you can follow the Wonderland Trail 6.3 miles back to Longmire via Rampart Ridge (Hike 57).

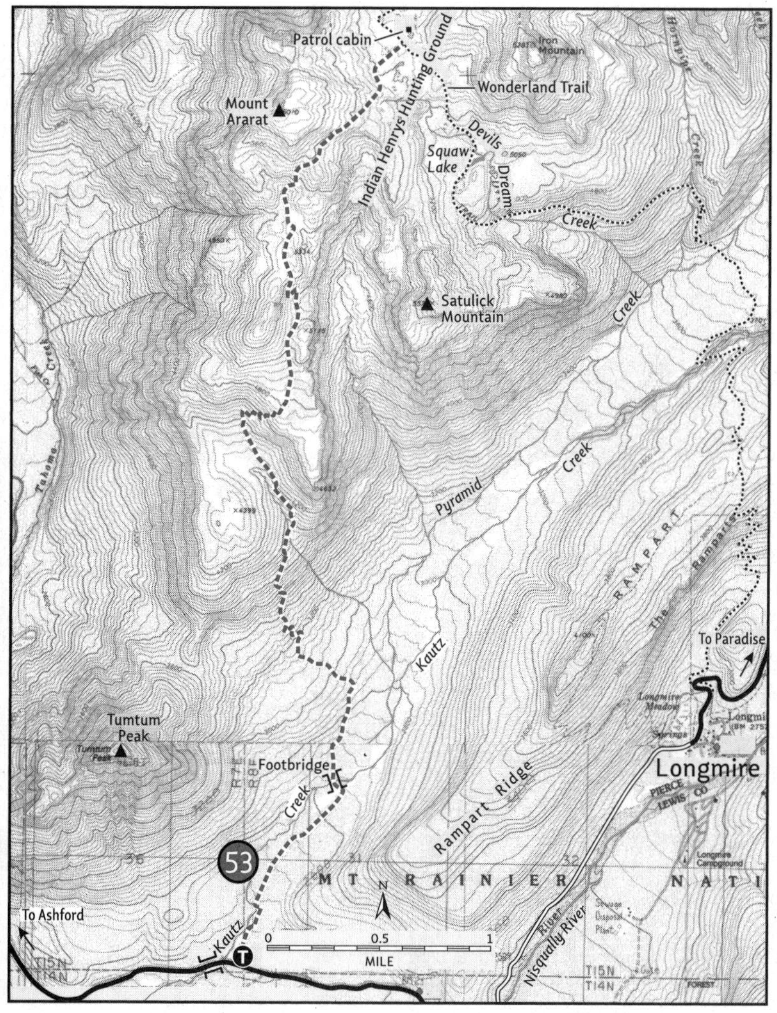

Opposite: Footlog crossing across Kautz Creek—make sure the crossing is in place and safe before heading out in late spring!

54 Twin Firs Loop

RATING/ DIFFICULTY	LOOP	ELEV GAIN/ HIGH POINT	SEASON
**/1	0.5 mile	50 feet/ 2550 feet	May–Oct

The old and the young: a small grand fir tree is dwarfed by its ancient ancestor growing directly behind it.

Maps: Green Trails Mount Rainier West, No. 269 and Green Trails Randle, No. 301; **Contact:** Longmire Wilderness Information Center, (360) 569-4453; **GPS:** N46 44.062, W121 50.327

Massive old trees, both standing and dead, are the key features of this interpretive loop hike. The ancient forest stands as a living cathedral, while the fallen old trees have become givers of new life. The large old logs on the ground that serve as nurseries to new trees are known as nurse logs. The trail weaves through this lush ecosystem, offering a cool walk on a hot summer day, with plenty of opportunities not only to exercise the kids but to give them a few lessons in forest ecosystems along the way.

GETTING THERE

From Tacoma, drive east on State Route 7 to Elbe, then veer left onto SR 706 to enter the park at the Nisqually Entrance near Ashford. Continue east toward Longmire. Just past the Kautz Creek basin, look for a small parking area and interpretive sign on the left (north) side of the road.

ON THE TRAIL

The trail cuts behind a pair of massive firs (hence the name Twin Firs) to start the loop clockwise. The path crosses a couple small freshets as it winds through the ancient grove.

Note the old nurse logs that sprout not only new young trees but a variety of ferns and wildflowers too. These massive logs offer a near-endless supply of nutrients to the new growth, providing a secure future for the next generation of forest.

The trail curls for 0.5 mile through the woods before ending where it started.

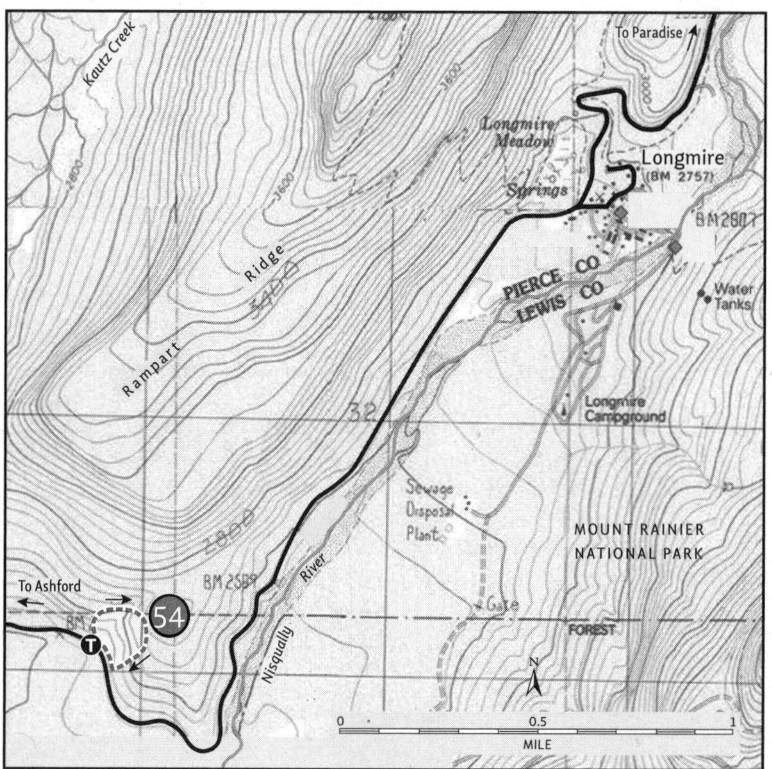

55 Eagle Peak

RATING/ DIFFICULTY	ROUND-TRIP	ELEV GAIN/ HIGH POINT	SEASON
***/4	7 miles	2950 feet/ 5650 feet	May–Oct

One-way
6000'
5000'
4000'
3000'
2000'
0 mile
1.75
3.5

Maps: Green Trails Mount Rainier West, No. 269 and Green Trails Randle, No. 301; **Contact:** Longmire Wilderness Information Center, (360) 569-4453; **GPS:** N46 44.909, W121 48.468

This trail is threatened by lack of use as well as perpetual flooding of the Nisqually River. The flooding doesn't affect the trail itself, but it does potentially block access to the trail. In fact, the access road was lost in the 2006 floods, so before heading out, be sure to check with the

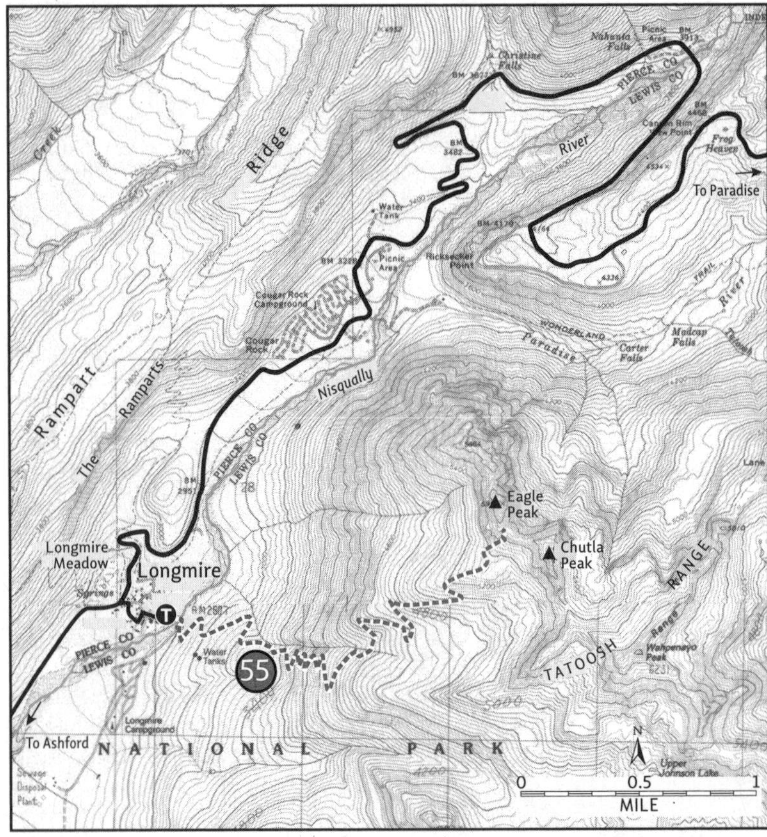

ranger to make sure this route is accessible. If it is, you'll find a long climb through forests leading to stellar views.

GETTING THERE

From Tacoma, drive east on State Route 7 to Elbe, then veer left onto SR 706 to enter the park at the Nisqually Entrance near Ashford. Continue east to Longmire and pull into the parking area. Drive past the ranger station to the bridge over the Nisqually River, found behind the staff housing. Check with the ranger to make sure this bridge is passable. If the road to the bridge is closed, park in the lot behind the Longmire hotel and walk to the bridge to find the trail on the far side.

ON THE TRAIL

Start up the trail as it angles away from the access road. The trail climbs steadily but moderately through pristine forests for the first 2 miles. At this point, the trail crosses a small stream and starts up the flank of Chutla Peak. The trail stays under a forest canopy, but once you're over the creek the forest's understory begins to open up, providing light as well as more views between the trees.

At 3.5 miles, the trail rolls into a hillside meadow just below the saddle separating Eagle and Chutla peaks. At the saddle, look northeast around the shoulder of Eagle to find impressive views of Mount Rainier. The maintained trail ends here, and while a climbers track continues upward, I recommend that anyone not equipped with climbing gear (and the associated skills) turn back here.

The last few rock steps to gain the ridge below Eagle Peak and your reward of vast Mount Rainier views!

MOUNT RAINIER: THE WEATHER-MAKER

Standing nearly 8000 feet above its neighbors, Mount Rainier alters the local atmospheric conditions enough to create its own weather patterns.

High-altitude winds that stream a mile or more above the rest of the Cascades slam into the jutting summit of Rainier. The mountain's great prominence captures high-altitude systems and contributes to the formation of local cumulus clouds, creating rain- and/or thunderstorms at any time. Because the peak can also draw down cold air from high in the atmosphere, snow is also a possibility at any time—while researching these routes, I experienced snowfall in every month of the year.

Like the rest of Western Washington, Mount Rainier gets most of its weather directly from the Pacific, just 100 miles west. The wet marine air keeps the park cool and well watered. The local climate in the park generally presents cool days, with summer highs in the 60s and 70s, though temperatures may infrequently climb into the 80s and 90s during the sunniest months (July and August). Rain can fall on any day, with spring being the wettest season.

Winter comes early most years, with snow starting to accumulate at higher elevations (above 5500 feet) by early October and at lower parts of the park in November. Mount Rainier competes with its northerly neighbor, Mount Baker, for the title of heaviest annual snowfall. For many years, Rainier was the champion, with more than 1122 inches (93.5 feet) of snowfall recorded during the 1971–72 season. That title was lost to Mount Baker in 1998–99 when that peak recorded 1140 inches! Rainier received a "mere" 1035 inches that year.

All that snow means great fun for skiers, snowshoers, and other winter recreationists. It also affects hikers during the summer months. The generally cool temperatures mean snowpacks can linger well into the summer, with some areas never fully melting out. Most years, snow will remain on trails in the 5000- to 7000-foot elevation range well into mid-July, and fresh snow will start falling in those same areas by late September.

In short, Mount Rainier is a weather-making wonderland. Hikers should be prepared for an array of weather, even when out on just a short day hike. Weather conditions change rapidly on Rainier. It's in its own world.

56 Trail of the Shadows

RATING/ DIFFICULTY	ROUND-TRIP	ELEV GAIN/ HIGH POINT	SEASON
**/1	1 mile	20 feet/ 2770 feet	May–Oct

Maps: Green Trails Mount Rainier West, No. 269; **Contact:** Longmire Wilderness Information Center, (360) 569-4453; **GPS:** N46 44.980, W121 48.639

This self-guided interpretive trail presents grand learning experiences for youngsters and adults alike. The trail loops through the old forests and wetlands that help make Longmire such a rich natural area. It also provides great lessons in human history in the park, passing the very mineral springs that were first promoted by James Longmire in his original hotels and spa. The route even

explores an old logging cabin erected in 1888 by James Longmire's son.

GETTING THERE

From Tacoma, drive east on State Route 7 to Elbe, then veer left onto SR 706 to enter the park at the Nisqually Entrance near Ashford. Continue east to Longmire. Park in the large lot behind the hotel, and find the trailhead on the north side of the road.

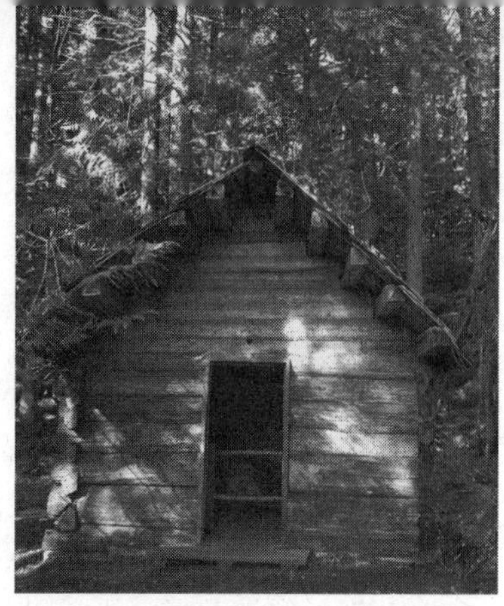

The historic Longmire cabin along the Trail of Shadows loop

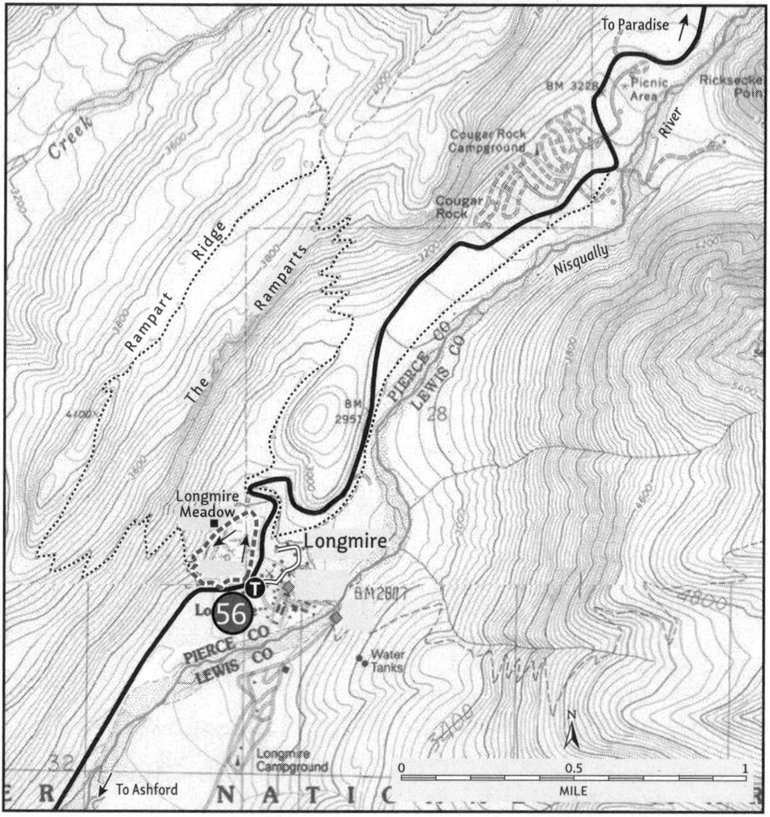

The ponds and streams that fill the meadows along the Trail of Shadows

ON THE TRAIL

The trail begins directly across the road from the Longmire hotel. Before starting the hike, pick up a copy of the trail-guide booklet from the box at the trailhead. This booklet provides details about the numbered features scattered around the loop. To use the booklet effectively, you'll want to hike the loop in a counterclockwise direction.

The trail loops around a marshy bog created by the mineral springs that burble out of the meadow. The trail brings you close to a couple of the springs. When the trail nears the stream alongside the meadow, you'll find a few beaver dams and—if visiting in the early morning or evening hours—you might even see one of those dam animals.

Halfway through the loop, the trail passes in front of a tiny log cabin, built in 1888 by Elcaine Longmire, James's son. The trail passes a junction with the Rampart Ridge Trail on the right just before closing the mile-long loop.

57 Rampart Ridge Loop

RATING/ DIFFICULTY	LOOP	ELEV GAIN/ HIGH POINT	SEASON
***/3	4.5 miles	1300 feet/ 4080 feet	June–Oct

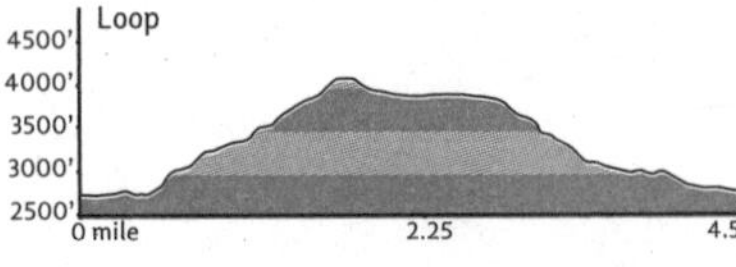

Maps: Green Trails Mount Rainier West, No. 269; **Contact:** Longmire Wilderness Information Center, (360) 569-4453; **GPS:** N46 44.980, W121 48.639

This is the perfect early-season hiking adventure. The loop route keeps you exploring new trail from start to finish, and there's a lot to explore here. The trail climbs through lush old forests, skirts along the view-rich rims of high cliffs, and weaves through a rich wetland environment along the river-side meadows.

GETTING THERE

From Tacoma, drive east on State Route 7 to Elbe, then veer left onto SR 706 to enter the park at the Nisqually Entrance near Ashford. Continue east to Longmire. Park in the large lot behind the hotel and find the trailhead at the northeast end of the building complex, next to the road on the south side.

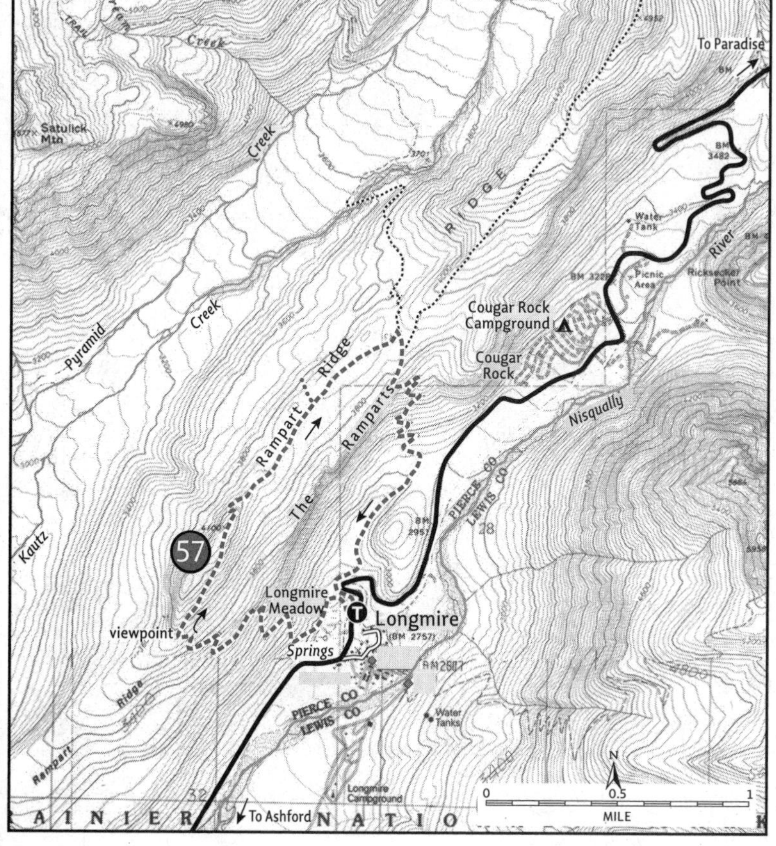

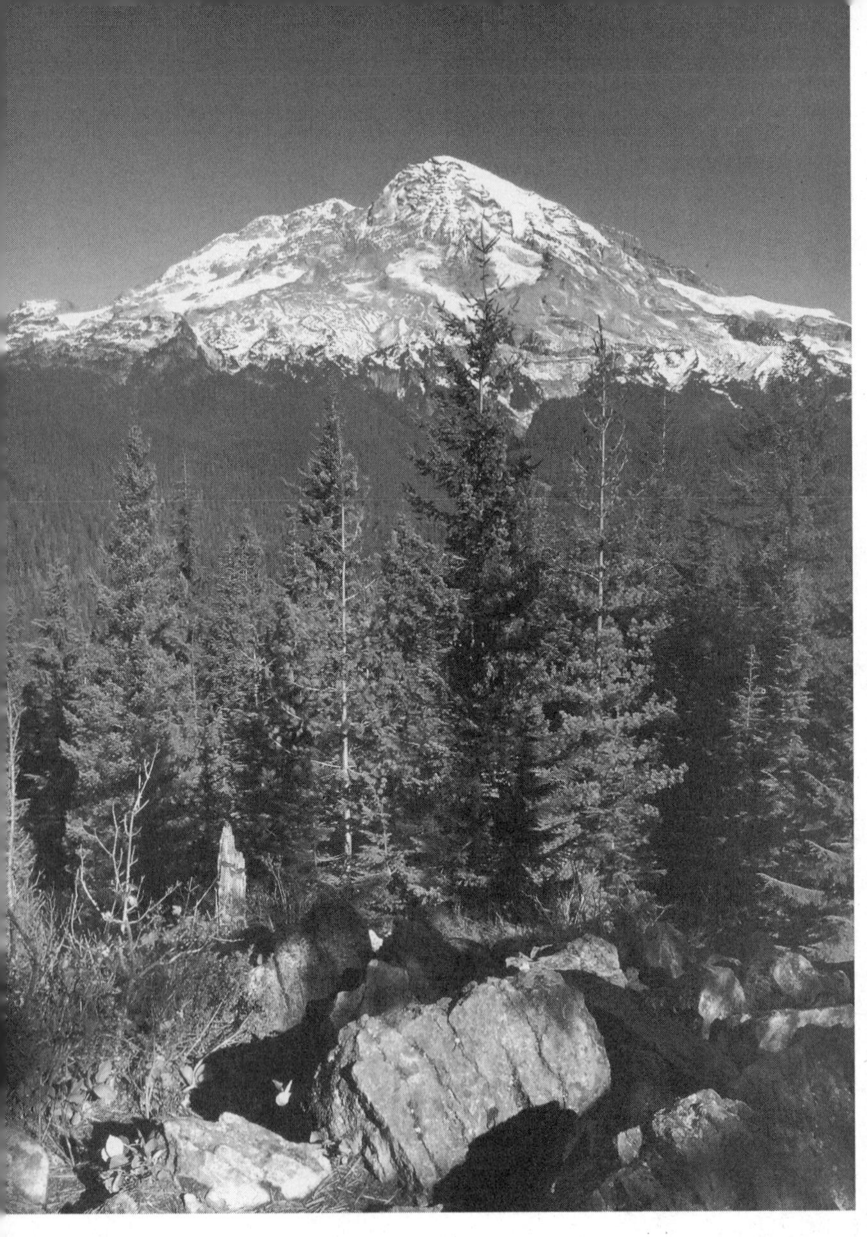

Mount Rainier views from the northeast end of Rampart Ridge before dropping down to join the Wonderland Trail

ON THE TRAIL

Start your hike on the Trail of the Shadows Nature Trail (Hike 56) on the north side of the road. From the start of the nature trail loop, go left for about 250 yards to cross the spring-fed creek, then turn left onto the Rampart Ridge Trail. This trail climbs gently for the first 0.5 mile, then steepens as it weaves through a series of switchbacks. The trail stays under dense forest canopy for the first 2 miles before reaching a small viewpoint at 3700 feet. From here you can look west across the valley to the cone-shaped Tumtum Peak.

Moving on another 0.25 mile leads to grander views as the trail skirts along the rim of the Ramparts' tall cliff band. Look down to Longmire and its historic buildings and broad meadows, with Eagle Peak beyond. For the next 0.75 mile, the trail runs along the ridge crest, descending gradually to a junction with the Wonderland Trail. About halfway down that section, about 2.6 miles from the start, turn off the trail onto a short spur on the left to find a good view of Mount Rainier.

At the junction with the Wonderland, turn right and descend 1000 feet in 1.5 miles to return to Longmire.

Crossing the vast rock-land bed of Kautz Creek heading toward Pyramid Creek Camp

58 Pyramid Creek Camp

RATING/ DIFFICULTY	ROUND-TRIP	ELEV GAIN/ HIGH POINT	SEASON
**/3	6.6 miles	1060 feet/ 3860 feet	June–Oct

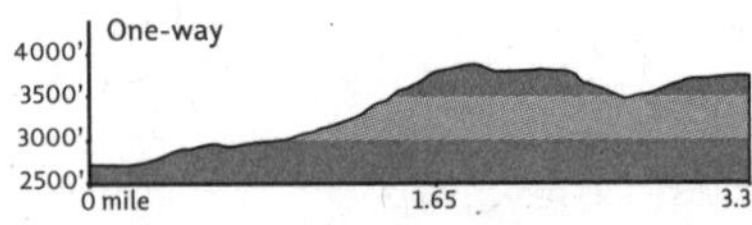

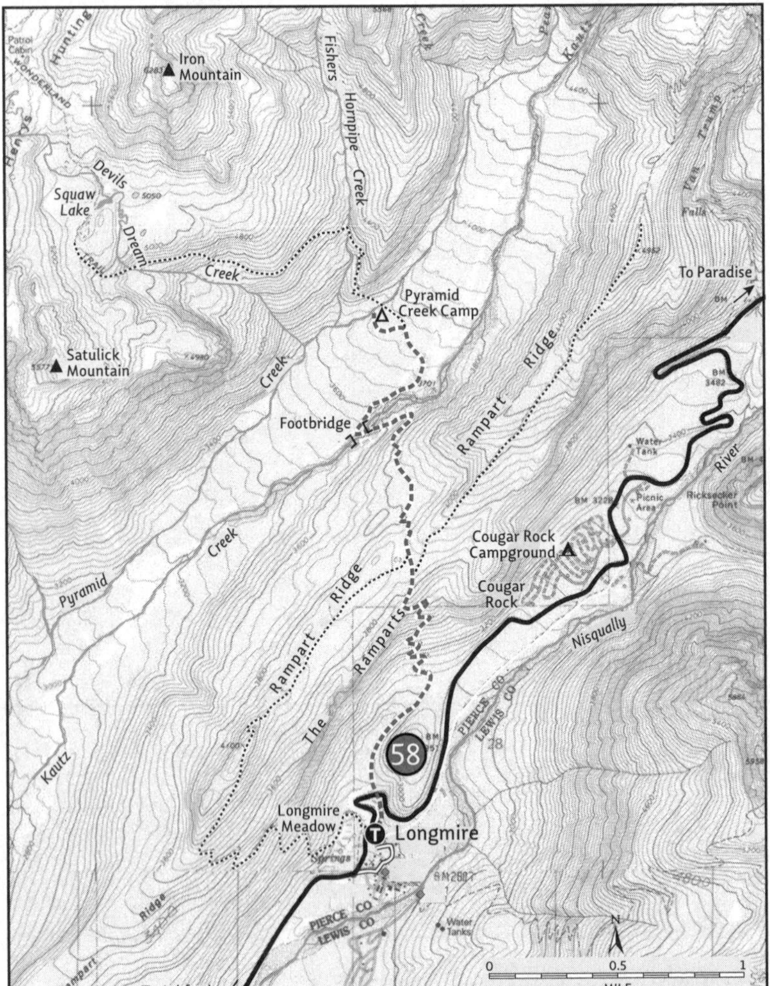

Maps: Green Trails Mount Rainier West, No. 269; **Contact:** Longmire Wilderness Information Center, (360) 569-4453; **GPS:** N46 44.980, W121 48.639

The Wonderland Trail wraps around Mount Rainier, delving into every ecological zone on the mountain. This section carries you through several of those zones, including low-elevation old-growth forests, rich riparian zones, and higher-altitude fir and hemlock forests. You'll also explore an old forest fire site and check out one of the park's established backcountry camps. It's a wonderful route for early-summer exploration. Note: Check with the ranger before heading out to make sure the footbridge across Kautz Creek is intact, especially if you are doing an early-season hike.

GETTING THERE

From Tacoma, drive east on State Route 7 to Elbe, then veer left onto SR 706 to enter the park at the Nisqually Entrance near Ashford. Continue east to Longmire. Park in the large lot behind the hotel, and find the trailhead at the northeast end of the building complex, next to the road on the south side.

ON THE TRAIL

Head northeast from the ranger station–museum to find the Wonderland Trail. Hike about 0.25 mile on it along the near road, and then cross the road to the north side. For 1.5 miles, you climb gradually through ancient forests to a low saddle on Rampart Ridge (3860 feet). The trail rolls over the ridge and descends on a traverse into the Kautz Creek valley. Pass the side trail to Van Trump Park and shortly afterwards reach a three-way trail intersection. Continue straight ahead. Along the way, you'll run through an old skeletal forest—the remnants of a decades-old forest fire.

Cross Kautz Creek at 2.5 miles (be sure to check with the ranger to make sure the bridge here is intact, especially early in the season). The first Wonderland Camp, Pyramid Creek Camp, is reached at 3.3 miles alongside Pyramid Creek. After enjoying the riparian area, turn around to return the way you came.

59 Indian Henrys Hunting Ground

RATING/ DIFFICULTY	ROUND-TRIP	ELEV GAIN/ HIGH POINT	SEASON
*****/5	12.6 miles	2500 feet/ 5300 feet	July–Oct

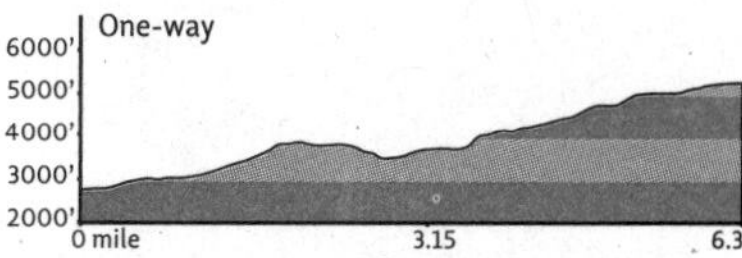

Maps: Green Trails Mount Rainier West, No. 269; **Contact:** Longmire Wilderness Information Center, (360) 569-4453; **GPS:** N46 44.980, W121 48.639

Indian Henrys Hunting Ground is one of those place names given by someone with no creativity. That is, this area was actually the favorite hunting ground of Indian Henry, an early mountain guide. The fact that it was a popular hunting area, however, suggests that hikers might enjoy it as a wildlife viewing area today. The meadows surrounding the old historic cabin in the Hunting Ground are wonderfully diverse in both flora and fauna. The meadows also provide glorious views of Mount Rainier and the lesser summits of Copper Mountain, Pyramid Peak, and Iron Mountain. Note: Check with the ranger before heading out to make sure the footbridge across Kautz Creek is intact, especially if you are doing an early-season hike.

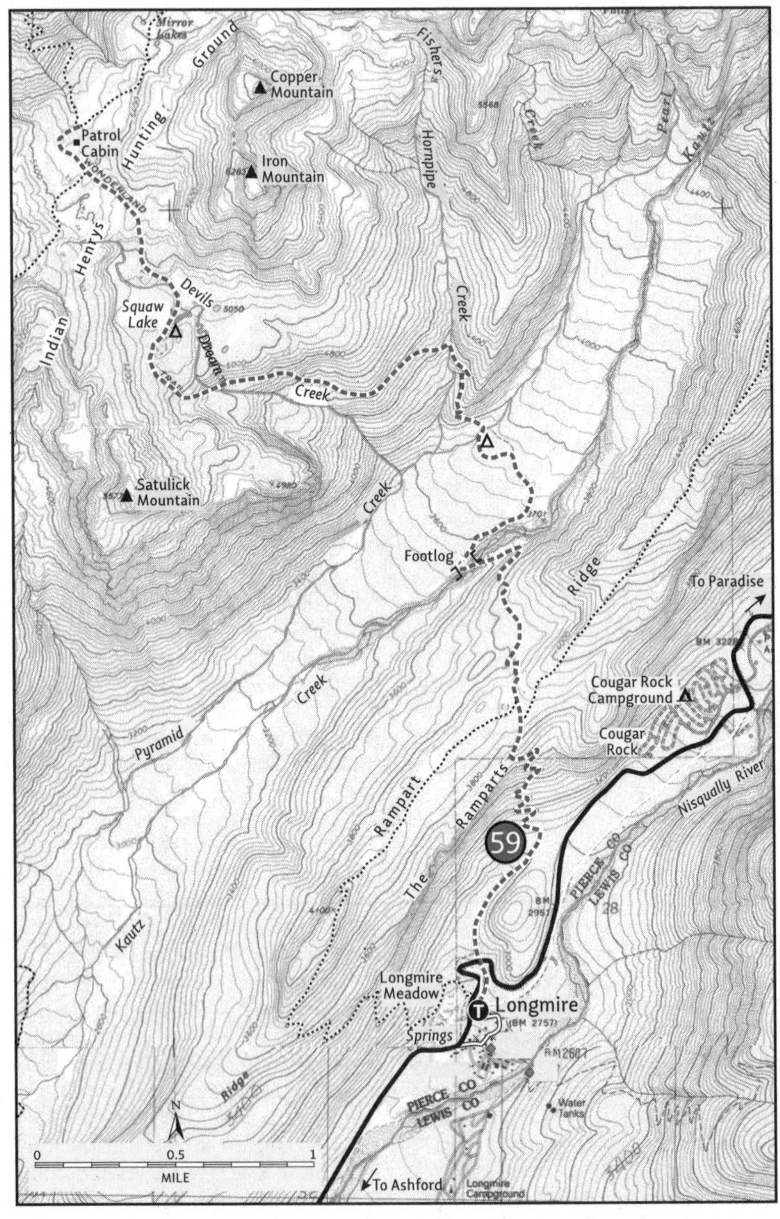
Mirror Lakes
Copper Mountain
Fishers
Hornpipe
Creek
Pearl
Kautz
Patrol Cabin
Hunting
Ground
Iron Mountain
WONDERLAND
Henrys
Indian
Squaw Lake
Devils
Dream
Creek
5050
Creek
Satulick Mountain
Creek
Footlog
Ridge
To Paradise
Cougar Rock Campground
Cougar Rock
Pyramid
Creek
Rampart
The
Ramparts
59
Nisqually River
PIERCE CO
LEWIS CO
Kautz
Longmire Meadow
Longmire
Springs
Ridge
PIERCE CO
LEWIS CO
Water Tanks
0
0.5
1
MILE
To Ashford
Longmire Campground

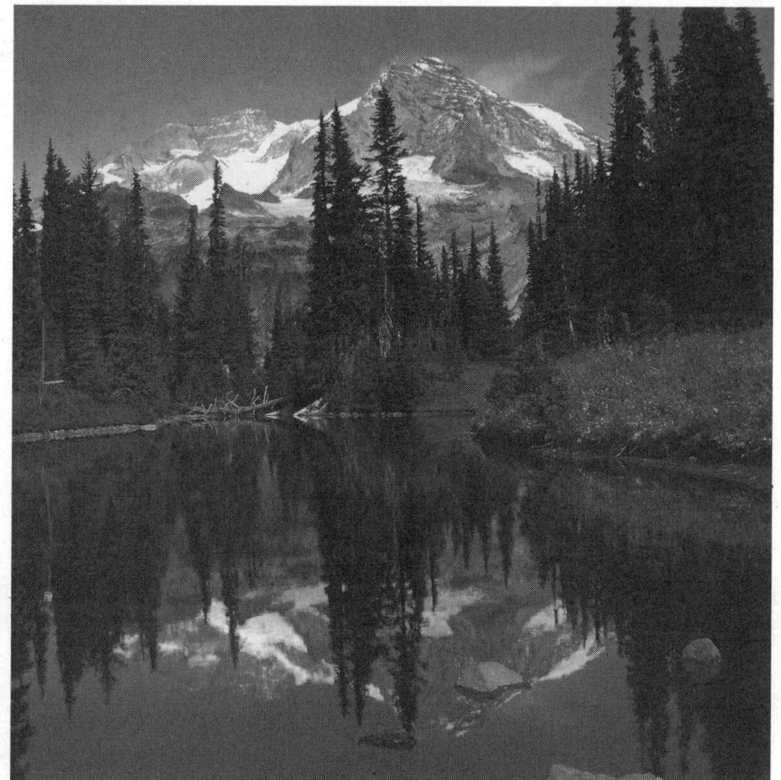

Reflection in Mirror Lake near Indian Henrys Hunting Ground

GETTING THERE

From Tacoma, drive east on State Route 7 to Elbe, then veer left onto SR 706 to enter the park at the Nisqually Entrance near Ashford. Continue east to Longmire. Park in the large lot behind the hotel and find the trailhead at the northeast end of the building complex, next to the road on the south side.

ON THE TRAIL

The trail follows the route described in Hike 58 (Pyramid Creek Camp) for the first 3.3 miles. That is, it ascends along the Wonderland Trail, crossing over Rampart Ridge at 1.5 miles, then descending through forest to Kautz Creek at 2.5 miles (before heading out, check with the ranger whether the footbridge across Kautz Creek is intact) and Pyramid Creek at 3.3 miles.

From Pyramid, the Wonderland climbs a steep, tight series of switchbacks before traversing into the Devils Dream Creek valley, reaching Devils Dream Camp at 5 miles. This forested camp provides cool relief from the midsummer sun, but the abundance of water around the camp also makes it a haven for mosquitoes. Don't linger here if the bugs are bad—just a few hundred yards up the trail, the forest opens a bit and a refreshing breeze sweeps the 'skeeters away.

Beyond Devils Dream, the trail flattens out as it weaves past Squaw Lake and up into increasingly open meadows of Indian Henrys Hunting Ground. You'll find the ranger cabin in the heart of the meadows at 6.3 miles. You can relax at the cabin's picnic table while soaking in the beauty around you. Once you've had your fill, return the way you came.

EXTENDING YOUR TRIP

If you have a shuttle vehicle, you can follow the Kautz Creek trail 6 miles to the Longmire Road trailhead (Hike 53).

60 Carter Falls

RATING/ DIFFICULTY	ROUND-TRIP	ELEV GAIN/ HIGH POINT	SEASON
***/2	7.2 miles	900 feet/ 3650 feet	May–Oct

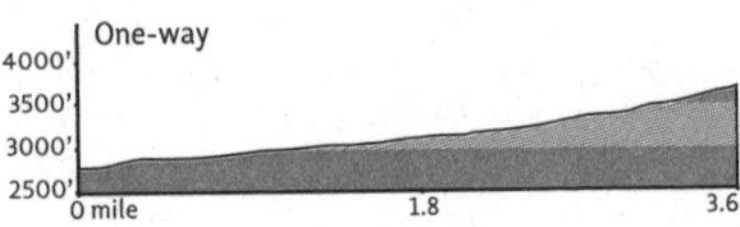

Maps: Green Trails Mount Rainier West, No. 269; **Contact:** Longmire Wilderness Information Center, (360) 569-4453; **GPS:** N46 44.980, W121 48.639

After the November 2006 floods took out the main Nisqually bridge, a footlog replacement has snowmelt splashing over it as hikers head to Carter Falls.

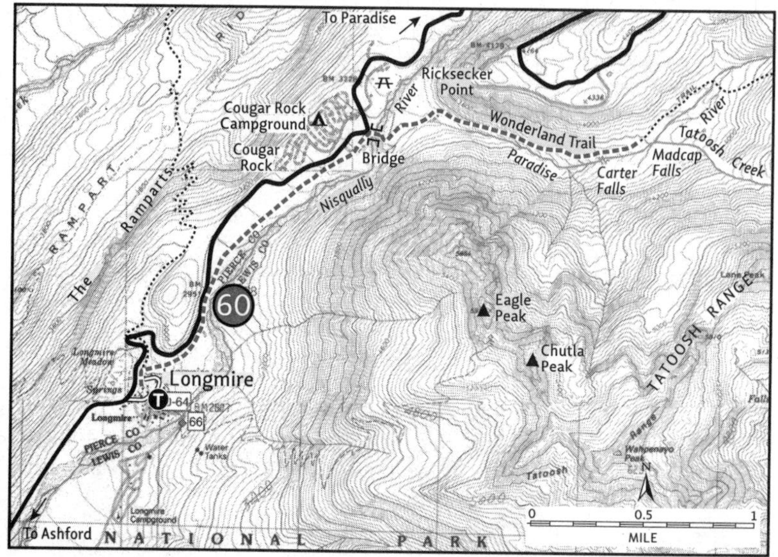

This route follows the Wonderland Trail east of Longmire through some of the oldest, most beautiful ancient forest left in Washington's Cascades, while providing views of the crashing waters of the milky Nisqually River. Families appreciate the nearly flat, easy trek through the trees along the first half of the route, while those with an appetite for more adventure enjoy the last half of the hike as it turns to follow the Paradise River upstream to a pair of pretty waterfalls. Note: The bridge over the Nisqually River was completely wiped out by the 2006 floods. A footlog was put in place in July 2007, but always check with the ranger before venturing out to make sure you can safely cross the river.

GETTING THERE

From Tacoma, drive east on State Route 7 to Elbe, then veer left onto SR 706 to enter the park at the Nisqually Entrance near Ashford. Continue east to Longmire. Park in the large lot behind the hotel, and find the trailhead on the south side of the road.

ON THE TRAIL

Find the trailhead to the right; you want the path that heads east on the Wonderland. The trail is nestled alongside Paradise Road for the first 0.5 mile and then is pinched tight between the road and the Nisqually River for a few hundred feet before the road angles left away from the river and trail. The forest around the trail is Douglas fir and cedar.

An assortment of wildlife thrives in this rich forest environment, and the most visible member of the forest community is the fearless gray jay, a.k.a. camp-robber jay, a.k.a. whiskey jack. These birds act as if they are all starving as they flit from limb to limb in the trees around the trail whenever hikers are near. The brazen beggars will even go so far as to land on a raised arm, a shoulder, or a head if there is a chance of a quick bite of bread or granola. The chittering, flittering chaps are harmless, and if you can resist their piteous begging, they will leave you alone. But be warned: feed one, and all will want a bite.

At 0.75 mile, the trail skirts the line between forest and riparian environments, with the Nisqually River just a stone's throw away to the right. The trail stays fairly level alongside the river to the 2-mile mark, where it passes the picnic area of Cougar Rock Campground. This is the last time the trail approaches the road, because the trail crosses the wide Nisqually on a stout bridge or footlog and climbs up the Paradise River valley, while the road sticks to the Nisqually valley. (Be sure to check with the ranger to make sure the Nisqually River bridge safely crosses the river.)

Comet Falls

The Paradise River is a smaller, more scenic stream, and the trail sticks close to its banks as it skirts along the base of the steep slope of a narrow gorge for 0.5 mile. The gorge slowly opens up; at 3.3 miles, the trail passes Carter Falls and at 3.6 miles, Madcap Falls. Both cascades are pretty plunges of the Paradise and are worthy of a photo and leisurely contemplation. Turn around after visiting Mapcap for a modest day's outing.

61 Comet Falls

RATING/ DIFFICULTY	ROUND-TRIP	ELEV GAIN/ HIGH POINT	SEASON
****/4	5 miles	1200 feet/ 4875 feet	July–Oct

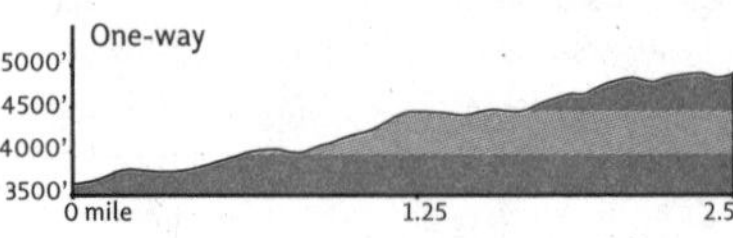

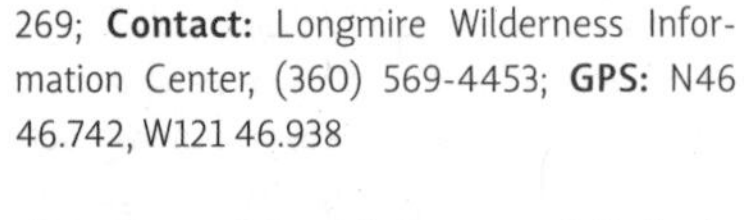

Maps: Green Trails Mount Rainier West, No. 269; **Contact:** Longmire Wilderness Information Center, (360) 569-4453; **GPS:** N46 46.742, W121 46.938

Many claim this two-step falls is the most beautiful waterfall in the park. The 320-foot cascade fans out as it crashes down the basalt cliffs, providing a spectacular show of force and beauty. The trail to this natural wonder climbs the steep valley of Van Trump Creek, offering little along the way other than an experience in the forest primeval. But once you reach the waterfall basin, that overly average trail suddenly seems exceptional.

GETTING THERE

From Tacoma, drive east on State Route 7 to Elbe, then veer left onto SR 706 to enter the park at the Nisqually Entrance near Ashford. Continue east 10 miles to the parking area on the left (north) side of the road, found just before the road passes over Christine Falls bridge.

ON THE TRAIL

The trail climbs steeply away from the road, piercing the dense old-growth forest of the Van

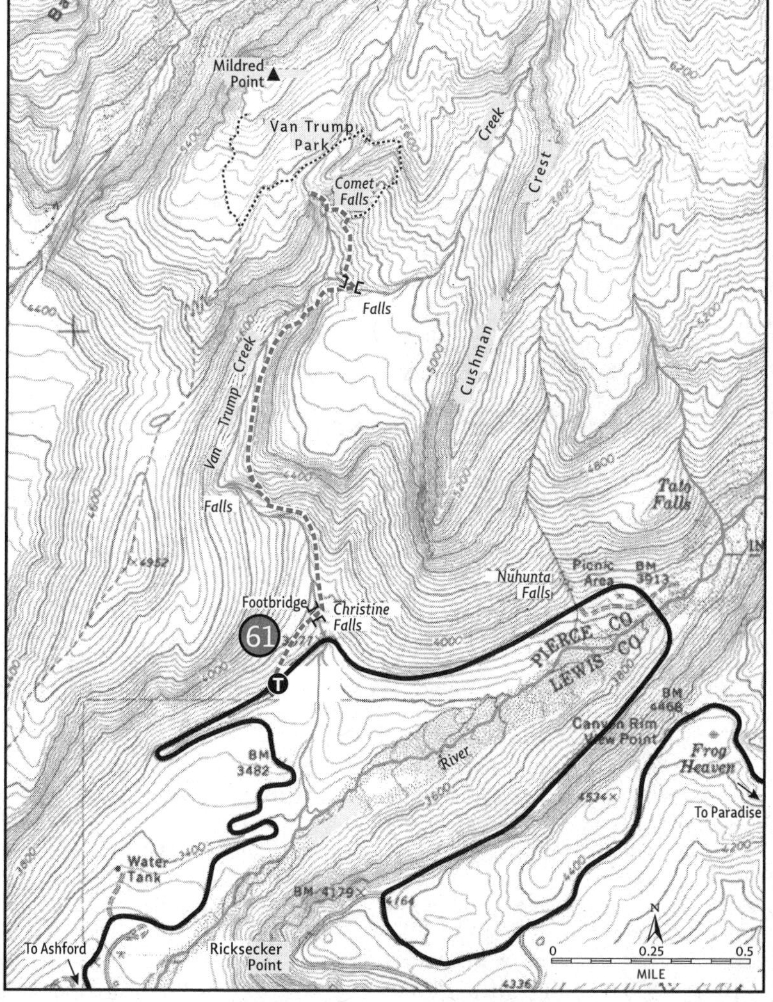

Mount Rainier rises above the beautiful meadows around Van Trump Park.

Trump valley. In 0.5 mile, the trail crosses Van Trump Creek—beyond that point, the pitch eases a bit. The trail continues to climb, just not as steeply as during that initial 0.5 mile.

Beyond the creek crossing, the trail traverses across the base of a few active avalanche chutes. Each year, snowslides scour these slopes, creating new and unique challenges for hikers each spring. You might find yourself hopping through downed trees or scrambling over jumbled rocks if you visit before the trail crews get in to repair the damage.

You cross Falls Creek at around 2.3 miles, and just past this point you'll see the lower cascade of Comet Falls. At about 2.5 miles, leave the main trail and angle off onto a side track on the left to access the plunge pool at the base of the falls. Enjoy the view before returning the way you came.

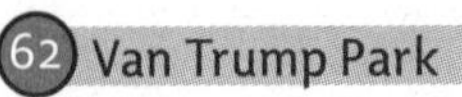

62 Van Trump Park

RATING/ DIFFICULTY	ROUND-TRIP	ELEV GAIN/ HIGH POINT	SEASON
*****/5	7 miles	2300 feet/ 5900 feet	July–Oct

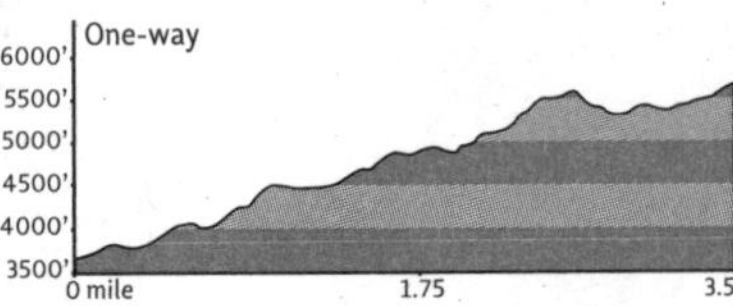

Maps: Green Trails Mount Rainier West, No. 269; **Contact:** Longmire Wilderness Information Center, (360) 569-4453; **GPS:** N46 46.742, W121 46.938

Van Trump Park, named for the first man to reach the summit of Mount Rainier, stretches across the ridges above Comet Falls. Vast wildflower fields comprise the parklands, and these fields are popular with foraging deer and mountain goats. Van Trump Park requires a good deal of effort to reach, but once it's attained, the rewards are boundless. Grand views accompanied by a plethora of local flora and fauna create a truly special wilderness experience.

GETTING THERE

From Tacoma, drive east on State Route 7 to Elbe, then veer left onto SR 706 to enter the park at the Nisqually Entrance near Ashford. Continue east 10 miles to the parking area on the left (north) side of the road, found just before the road passes over Christine Falls bridge.

ON THE TRAIL

Take time to stretch before starting up the trail, because once you're on the trail, you'll get a workout. The first 0.5 mile climbs brutally, though after the trail crosses Van Trump Creek the ascent moderates a bit. The next 2 miles continue to climb, but at a reasonable rate.

At 2.5 miles, pause and enjoy the incredible views of the 320-foot Comet Falls as it pounds into a deep slash pool, then rolls out of that pool to drop off another 40-foot cascade.

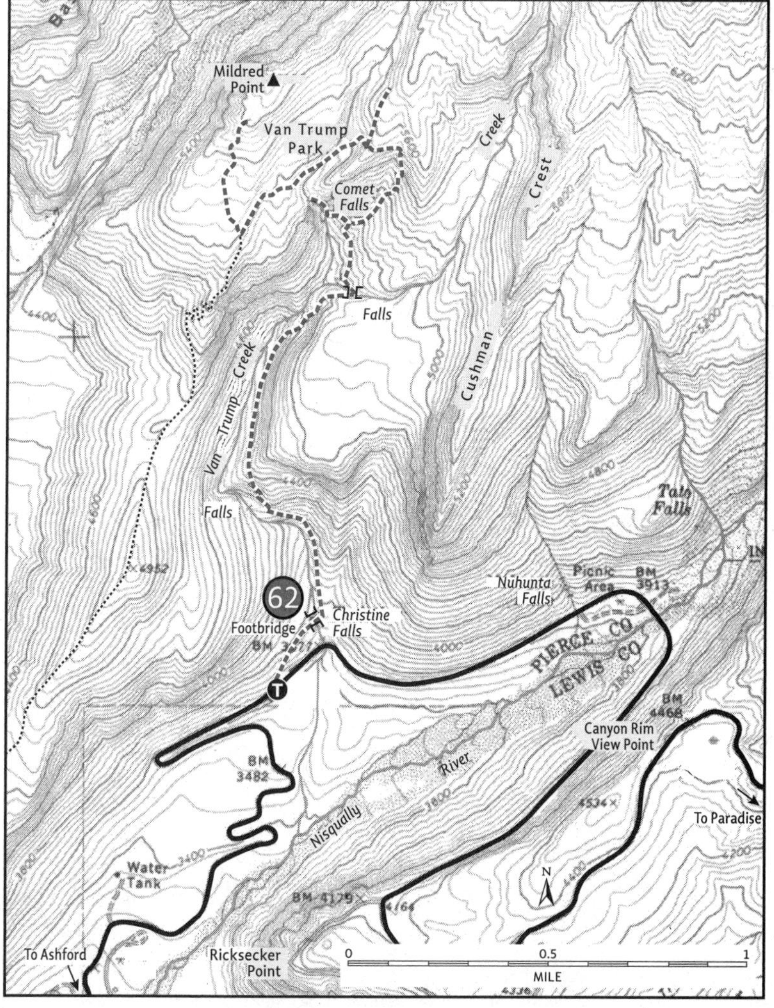

From the falls, the trail climbs steeply for 0.5 mile, switching back and forth to reach the top of the falls and the meadows beyond.

At 3 miles, the trail recrosses Van Trump Creek, above the falls this time. In early summer, the crossing can be dangerous—rather than risk the ford, find the faint way trail on the right and climb through the meadows on the east side of the creek to reach a high vantage point with grand views, then return as you came.

If the water level is low, however, better to cross the creek and continue up the main trail another 0.5 mile, turning right at a junction to reach Mildred Point in upper Van Trump Park. Here, you can enjoy the broad meadows at your feet and the sweeping vista stretching out in front of you. Return the way you came.

Oppposite: Winter view from Mazama Ridge south toward the Tatoosh Range

paradise

The awesome splendor of this region earned its name in 1885, when James Longmire's daughter-in-law Martha first ventured into the meadows and declared, "Oh, it looks just like Paradise." The name stuck, and though the area has its ups and downs—the downs include having had the meadows overrun by early car campers and the indignity of housing a golf course—the meadows today are just as spectacular as they were 130 years ago. Trails in the region explore the rich meadows, as well as the rocky slopes above and icy rivers of the surrounding glaciers.

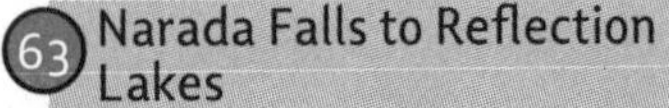

63 Narada Falls to Reflection Lakes

RATING/ DIFFICULTY	ROUND-TRIP	ELEV GAIN/ HIGH POINT	SEASON
**/3	3 miles	500 feet/ 4900 feet	July–Sept

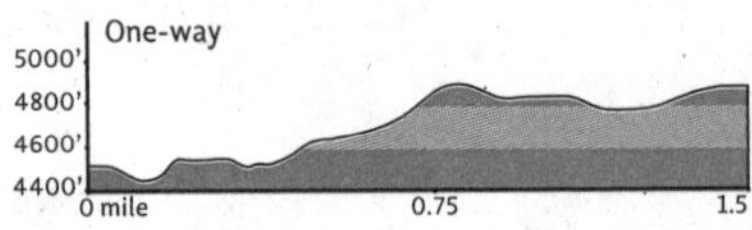

Maps: Green Trails Paradise, No. 270S; **Contact:** Longmire Wilderness Information Center, (360) 569-4453; **GPS:** N46 46.516, W121 44.793

Narada Falls in the midst of the Paradise River pounds down into a deep plunge pool, sending out a curtain of spray that provides a refreshingly cool breeze to hikers on this route. You hike the falls from top to bottom before climbing through salmonberry brambles and rich forest ecosystems to reach the upper trailhead at Reflection Lakes. This section of the Wonderland Trail gets relatively little use, so even though it's so close to the maddening crowds of Paradise tourists, the odds are

Sunrise at Reflection Lakes

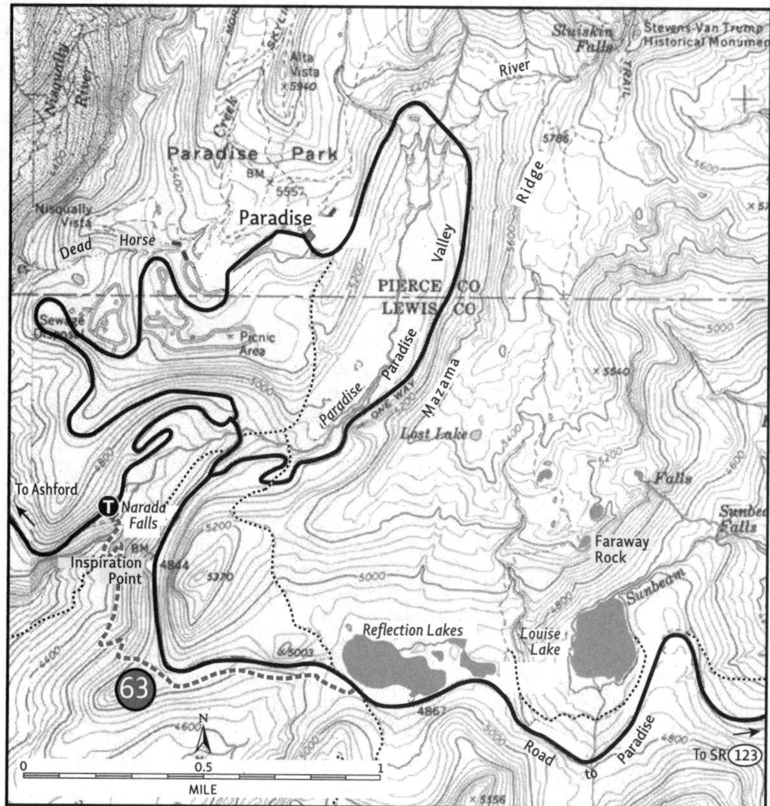

good that you'll share the trail with few other hikers.

GETTING THERE

From Tacoma, drive east on State Route 7 to Elbe, then veer left onto SR 706 to enter the park at the Nisqually Entrance near Ashford. Continue east along the Nisqually Road to the Narada Falls parking area found on the right.

ON THE TRAIL

From the parking lot, cross the river above the thundering falls on the large stone bridge. Once over the river, descend along the trail leading downstream. In about 0.1 mile, you skirt along the lower reaches of the plunge pool at the base of the falls. Another 0.1 mile farther on, you hit a junction with the Wonderland Trail.

Turn left onto the Wonderland and begin climbing through sun-dappled slopes above the river. Juicy orange salmonberries can be found here in mid-July.

At about 0.75 mile, the trail swings into a series of switchbacks and climbs into a rich forest zone before cresting the ridge and starting a 0.5-mile-long traverse parallel to and below the Road to Paradise. The trail pops

A colorful sunset on Mount Rainier and autumn colors in the meadows around the Nisqually Vista Loop trail

out of the woods onto the road at 1.5 miles at the western end of the Reflection Lakes.

Turn around at the lakes and return to Narada Falls.

EXTENDING YOUR TRIP

You could also return by crossing the road and heading northwest on a trail climbing about 200 feet to a saddle, then descending in about 0.8 mile to the Paradise Road. Cross it at a hairpin turn and at a trail junction shortly after, go left to descend to Narada Falls in about 1.6 miles from Reflection Lakes.

64 Nisqually Vista Loop

RATING/ DIFFICULTY	LOOP	ELEV GAIN/ HIGH POINT	SEASON
***/1	1.4 miles	200 feet/ 5400 feet	July–Oct

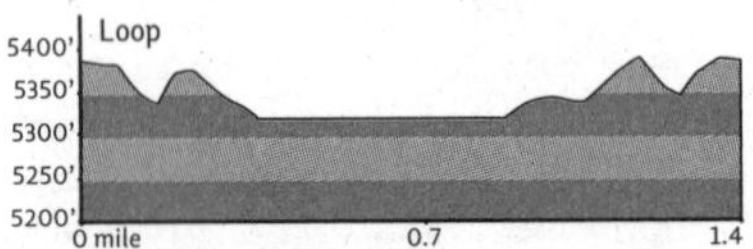

Maps: Green Trails Paradise, No. 270S; **Contact:** Longmire Wilderness Information Center, (360) 569-4453; **GPS:** N46 47.088, W121 44.487

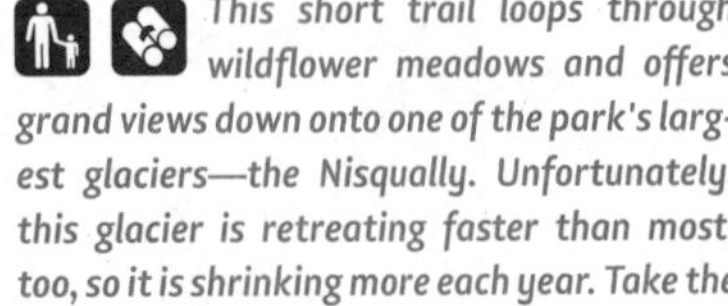

This short trail loops through wildflower meadows and offers grand views down onto one of the park's largest glaciers—the Nisqually. Unfortunately, this glacier is retreating faster than most, too, so it is shrinking more each year. Take the kids to show them this changing landscape—it's a great lesson in climate change.

GETTING THERE

From Tacoma, drive east on State Route 7 to Elbe, then veer left onto SR 706 to enter the park at the Nisqually Entrance near Ashford. Continue east along the Nisqually Road to the Paradise visitor center. Park in the lot behind the visitor center and find the trail at the northern edge of the parking lot.

ON THE TRAIL

To ensure you find the proper trail, when you leave the visitor center stay left at any trail

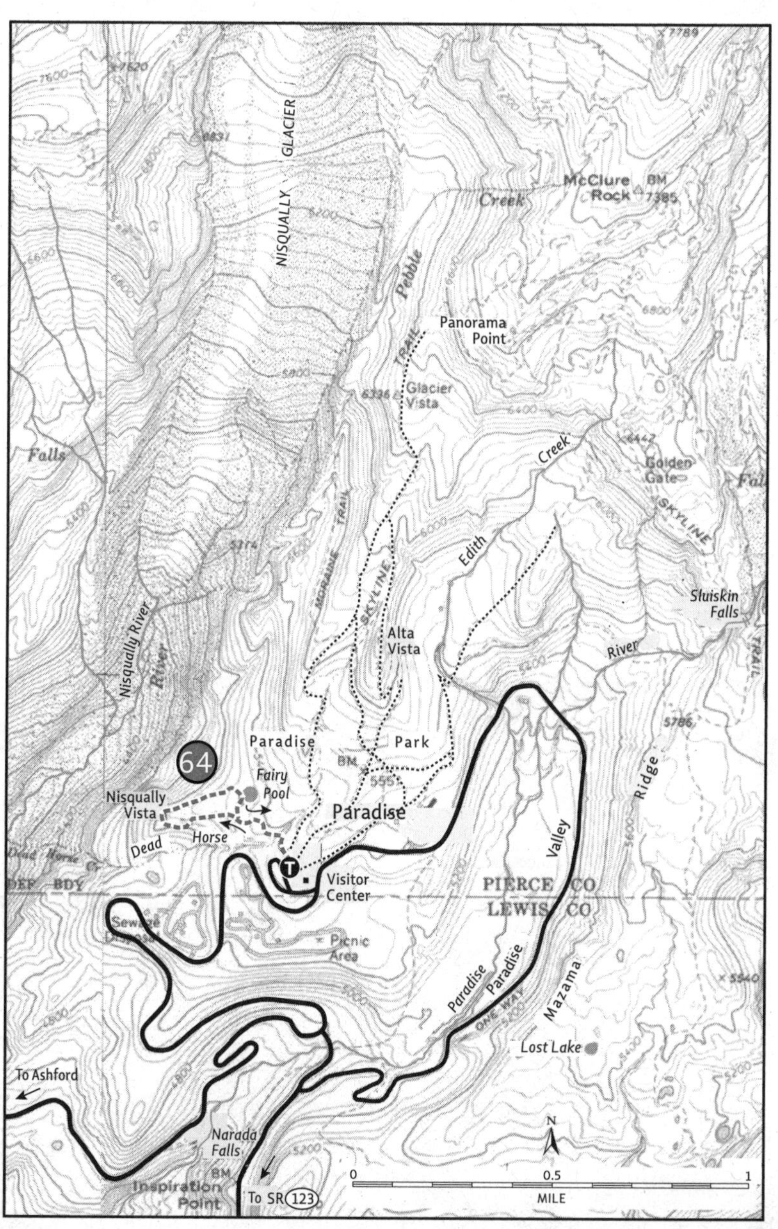
NISQUALLY GLACIER
McClure Rock
Pebble Creek
Panorama Point
Glacier Vista
Falls
Golden Gate
SKYLINE
Edith Creek
Sluiskin Falls
Alta Vista
SKYLINE TRAIL
MORAINE TRAIL
Nisqually River
River
64
Paradise Park
Fairy Pool
Nisqually Vista
Paradise
Dead Horse
Visitor Center
PIERCE CO
LEWIS CO
Valley
Ridge
Picnic Area
Paradise
Paradise
Mazama
ONE WAY
Lost Lake
To Ashford
Narada Falls
Inspiration Point
To SR 123
0
0.5
1
MILE

junction you come to (unless that trail obviously drops straight back to the parking lot). The Nisqually Vista Trail leads west away from the visitor center, climbing a gentle slope through flower fields for 0.3 mile.

The trail splits here. Go left to do the loop section in a clockwise direction. The trail angles out along a ridge crest before turning north to reach the rim of the tall wall above the Nisqually Glacier. Or it used to be above the glacier. The retreating ice field now resides farther up the valley—directly below your vantage point are vast mounds of moraine and the milky waters of the Nisqually River.

The trail follows the rim of this steep slope for a short distance before curving back to the east, passing a small tarn (Fairy Pool) before rejoining the initial trail to close the 0.8-mile loop. Follow the trail 0.3 mile back to the visitor center.

65 Alta Vista Loop

RATING/ DIFFICULTY	LOOP	ELEV GAIN/ HIGH POINT	SEASON
***/1	1.5 miles	540 feet/ 5940 feet	July–Oct

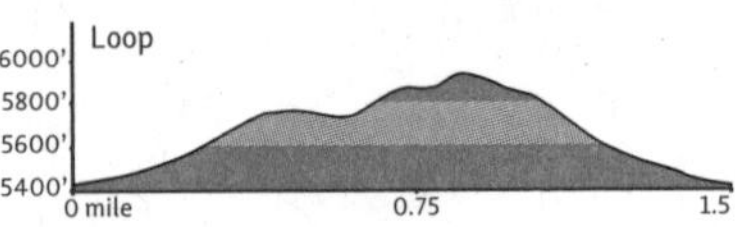

Maps: Green Trails Paradise, No. 270S; **Contact:** Longmire Wilderness Information Center, (360) 569-4453; **GPS:** N46 47.162, W121 44.099

This little loop explores some of the most spectacular wildflower fields on the continent. These glorious meadows of flowers are lined with trails, most of which

A lovely doe enjoys the huckleberries and crimson fall colors in the meadows by Alta Vista.

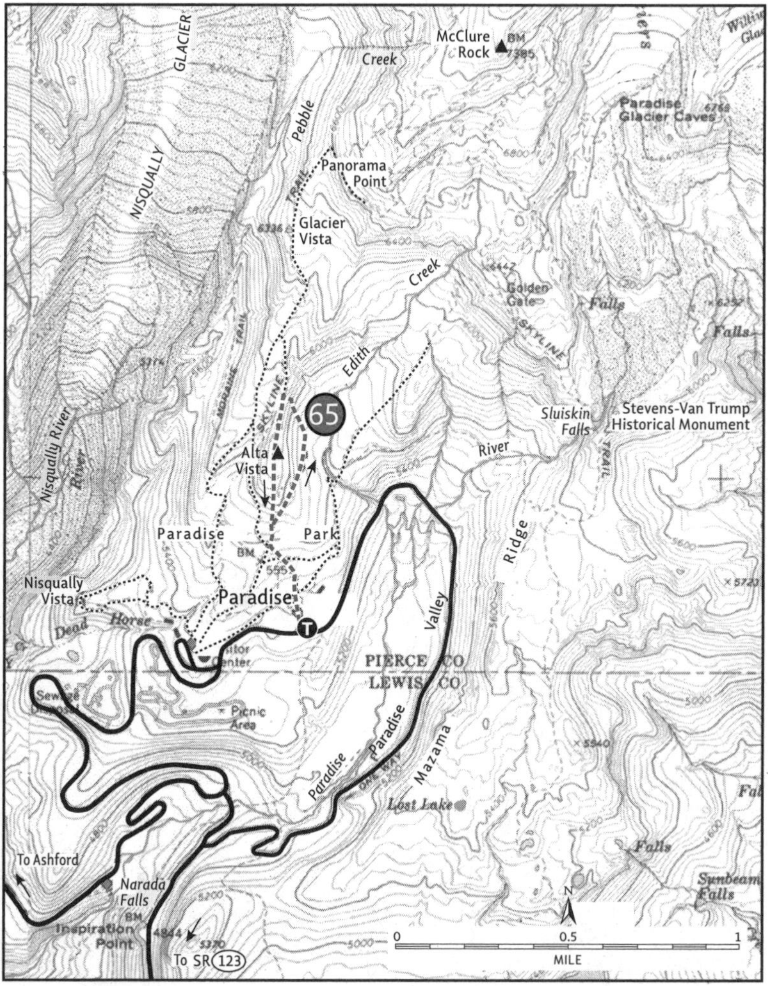

are paved—at least along their lower reaches. This is an unfortunate but necessary fact. These high-altitude meadows are so fragile, and so popular, that the hardened trail surfaces are needed to prevent the fields from being loved to death.

GETTING THERE

From Tacoma, drive east on State Route 7 to Elbe, then veer left onto SR 706 to enter the park at the Nisqually Entrance near Ashford. Continue east along the Nisqually Road to the Paradise Lodge parking area. Park in the large parking lot and find the trail near the climbers hut on the north side of the parking lot.

ON THE TRAIL

The paved trail climbs steeply through the wildflowers that grow right down the verge of the parking lot. The network of trails in the lower meadows can be a bit confusing, but to make your routefinding easier, simply keep your goal in sight. Alta Vista is the tall fin of tree-covered rock due north of the parking lot. At each intersection, pick the trail that leads north toward this fin.

For the best experience, angle toward the

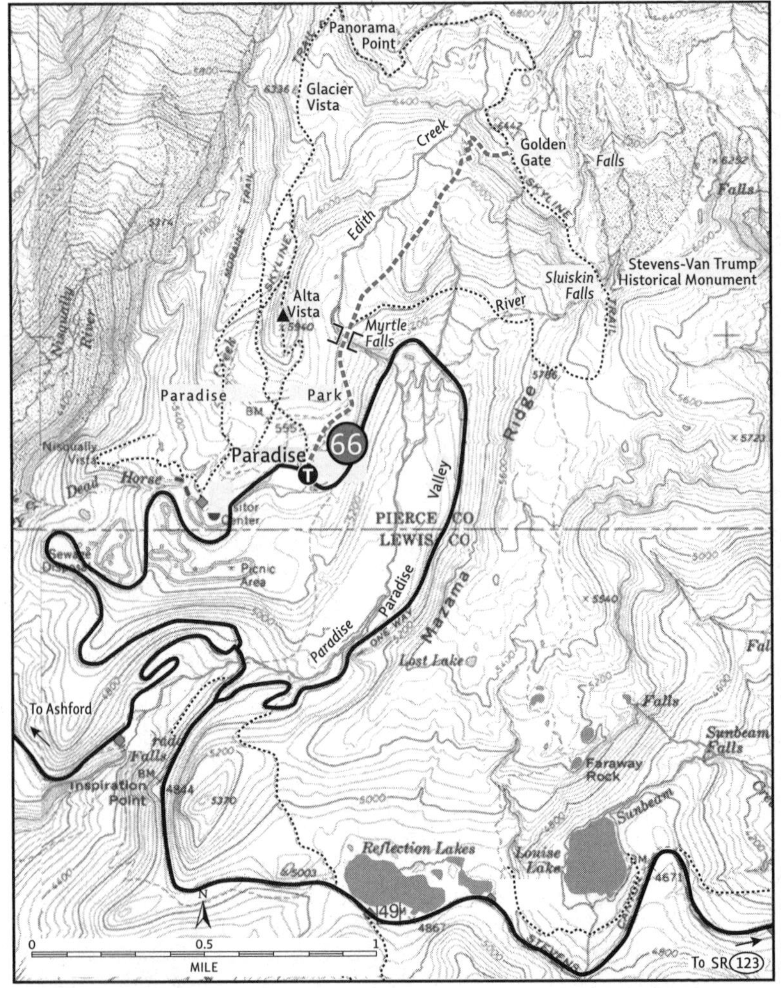

Open meadows, fall colors, and The Mountain comes out to play for photos. Another great day!

east side of the Alta Vista summit, following a steep dirt trail along the precipitous wall above Edith Creek basin. This deep, green valley is typically awash in wildflowers from late July through August.

At about 0.7 mile, the trail—now on the northern flank of Alta Vista—reaches a four-way junction. The Skyline Trail leads farther north, as well as southwest toward the Paradise visitor center. The other forks are the one you came up and the return left across the crest of Alta Vista. Take this path back.

Stop periodically to look behind you at the monolith of Mount Rainier. The trail drops off the southern end of Alta Vista and descends steeply back into the Paradise meadows to close your loop. Wander back to where you started.

66 Golden Gate

RATING/ DIFFICULTY	ROUND-TRIP	ELEV GAIN/ HIGH POINT	SEASON
****/3	3.2 miles	1000 feet/ 6400 feet	July–Sept

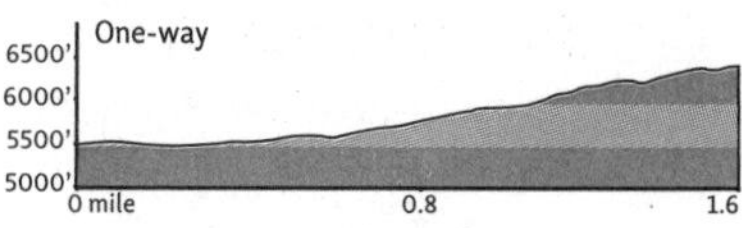

Maps: Green Trails Paradise, No. 270S; **Contact:** Longmire Wilderness Information Center, (360) 569-4453; **GPS:** N46 47.162, W121 44.099

  ***This route offers the most direct route from Paradise to the rock-and-ice world of the upper mountain's lower reaches, with wonderful views of the Tatoosh Range and the expansive Paradise Valley spread out at your feet. Thrown in for good measure is Myrtle Falls, right alongside the trail.***

GETTING THERE

From Tacoma, drive east on State Route 7 to Elbe, then veer left onto SR 706 to enter the park at the Nisqually Entrance near Ashford. Continue east along the Nisqually Road to the Paradise Lodge parking area. Park in the large parking lot and find the trail near Paradise Lodge.

ON THE TRAIL

Head northeast from the lodge into the lower reaches of Edith Creek basin on the Skyline Trail. The paved trail leads to Myrtle Falls at 0.6 mile. Enjoy the views of the falls from the bridge, then move on up the trail. At the trail fork just beyond the bridge, veer left to climb the Golden Gate Trail through Edith Basin; the right-hand Skyline Trail heads east (Hike 68).

The Golden Gate trail cuts through the flower fields of the basin floor before turning steeply upward. Climb directly up the headwall of the valley. At about 1.3 miles, the slopes turn steep enough that the trail has to switchback up the final 0.3 mile to reach the viewpoint known as Golden Gate (6400 feet), at the junction with the Skyline Trail.

Stop here to rest and recover from the steep ascent, and enjoy the panoramic views spread out before you. Look south over the long finger of the Paradise Valley to the craggy fence of the Tatoosh Range. Behind you, Mount Rainier dominates the northern horizon. Return as you came.

EXTENDING YOUR TRIP

You can return via either branch of the Skyline Trail (Hike 68) for a longer loop; that trail to the south heads past Sluiskin Falls for a 4-mile loop; to the north, Panorama Point for a 5-mile loop.

67 Mazama Ridge

RATING/ DIFFICULTY	ROUND-TRIP	ELEV GAIN/ HIGH POINT	SEASON
****/3	7 miles	600 feet/ 5850 feet	July–Sept

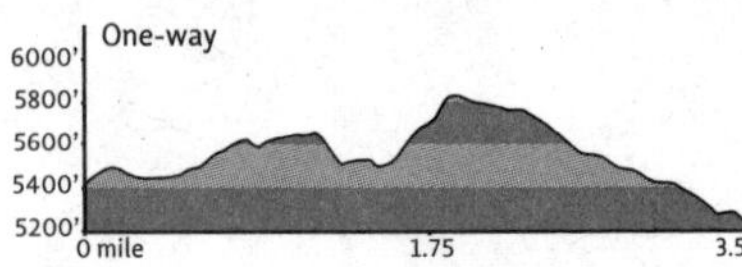

Maps: Green Trails Paradise, No. 270S; **Contact:** Longmire Wilderness Information Center, (360) 569-4453; **GPS:** N46 47.162, W121 44.099

   ***The long ridge to the east of Paradise offers a grand adventure through the varied ecosystems of the alpine wonderland of this region. The route described here is a simple out-and-back walk but with a little planning, hikers can create their own itinerary, utilizing the multitude of trails in the area to link together loops of various lengths. But that's too much work when all we want to do is tiptoe through the lupine.***

GETTING THERE

From Tacoma, drive east on State Route 7 to Elbe, then veer left onto SR 706 to enter the park at the Nisqually Entrance near Ashford. Continue east along the Nisqually Road to the Paradise Lodge parking area. Park in the large parking lot and find the trail near the climbers hut on the north side of the parking lot.

ON THE TRAIL

Follow the Skyline Trail (Hike 68) northeast

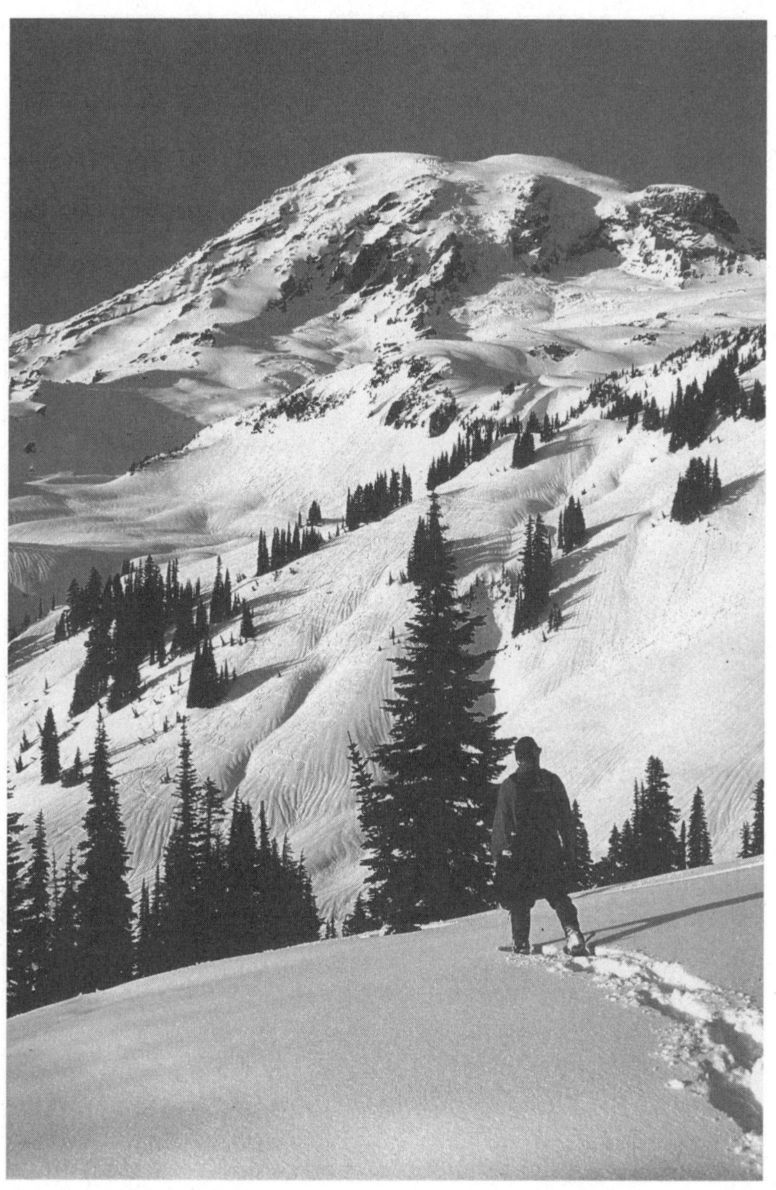

Craig snowshoes down the slopes of Mazama Ridge on a rare clear-day winter visit.

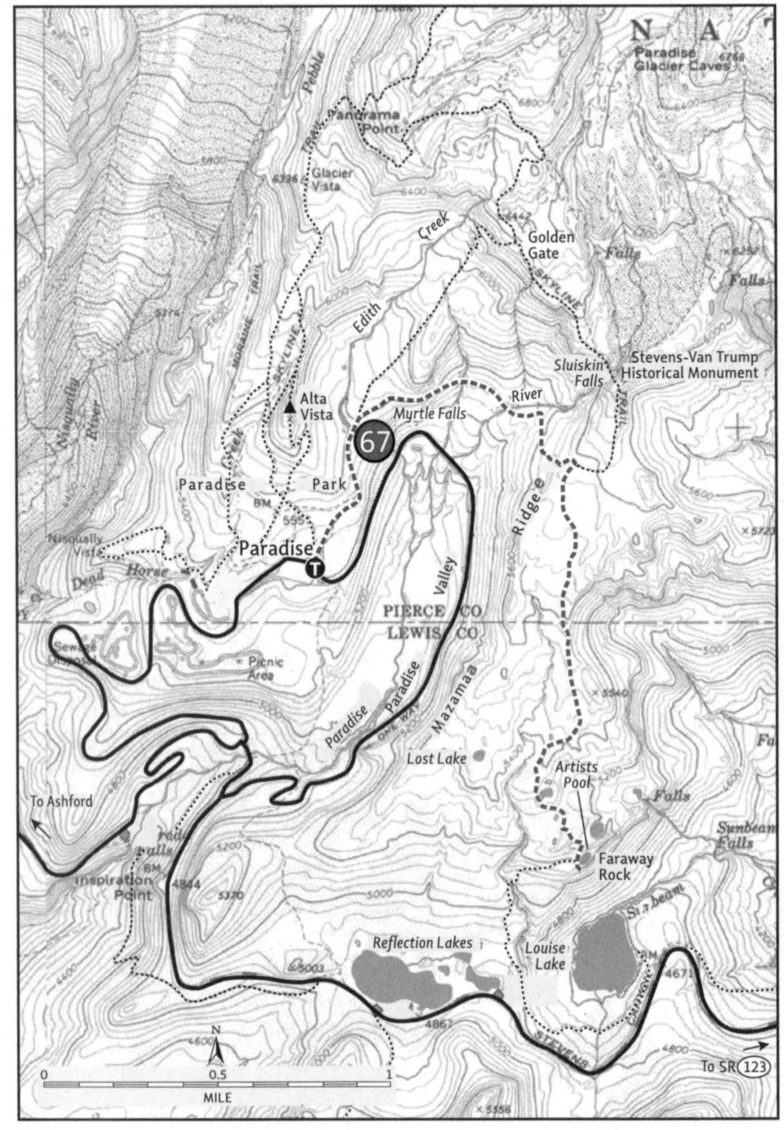
Paradise Glacier Caves
Panorama Point
Glacier Vista
Golden Gate
Edith Creek
Stevens-Van Trump Historical Monument
Sluiskin Falls
River
Myrtle Falls
Alta Vista
67
Paradise Park
Nisqually Vista
Paradise
Dead Horse
Ridge
Valley
PIERCE CO
LEWIS CO
Sewage Disposal
Picnic Area
Paradise
Paradise
Mazamaa
ONE WAY
Lost Lake
Artists Pool
To Ashford
Faraway Rock
Sunbeam Falls
Inspiration Point
Reflection Lakes
Louise Lake
STEVENS
To SR 123
0
0.5
1
MILE

from the parking lot, passing Myrtle Falls at 0.6 mile and a trail junction shortly after; stay right on your way to the crest of Mazama Ridge at 2 miles out. At the trail junction atop the ridge, veer right and start the gradual descent along the spine of the ridge, weaving through meadows and stands of old alpine fir.

A gaggle of birds will likely keep you and your kids company as you hike. Immense ravens soar on the valley thermals while gray jays (a.k.a. camp robbers) and Clark's nutcrackers dart to and fro around you, looking for dropped granola and other handouts. Indeed, the local camp robbers are so bold, they will at times even land on your pack as you hike, looking for an easy snack.

About 0.75 mile after the last trail junction, you pass the first of the series of small tarns that dot the ridge top. These pools are frequented by the resident black-tailed deer, and marmots can frequently be found scurrying around the meadows near them. Continuing south along the ridge, enjoy the views of the Tatoosh Range before you, with the tall spires of Pinnacle Peak, Plummer Peak, The Castle, and Unicorn Peak marking the ridgeline.

At 3.5 miles, the trail reaches Artists Pool—a small reflective pool near Faraway Rock high above Louise Lake. This makes a good turnaround point.

EXTENDING YOUR TRIP

If you arrange a shuttle vehicle, you can continue south from Faraway Rock (Hike 48) to the trailhead near Reflection Lakes.

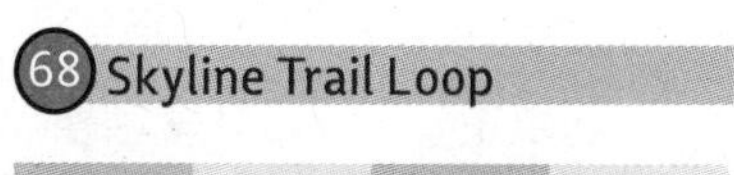

68 Skyline Trail Loop

RATING/ DIFFICULTY	LOOP	ELEV GAIN/ HIGH POINT	SEASON
****/4	6 miles	1400 feet/ 6800 feet	July–Sept

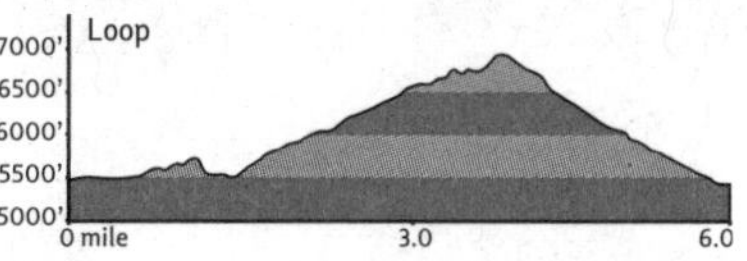

Maps: Green Trails Paradise, No. 270S; **Contact:** Longmire Wilderness Information Center, (360) 569-4453; **GPS:** N46 47.162, W121 44.099

This route loops around the broad Edith Creek basin, leading through alpine flower fields, past thundering waterfalls, and over high, craggy peaks. In this one loop, you'll experience the best the Paradise region has to offer in terms of scenic beauty, rugged hiking, and varied terrain and ecosystems. You'll also find a memorial marking an important event in park history!

GETTING THERE

From Tacoma, drive east on State Route 7 to Elbe, then veer left onto SR 706 to enter the park at the Nisqually Entrance near Ashford. Continue east along the Nisqually Road to the Paradise Lodge parking area. Park in the large parking lot and find the trail near Paradise Lodge.

ON THE TRAIL

Head northeast from the lodge, entering the lower reaches of Edith Creek basin on the Skyline Trail. At 0.6 mile, the trail crosses directly above the crashing cascade of Myrtle Falls. The best views are from the trail bridge, looking directly down the falls.

Continuing past the falls, the trail splits almost immediately. Stay right; the left-hand trail heads steeply northeast toward Golden Gate, but you'll get there on a different route.

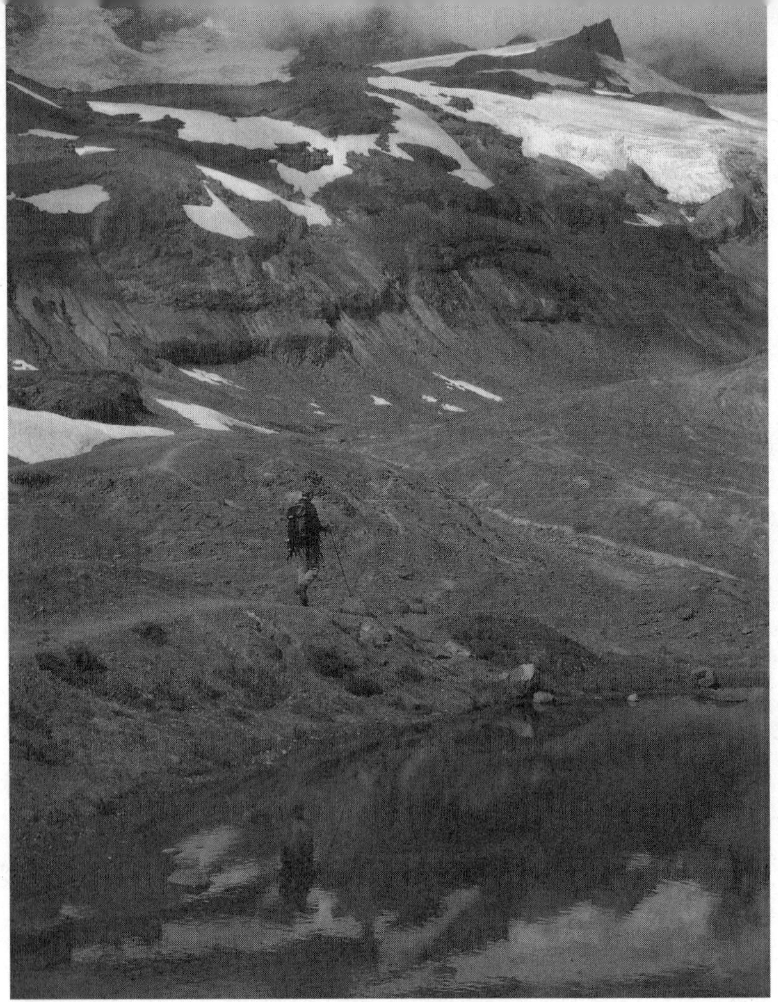

Opposite: A hiker passes a reflective tarn near the Paradise Glacier

Hike east on the trail that traverses out of the Edith Creek basin and loops around the head-wall of the adjacent Paradise Valley.

On the east side of the basin, reach another trail junction at 1.5 miles. Stay left; the right-hand trail heads south down to the Paradise Valley Road in the Paradise valley. Start the steep climb up the side of Mazama Ridge. You attain the ridge crest in 0.5 mile, where the trail forks once more. Again, stay left to continue moving north. At this junction at 2 miles, the trail passes the Stevens–Van Trump Historical Monument above Sluiskin Falls. The memorial is a stone and concrete bench placed to honor the first two climbers to ascend Mount Rainier. The placement of the memorial, above

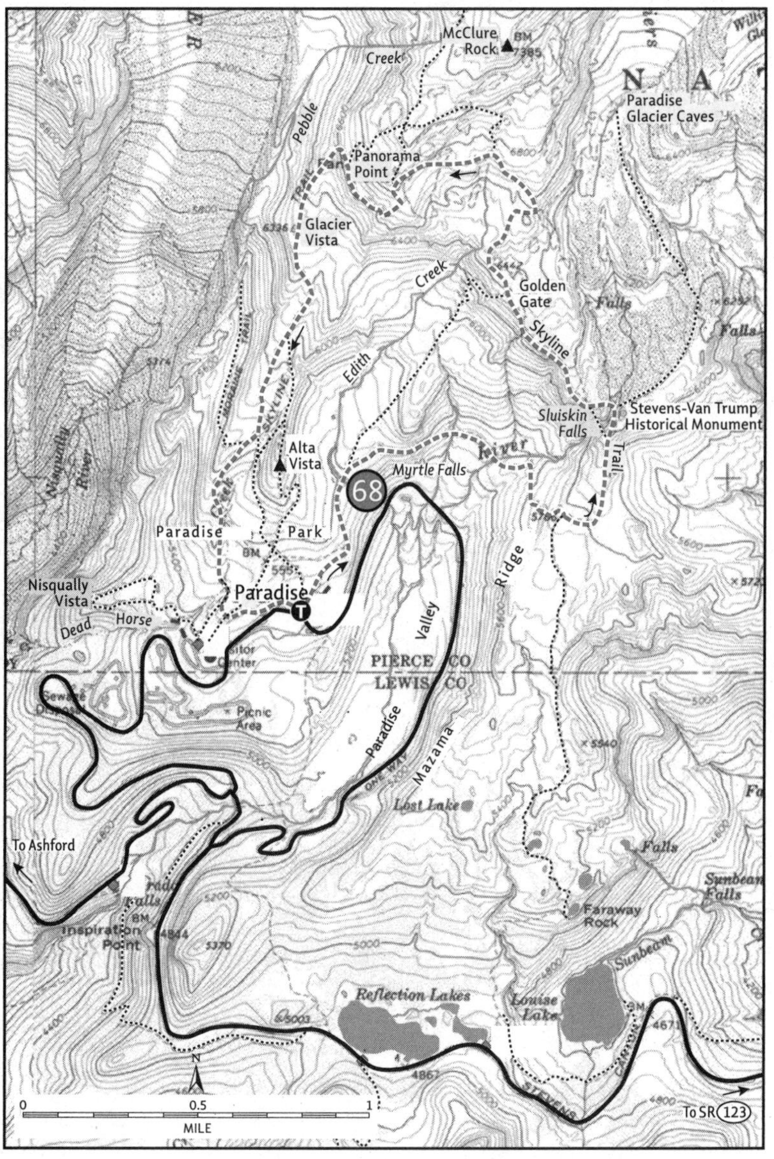
McClure
Rock
Creek
Paradise
Glacier Caves
Pebble
Panorama
Point
Glacier
Vista
Creek
Golden
Gate
Skyline
Edith
Sluiskin
Falls
Stevens-Van Trump
Historical Monument
Trail
Alta
Vista
Myrtle Falls
68
Paradise
Park
Ridge
Nisqually
Vista
Paradise
Dead
Horse
Valley
PIERCE CO
LEWIS CO
Picnic
Area
Paradise
Mazama
Lost Lake
To Ashford
Inspiration
Point
Reflection Lakes
Faraway
Rock
Sunbeam
Falls
Louise
Lake
0
0.5
1
MILE
To SR 123

LOW-IMPACT RECREATION

In days gone by, wilderness travelers did as they pleased when hiking through the backcountry. If a trail got muddy or wet, a new one was created parallel to the first. If folks wanted a warm drink with lunch, they'd start a campfire. And campers would cut young, fragrant pine boughs to create soft bedding.

As more and more people took to the hills, those actions began to leave large, noticeable scars on the land. Today, with millions of hikers flocking to the backcountry, these kinds of intrusive practices would leave the wilderness blighted for decades to come. To ensure that we don't destroy the essence of the wild country we all enjoy visiting, hikers today are encouraged to employ the Leave No Trace (LNT) principles.

In short, these principles and practices are built around the idea that human visitors to the backcountry should "leave only footprints, take only pictures." In fact, done right, even the footprints will be minimized.

Hikers who encounter mudholes in the middle of trails should suck it up and stride through the puddle rather than stomp down the vegetation around the edge of the mud. Each passing hiker skirts wider and wider around the ever-growing mudhole, until the trail is wide enough to drive a truck on and the vegetation is stomped into oblivion. If you've planned ahead, you're likely wearing hiking boots appropriate for your trail experience, and in Washington that generally means they are waterproof. So stepping in mud does you no harm and helps prevent trail erosion.

Likewise, hikers should resist creating new trails. This doesn't mean you should never step off-trail. By all means, hikers should explore off-trail if they're comfortable doing so. But when you step off the established trail, you should do it in a place that won't leave a permanent scar, and once you're off-trail, you need to move well away from the trail. There's no reason to explore off-trail if you're going to be only 20 feet away from that established path.

As well, cutting across a switchback turn yields you nothing (maybe shaving a couple of seconds off your travel time), but it does lasting damage to the trail and the environment around the trail. Cutting switchbacks leads to loss of vegetation and establishment of "cut trails" that channel rainwater and snowmelt. This leads to erosion of the hillside and trail tread.

A willingness on the part of all hikers to practice a little patience and to put up with a little discomfort (such as getting a touch muddy) will help keep our trails open and enjoyable for everyone.

Sluiskin Falls, is said to be at the spot where Chief Sluiskin waited for the climbers to return from their summit bid.

From this point, the trail angles northwest, climbing gradually to Golden Gate (Hike 66) at 2.5 miles, where a trail leads left back to Myrtle Falls; stay straight ahead. Then climb more steeply, staying left at trail junctions, to Panorama Point (6800 feet) at 3.5 miles. From Panorama Point, descend past Glacier

Views up the Nisqually Glacier and the entirety of Mount Rainier from near Panorama Point

Vista (Hike 69), staying right at trail junctions above Alta Vista, then taking the east-bound trail below Alta Vista to return to the trailhead parking lot at 6 miles.

69 Glacier Vista–Panorama Point

RATING/ DIFFICULTY	ROUND-TRIP	ELEV GAIN/ HIGH POINT	SEASON
****/3	5 miles	1300 feet/ 6700 feet	June–Oct

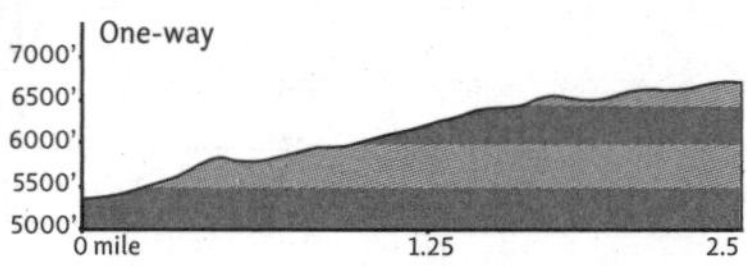

Maps: Green Trails Paradise, No. 270S; **Contact:** Longmire Wilderness Information Center, (360) 569-4453; **GPS:** N46 47.162, W121 44.099

The open meadows above Paradise draw hikers from around the world. Countless opportunities for enjoying these flowers can be found in the maze of meadow trails, but heading up toward Panorama Point and beyond on the Glacier Vista Loop is the best of the bunch.

GETTING THERE

From Tacoma, drive east on State Route 7 to Elbe, then veer left onto SR 706 to enter the park at the Nisqually Entrance near Ashford. Continue east along the Nisqually Road to the Paradise Lodge parking area. Park in the large parking lot and find the trail near the climbers hut on the north side of the parking lot. .

ON THE TRAIL

Hike up the steep meadow trail behind the climbers lodge. The network of trails in the lower meadows can be a bit confusing, but to make your routefinding easier, stay along the

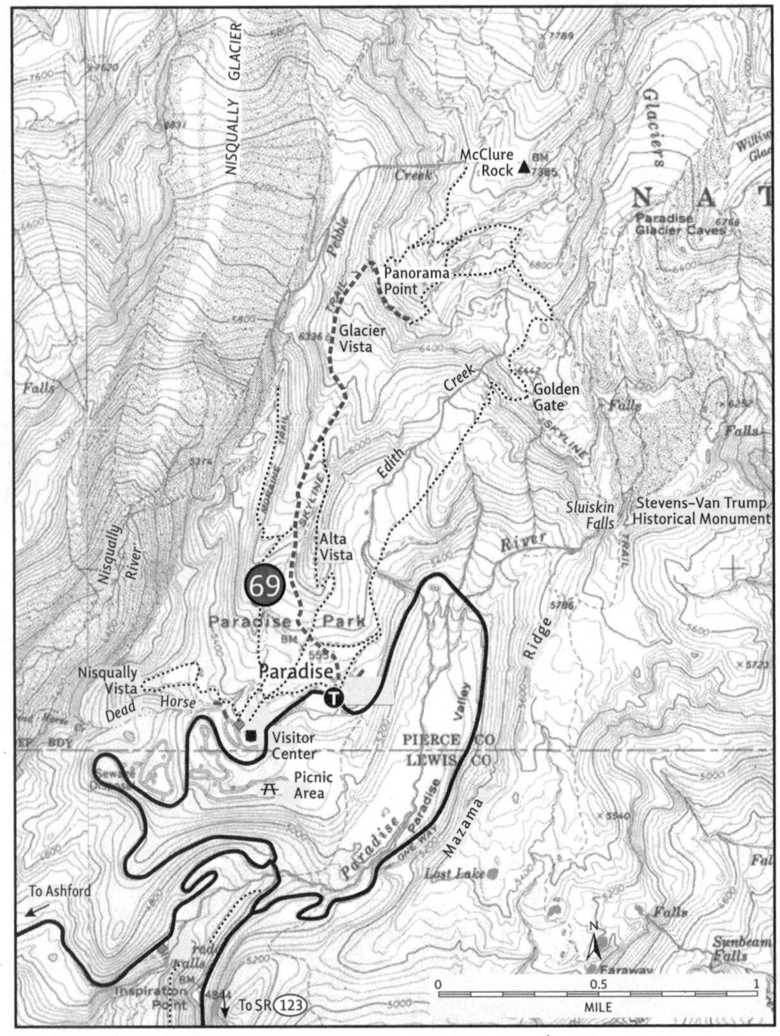

west side of the tree-covered crown of Alta Vista peak (see Hike 65). The route rolls uphill through meadows and thin tree cover, with excellent views of the mountain when the weather is clear.

From the small saddle on the north side of Alta Vista, climb along the prominent ridge crest as it leads straight toward Mount Rainier. If you somehow get onto the Skyline Trail, that's okay; it rejoins your path. The route parallels the massive finger of Nisqually Glacier and, at 1.5 miles, crosses a flat bench aptly named Glacier Vista. This is the best place to find a panoramic view of the sprawling glacier as it stretches from high on the flank of the mountain nearly to the road to Paradise.

From Glacier Vista, the route climbs steeply northeast through open hillside meadows, with a few thin stands of wind-savaged alpine trees, reaching another broad bench nearly 1 mile farther up the mountain. Panorama Point lives up to its name, with grand views of the mighty mountain, its lower flanks, and the serrated ridge line of the Tatoosh Range to the south. On clear days, the rocky spires of the Goat Rocks Wilderness Area as well as the perfect cone of Mount Adams are visible to the southeast.

To return to Paradise, descend along the route you climbed.

EXTENDING YOUR TRIP

You can also continue east across snowfields, crossing the headwaters of Edith Creek and then turning southwest to return alongside and below the creek.

70 Camp Muir

RATING/ DIFFICULTY	ROUND-TRIP	ELEV GAIN/ HIGH POINT	SEASON
*****/5	10 miles	4600 feet 10,000 feet	July–Sept

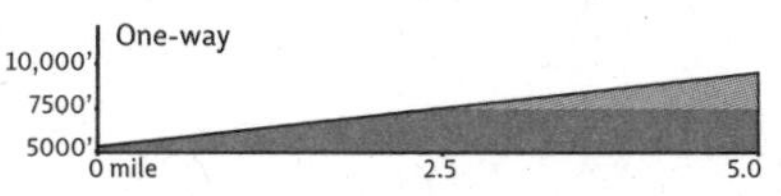

Maps: Green Trails Paradise, No. 270S; **Contact:** Longmire Wilderness Information Center, (360) 569-4453; **GPS:** N46 47.162, W121 44.099

The route to Camp Muir gives hearty hikers a small taste of what alpine climbers experience. The trail stretches high up the flank of Rainier, toward the upper mountain where alpine climbers play. This route isn't for everyone since it does entail substantial snow travel and may require good routefinding skills. But on a clear summer day, hikers in excellent physical condition might consider this most strenuous trek into the world of rock and ice.

Hiking up past Pebble Creek toward the snowfields that lead toward Camp Muir while the Nisqually Glacier always dominates the nearby view

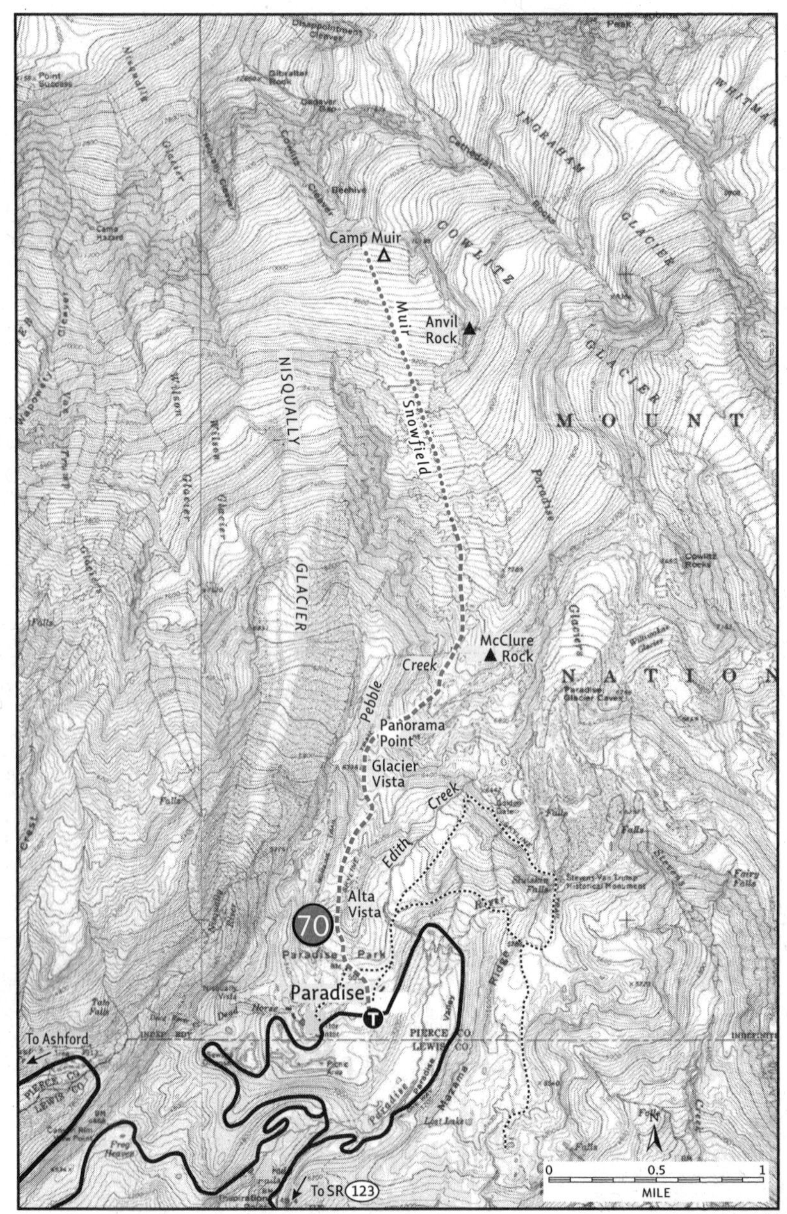
Camp Muir
Muir Snowfield
Anvil Rock
NISQUALLY GLACIER
COWLITZ
INGRAHAM GLACIER
MOUNT
NATION
McClure Rock
Creek
Pebble
Panorama Point
Glacier Vista
Edith Creek
Alta Vista
70
Paradise
To Ashford
To SR 123
0
0.5
1
MILE

GETTING THERE

From Tacoma, drive east on State Route 7 to Elbe, then veer left onto SR 706 to enter the park at the Nisqually Entrance near Ashford. Continue east along the Nisqually Road to the Paradise Lodge parking area. Park in the large parking lot and find the trail near the climbers hut on the north side of the parking lot.

ON THE TRAIL

Pick a path and head north from the parking lot. It doesn't matter which route you take—keep moving upward, and all trails eventually merge. At 1.5 miles, you pass the viewpoint at Glacier Vista (Hike 69), and 0.3 mile beyond that, you come to a trail fork. To the right is the Panorama Point Trail. Go left to continue your steep climb. In about 0.25 mile, the trail moderates a bit as it moves up through the rocky slopes above Panorama Point.

At 2.5 miles, the trail crosses a shallow ford of Pebble Creek and then fades away. From this point forward, the trail is merely a boot track through the snows of the Muir Snowfield. For 2.5 miles, you climb along the face of the snowfield, reaching the rocky spine that houses Camp Muir at 10,000 feet. A couple of rock shelters reside here—one is used as a communal bunkhouse, the other is assigned to the licensed climbing guide service.

Turn around here (if not before), making sure you have plenty of time and energy in reserve for the return trek. Use caution descending the snowfield.

Appendix: Conservation and Trail Organizations

Cascade Land Conservancy
615 Second Avenue, Suite 625
Seattle, WA 98104
(206) 292-5907
info@cascadeland.org
www.cascadeland.org

Conservation Northwest
1208 Bay Street, Suite 201
Bellingham, WA 98225
(360) 671-9950
www.conservationnw.org

Issaquah Alps Trail Club
P.O. Box 351
Issaquah, WA 98027
www.issaquahalps.org

The Mountaineers
300 Third Avenue West
Seattle, WA 98119
206-284-6310
clubmail@mountaineers.org
www.mountaineers.org

Mountains to Sound Greenway
911 Western Avenue, Suite 523
Seattle, WA 98104
(206) 382-5565
info@mtsgreenway.org
www.mtsgreenway.org

Sierra Club, Cascade Chapter
180 Nickerson Street, Suite 202
Seattle, WA 98109
(206) 378-0114
cascade.chapter@sierraclub.org
www.cascade.sierraclub.org

Volunteers for Outdoor Washington
8511 Fifteenth Avenue NE, Room 206
Seattle, WA 98115-3101
(206) 517-3019
info@trailvolunteers.org
www.trailvolunteers.org

Washington Trails Association
2019 Third Avenue, Suite 100
Seattle, WA 98121
(206) 625-1367
info@wta.org
www.wta.org

Index

About the Author

Dan Nelson's personal and professional life has long focused on the great outdoors of the Pacific Northwest. After a short stint as a newspaper reporter, Dan joined the staff of the Washington Trails Association (WTA), where he worked and played for eleven years as the editor of *Washington Trails* magazine. Currently, Dan serves as the public information officer for the Olympic Region Clean Air Agency—an agency charged with ensuring the air remains clean, clear, and healthy on the beautiful Olympic Peninsula. In addition to loving to walk the wild country, Dan is an avid fly fisher, canoeist, snowshoer, telemark skier, and paraglider pilot. If he's not out enjoying the backcountry, he's indoors writing about it.

In addition to his past work at the WTA, Dan continues as a regular contributor to the *Seattle Times*, *Backpacker* magazine, and *Hooked on the Outdoors* magazine. He specializes in Northwest destinations and outdoor-equipment reviews. He is also author or editor of several outdoor guidebooks published by The Mountaineers Books. He lives in Puyallup with his partner, Donna, and their yellow lab, Parka (co-researcher for *Best Hikes with Dogs in Western Washington*).

About the Photographer

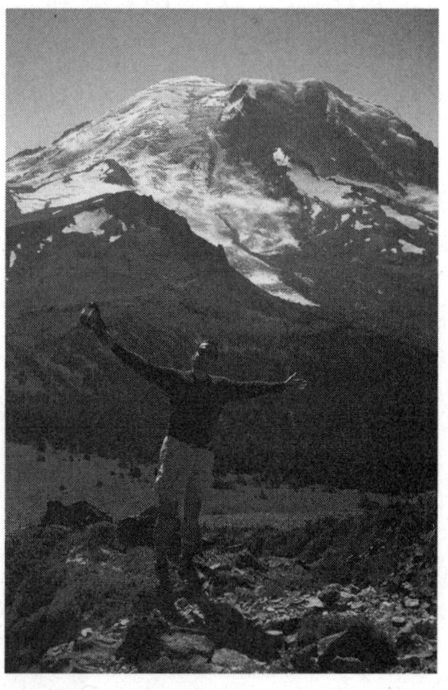

Alan L. Bauer is a professional freelance photographer specializing in the natural history of the Pacific Northwest and coverage of local history. He is a lifelong resident of the Pacific Northwest, having grown up on a large family farm in Oregon's Willamette Valley and now calling Washington State his home for the past twenty years. Much of his love for the outdoors can be traced back to his being outside on the farm working and playing—an experience he wouldn't trade for anything!

His work has been published in *Backpacker, Odyssey, Northwest Runner, Oregon Coast*, and *Northwest Travel* magazines as well as numerous publications and books across fourteen countries. He regularly provides images for projects including CD covers, textbooks, websites, presentations, research, and corporate materials. Prior to his involvement with this new book series, he was co-author of *Best Desert Hikes: Washington* and *Best Dog Hikes: Inland Northwest* with The Mountaineers Books.

He resides happily in the Cascades foothills east of Seattle with his caring family and border collie. For further information and to see samples of his work, please visit *www.alanbauer.com.*

1% for Trails and Washington Trails Association

Your favorite Washington hikes, such as those in this book, are made possible by the efforts of thousands of volunteers keeping our trails in great shape and by hikers like you advocating for the protection of trails and wildlands. As budget cuts reduce funding for trail maintenance, Washington Trails Association's volunteer trail maintenance program fills this void and is ever more important for the future of Washington's hiking. Our mountains and forests can provide us with a lifetime of adventure and exploration—but we need trails to get us there. One percent of the sales of this guidebook goes to support WTA's efforts.

Spend a day on the trail with Washington Trails Association, and give back to the trails you love. WTA hosts more than 750 work parties throughout Washington's Cascades and Olympics each year. Volunteers remove downed logs after spring snowmelt, cut away brush, retread worn stretches of trail, and build bridges and turnpikes. Find the volunteer schedule, check current conditions of the trails in this guidebook, and become a member of WTA at *www.wta.org* or (206) 625-1367.

THE MOUNTAINEERS, founded in 1906, is a nonprofit outdoor activity and conservation club whose mission is "to explore, study, preserve, and enjoy the natural beauty of the outdoors...." Based in Seattle, Washington, the club is now the third-largest such organization in the United States, with seven branches throughout Washington State.

The Mountaineers sponsors both classes and year-round outdoor activities in the Pacific Northwest, which include hiking, mountain climbing, ski-touring, snowshoeing, bicycling, camping, kayaking, nature study, sailing, and adventure travel. The club's conservation division supports environmental causes through providing educational activities, sponsoring legislation, and presenting informational programs.

All club activities are led by skilled, experienced instructors who are dedicated to promoting safe and responsible enjoyment and preservation of the outdoors.

If you would like to participate in these organized outdoor activities or the club's programs, consider a membership in The Mountaineers. For information and an application, write or call The Mountaineers, Club Headquarters, 300 Third Avenue West, Seattle, WA 98119; 206-284-6310. You can also visit the club's website at www.mountaineers.org or contact The Mountaineers via email at clubmail@mountaineers.org.

The Mountaineers Books, an active, nonprofit publishing program of the club, produces guidebooks, instructional texts, historical works, natural history guides, and works on environmental conservation. All books produced by The Mountaineers Books fulfill the club's mission.

The Mountaineers Books is proud to be a corporate sponsor of the Leave No Trace Center for Outdoor Ethics, whose mission is to promote and inspire responsible outdoor recreation through education, research, and partnerships. The Leave No Trace program is focused specifically on human-powered (nonmotorized) recreation.

Leave No Trace strives to educate visitors about the nature of their recreational impacts, as well as offer techniques to prevent and minimize such impacts. Leave No Trace is best understood as an educational and ethical program, not as a set of rules and regulations.

For more information, visit *www.LNT.org,* or call 800-332-4100.

OTHER TITLES YOU MIGHT ENJOY FROM THE MOUNTAINEERS BOOKS

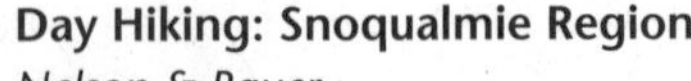

Day Hiking: Snoqualmie Region
Nelson & Bauer
Great hikes—done in a day!

Day Hiking: Olympic Peninsula
Romano
"... covers a lot of territory that other guidebooks have passed up"
—*Seattle P-I*

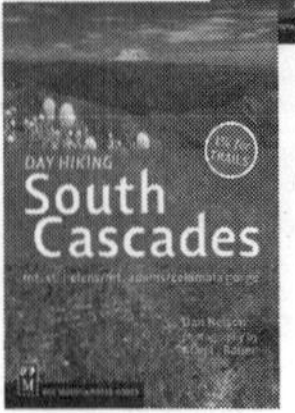

Day Hiking: South Cascades
Nelson & Bauer
Remote, pristine trails in rugged volcano country

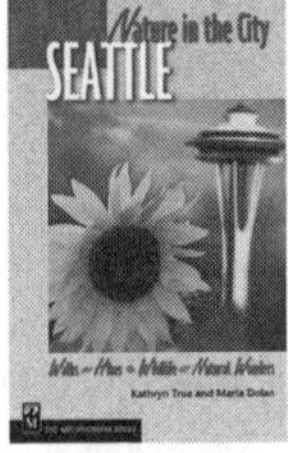

Nature in the City: Seattle
True & Dolan
The best places to experience wild-life and wild surroundings in the city

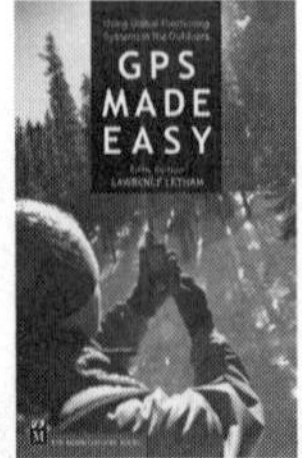

GPS Made Easy, 4E
Lethem
"Required reading for everyone who plans to leave the house with a GPS receiver in hand"
—*Cheyenne Wyoming Tribune-Eagle*

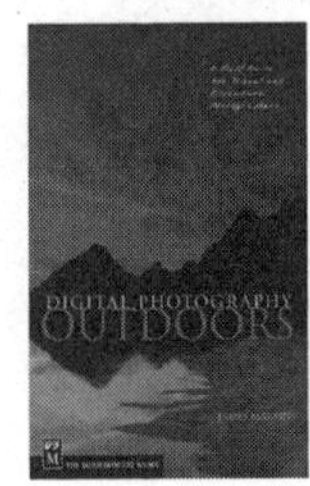

Digital Photography Outdoors, 2E
Martin
"A great all-in-one reference"
—*Digital Photography* magazine

The Mountaineers Books has more than 500 outdoor recreation titles in print.
Receive a free catalog at www.mountaineersbooks.org.